APR 1 1 2003

Sci ✓

1995
14X 3/09. 7/09
17X (6/10) 6/11

MAY 0 5 2003

When the Music's Over

When the Music's Over

MY

JOURNEY

INTO

SCHIZOPHRENIA

Ross David Burke

Edited by
Richard Gates
and Robin Hammond

BasicBooks
A Division of HarperCollins*Publishers*

Copyright © 1995 by Richard Gates and Robin Hammond.
Published by BasicBooks, A Division of HarperCollinsPublishers, Inc.

First published in 1993 by University of New England Press, Armidale, New South Wales, Australia.

Designed by Jessica Shatan

Library of Congress Cataloging-in-Publication Data

Burke, Ross.
    When the music's over : my journey into schizophrenia / Ross Burke ; edited by Richard Gates and Robin Hammond.
        p. cm.
    Includes bibliographical references.
    ISBN 0–465–09141–5
    1. Schizophrenia—Patients—Australia—Memoir.   I. Gates, Richard.   II. Hammond, Robin.   III. Title.   IV. Title: When the music's over.
PR9619.3.B8244W48   1995
823—dc20   94–27100
                                                                CIP

95 96 97 98 ❖/RRD 9 8 7 6 5 4 3 2 1

Contents

Foreword

This is an alarming, funny, sad, courageous book. I use all these adjectives deliberately and could find dozens more, because I write about the maelstrom of emotions that madness brings.

Ross David Burke, who wrote this book, had the guts and the tenacity to record his experiences with schizophrenia. Not many people have done so with quite such intensity and color. Yes, there have been numbers of people who have written either about schizophrenia or about manic depression, but usually passages about florid experiences are alternated with more lucid interpretations or commentary. Ross chose to write his book as a novel, and we are immediately plunged into psychotic chaos and stay there for most of the story. There is no respite and no escape—and for some people, this is how it is. Like my own son, Jonathan, Ross had little relief.

Much of the language is rich in metaphor and sharp in its brilliance. This is a world that glitters with the unexpected. The illness brings about a confusion and profusion of experiences, and as a reader I felt I was being taken on a roller-coaster ride of differing realities.

Ross's novel is autobiographical and is embedded within a broader book, in which Richard Gates and Robin Hammond describe to us the nature of schizophrenia and the background to Ross's life. The authors have done us a good service by taking this approach, because there are times when interpretation is required. Ross's story becomes even richer when it is understood, and all the more poignant when we learn that Ross made this request in one of several notes he left behind before he took his own life.

I commend the understanding, dedication, and skill that Richard

Gates and Robin Hammond have put into making this book happen. I salute Ross David Burke for his courage, his humor, and his considerable writing skills. He has left us a good and brave legacy.

ANNE DEVESON
Founder of Schizophrenia Australia,
author of *Tell Me I'm Here*

Preface

"The Truth Effect," the work that forms the core of this book, was written by Ross David Burke and is the fictionalized account of the last part of his life. At twenty-one he had been diagnosed schizophrenic and his experiences as a sufferer of this disease form the basis of this story. Shortly after its completion, Ross killed himself at the age of thirty-two.

Ross's life was relatively short but particularly colorful. He began writing his book as a means of therapy while serving a sentence in Long Bay jail for armed robbery, a crime he committed while in the grip of his schizophrenic delusions. By the time he completed his story, Ross realized it could be used to benefit others.

Ross was well known to one of us (Richard) as a psychology student at the University of New England at Armidale, New South Wales, during 1984–1985. Over that period he visited Richard regularly to talk over many things, but often he discussed the illness of schizophrenia and issues related to his own suffering with the disease. One morning, in November 1985, Richard received a telephone call from a university staff member informing him that Ross had killed himself the night before. He had left behind a note, one of several, in which he requested that Richard publish the story he had spent his last years writing: "I want the book published. I would like a separate reality besides my fantasy, a factual description. It's up to you. Thank you. Ross."

This volume, then, is an attempt to present not only Ross's story but that factual reality he spoke about in his suicide note. It is also his legacy to us, to help us understand the illness of schizophrenia. Many of us are afraid of people with schizophrenia because of the bad publicity some of them get for the unusual things they do. However, most of those suffering from this illness of the brain are not harmful to others. Richard was privileged to see schizophrenia first hand and learned from Ross to feel comfortable around this illness. Ross was often insightful and could convey his feelings, thoughts, and ideas about schizophrenia in a way that gave Richard a much better understanding than most people have had the opportunity to gain.

It is no doubt impossible for those of us without this illness to understand the suffering that those with schizophrenia endure. In his writing, Ross attempted to explain some of this suffering by taking the reader on a journey into his mind, into his delusions, hallucinations, and fantasies. His writing is frank and sometimes shocking, and, although the result is often disturbing, Ross also had a wry sense of humor which he used against himself to good effect. He was not afraid to laugh at himself. In many places his humor transforms an otherwise grim tale, lending it a particular poignancy. Certainly, while reading his story we frequently find ourselves unable to separate fact from fantasy—but that, after all, is precisely the experience of the individual with schizophrenia.

"Schizophrenia" is a wastebasket category for a number of diseases of the central nervous system. All the evidence now points to schizophrenia being a disease that has its origins in the effects on the fetus in utero. It is not a disorder that is caused by poor early learning experiences or poor parenting. It is time we stopped blaming families for their schizophrenic children, time we discarded the theory that families are responsible for causing the illness. Schizophrenia must be seen as a disorder of the central nervous system with some interesting and often complex psychological manifestations. Life stresses certainly play a part in expression of the illness, but should not be seen as its fundamental basis.

Ross hoped publication of his story might help others with schizophrenia to come to terms with their illness. The note found with his body asked that his mother be contacted for his case history. Unfortunately, his mother died before we were able to begin researching the book, and with her death much important information was lost. The manuscript itself posed more puzzles than answers. As a fictional account of his life, it obviously needed careful research but it was peopled with unidentifiable characters. In an apparent desire to preserve the anonymity of close friends and acquaintances, Ross had given them all pseudonyms and left behind no clues as to their real identities. Because we believed that many episodes in his book were products of his vivid imagination, we needed to talk to all these people, if indeed they existed, to try to piece together his life story as it actually happened.

Our subsequent search took us from Armidale in the northern tablelands of New South Wales to suburbs north, south, east, and west of Sydney, as well as the heart of the city itself. We also traveled to Brisbane and the Kerry Valley in Queensland, to townships on the north coast of New South Wales, to Long Bay jail, Wisemans Ferry, and Morisset Prison Hospital. Because the music of the 1960s and 1970s heavily influenced much of Ross's philosophy, we found ourselves listening to the Doors and other bands of that era, as well as reading the poetry of Jim Morrison. We ultimately succeeded in tracking down everyone mentioned in Ross's story who is still alive, from the parole officer he fell in love with and named (optimistically) "Surrender," to the enigmatic "Dr. Abraxas" and the elusive "Elysium Dream." We spoke at length with all these people and with Ross's remaining family members, who permitted us access to his medical and criminal records.

Because of the sensitivity of much of the material, we have promised to conceal the identities of Ross's characters. None we spoke to had read his story, so in that respect their recollections were unbiased. From our interviews the realization gradually unfolded that the events he wrote about had, in fact, taken place as he described them. Although he resorted to artistic license at times, this had been kept to a minimum and did not interfere in any way with the integrity of the narrative.

To help the reader set Ross's story in perspective, we have compiled an introduction from the information we obtained during our research. Of necessity we have relied on much verbal evidence and reminiscence, but this has been backed up, wherever possible, by independent confirmation from other sources, official documentation from government bodies, medical or psychiatric reports, or other documentary evidence.

We hope we have done justice to Ross's story and that in the writings you are now about to read, you will learn something of this interesting man and his life, and gain some insight into the workings of the schizophrenic mind.

Acknowledgments

We are grateful to many people for their invaluable assistance in the making of this book.

Thanks to the following friends and acquaintances of Ross for their personal reminiscences: Bernie, Jillian, Michelle, Dean Hartman, Ken Grey, Chris Stephens, Eve Kiernan, and Joe Massingham. We especially thank Ross's family members, William, Kerry, Shane, Frank, Kerry Ann, and Fiona Burke, Maryann Todman, and Mrs. Nelly Johnson, for talking to us with such frankness.

Our thanks also go to the following people who assisted us in gaining access to various records: Bernard McNair from St. John of God Hospital, Richmond, New South Wales (NSW), Australia; Brad Miles, Noel White, Denise Credaro, and Leanne Millard from the NSW Department of Corrective Services; Liang Soei from the Prison Medical Service at Long Bay jail; Terry Griffiths, Minister for Justice; David Edwards, solicitor; Dr. Hansen; and Dr. Tugwell. Thanks also to the staffs of the following: Armidale and New England Hospital, NSW; Armidale Court House; Morisset Hospital; NSW Courts; NSW Department of Health; NSW Police; and the University of New England, Armidale.

Identification of the various lyrics referred to in Ross's book would not have been possible without the help of Jon Fitzgerald and other staff and students of the University of New England–Northern Rivers, as well as Brewster Everett and Morgan Tucker. Tony Young lent us his expertise on the question of "blue meanies" and "goldtops" and Ned McCann talked to us about Folidol.

Our gratitude also to publisher Ken Shearman and editor Deb Brown for their hard work and faith in the success of this book.

We also wish to acknowledge the team at Basic Books, led by Jo Ann Miller, for their enthusiastic support of Ross's story.

When the Music's Over

Introduction

Ross David Burke was born on June 21, 1953, the third of four sons, his father a customs officer and his mother a nurse. Mr. Burke senior had been born near Tamworth in New South Wales and was living in Sydney when World War II broke out. He joined up and served as a machine gunner in the Middle East, Greece, Crete, New Guinea, and Borneo. On leave he met the woman who later became his wife and corresponded with her frequently until the war ended and he returned to Australia. Mrs. Burke had come to Sydney from the Kerry Valley, near Beaudesert in Queensland. Bright and active, she had wide-ranging interests and endeavored to live life to the fullest. In addition to her nursing work, she conducted a voluminous correspondence with many soldiers serving overseas. Her weekends were often spent bushwalking in the Blue Mountains and it was on one of these occasions that she first met her future husband. They married within two months of his homecoming and it was then that Mr. Burke joined the Customs Service, a job in which he spent almost forty years.

Ross spent his childhood in what, to many children, would have seemed like near-idyllic circumstances. In 1950, his parents had bought a century-old farmhouse at what is now Carlingford, then on the outskirts of Sydney. Set on fifteen acres, with an orchard, cows, fowl, pigs, geese, a dam, and plenty of bush and trees, it was an ideal spot for boyhood adventures. Ross and his brothers spent their early years roaming adjacent bushland, sailing homemade canoes on the dam, waging make-believe battles against neighborhood boys, and crayfishing in the nearby creek. Sitting up in their hideout among the branches of the coral trees, eating their cooked crayfish, Ross and his brothers must often have felt like kings of their little world.

Certain incidents in his early life later assumed great significance for Ross. One of these allegedly occurred when he was a few months old. According to his mother, Ross had always been a happy baby who rarely cried. This apparently changed when, one day, she left him with a female baby-sitter and returned to find him crying uncontrollably. Mrs. Burke referred to the incident many times within the family circle, but when pressed, would only say that the baby-sitter must have "done something" to Ross, for he was "never the same happy baby again." This incident was thought by some family members and Ross himself to have been a major cause in the development of his schizophrenic illness. It is not clear what, if anything, actually occurred; Ross himself seemed to believe he was sexually molested in some way.

In another significant incident, when he was of preschool age, Ross accidentally drank, or breathed the fumes from, some insecticide his father was using to spray the orchard. Ross was hospitalized in intensive care for a short period, his breathing assisted by an iron lung, and was released fully recovered. He and his parents always suspected, although it is highly unlikely, that this poisoning also had a direct bearing on the development of his illness.

Ross was a highly sensitive person and very close to his mother. He confided in her and she in him, so it is unfortunate we no longer have her memories upon which to draw. From our interviews with his surviving family members, however, we noted that she was obviously a major influence in his life and did everything in her power to love, protect, and care for him during his illness. The following words of one such family member are representative of everything we were told about her: "His mother cared deeply for Ross and she was very protective of him . . . whatever Ross did, she would always try to build him up and praise him for it. . . . I think she was a very good mother . . . she saw that as a very important role."

But Ross's parents' marriage was not stable. While his brothers and he enjoyed an active outdoor life and their father spent his days at work in the city, Mrs. Burke was left to manage house, farm, and family. The house was literally falling down around her: riddled with white ants, freezing in winter, with a leaking roof, no modern conveniences, and scanty or no floor coverings. Living conditions were at times almost unbearable. In addition to household chores, it was left to Mrs. Burke to milk the cows, feed the fowl, geese, and pigs, and perform many of the tasks in the orchard. Raising four active boys in such an environment, with her husband away working for long hours, and with the additional handicaps of no car or telephone, proved more than she could cope with. She left the home on at least one occasion for an extended period, supporting herself by working as a nurse's aide in a nursing home.

The family fortunes improved dramatically, however, when in the early 1960s the farm was subdivided and sold, the family retaining a block on which they built a modern brick home with all modern conveniences. Mrs. Burke at last had a comfortable living and working environment, and there is no doubt the boys benefited from the improved living standards. They now had all the material comforts they could require. At least one brother gives evidence of a huge improvement in school grades after the move. Funds from the sale were invested in more property, and Mr. Burke and his sons began to enjoy the luxury of frequent overseas and interstate holidays. Mrs. Burke usually visited her family in Queensland on these occasions for, although she had returned to live in the family home, she and her husband lived separate lives within the home for the remainder of their marriage.

Ross was evidently a reasonable scholar during his school years although, for reasons that are now obscure, he was made to repeat second grade at the Catholic school he attended. This apparently rankled deeply, for he refers to it often in his story, it is noted on a number of occasions in records of interviews in his hospital notes, and almost every remaining member of his family mentioned it to us in interviews.

His school years were apparently otherwise uneventful, except for an incident in 1971 when the school refused to allow him to return until his hair was cut. Ross and some of his friends had let their hair grow over the Christmas–New Year holiday period in accordance with the latest fashion. Ross actually returned to school wearing a short wig, but the authorities were not fooled and all boys with long hair were sent home. Refusing to give in, he was enrolled instead at the local state high school, where he completed his Higher School Certificate in 1972 at the age of nineteen.

It was at this point that many of Ross's problems appear to have begun, as he tried to live up to the conflicting expectations of his parents. His mother was highly intelligent, with a huge library of books. Her personal ambition to be a writer remained unfulfilled, but she tried to encourage her sons along that path. Ross was the only one to follow her lead, writing songs, poetry and stories and, finally, his book, much of which his mother typed for him from his handwritten draft. Always supportive, she encouraged him to learn musical instruments—drums, guitar, harmonica—to paint and to read widely. He began to collect records and developed a consuming passion for rock music, particularly that of the Doors, Frank Zappa, the Beatles, the Grateful Dead, and Jefferson Starship. With friends, he wrote songs which they played together as a band at each other's houses.

Mrs. Burke, after a lapse of many years, had returned to the Catholic faith in the mid-1960s. She had always sought to inculcate in her sons strong Christian principles, and they were regular churchgoers. Christianity was very important to Ross, particularly in the years during and after his imprisonment.

His father's support, by contrast, was along strictly practical lines, as he tried to guide Ross toward a career. A public servant himself, Mr. Burke thought it an ideal career for a lad like Ross. Ross's two older brothers had long since left school, one joining the Air Force, the other working and undertaking college study. There was pressure on Ross to "succeed" like his brothers and father. Mr. Burke told Ross he needed to have a goal, to have ambition, to earn plenty of money, to "make something of himself." Ross adopted his father's suggestion by joining the Post-Master General's Department in 1973 as a clerk. At the same time, he moved out of home and into a flat at Mosman, a Sydney suburb, with two friends from school, and enrolled in an evening accountancy course at technical college. The story he wrote begins with this period.

Ross, by then, had already experimented with drugs: from a trip to the Himalayas around 1969 he had brought back a quantity of hashish and Buddha sticks, which he distributed among his friends;

like many young people, he had been smoking marijuana at social gatherings for some years. During his final year at school he had met a new friend who easily persuaded him to play truant. They spent much of their time growing and nurturing a small marijuana patch near a shack they had built in bushland near his house and which they reached by rope ladders down a cliff face.

The two friends he set up house with in Mosman were cousins of each other: Uncle Cane Toad and Baron Wasteland in his story. All three roommates had full time jobs at this stage, Uncle Cane Toad as a public servant in the Taxation Department and Baron Wasteland as a postman. They began making frequent weekend trips to Wisemans Ferry to paddocks where hallucinogenic mushrooms grew. Up to this time, Ross is remembered by his family and friends as a cheerful, friendly, and witty person, good company, loving and loyal. At the same time, some of his friends considered him to be something of an outsider in the group. Uncle Cane Toad told us that from the late 1960s he and Ross were best friends for some years, sharing a common interest in music and other leisure activities. However, he gradually noticed Ross becoming a little "weird" and difficult to understand, frequently needing to escape reality with alcohol, marijuana, and hallucinogens.

In early 1974, Ross met Elysium Dream, who was introduced to him by her cousin, Magic Star Flower. Elysium Dream has told us that she was attracted to Ross because she "thought he was really sweet, . . . intellectually quite interesting and stimulating, [and that] . . . he had a bit of depth." He showed more political awareness than most of the others in their group and was more thoughtful about what was happening in the world in general. Their relationship lasted only a few weeks, however. Elysium was wary of a permanent liaison with Ross, who became, as the relationship progressed, increasingly possessive and obsessive about his love for her. She told us:

> Ross actually did worry me. He was incredibly intense. I just had the feeling if I gave Ross any hook into my life I would have had a lot of difficulty removing him. . . . Afterwards he wrote to me consistently for many years. I didn't answer his letters because he actually frightened me. . . . I don't think I appreciated Ross

particularly. The fact that he offered me somewhere to live and then accidentally fell in love with me—as far as I was concerned that was his fault, not mine. I just told him he was very silly.

Elysium left Ross and returned to her former partner, unaware at the time that she was carrying Ross's child.

Uncle Cane Toad also began to have a few qualms, arriving home one evening to find Ross stretched out on the floor, babbling incoherently about being the Antichrist, his ears stuffed with cotton and the record player turned down very low. Ross had taken a strange "turn" in a barber's chair about twelve months before, which they had attributed to the after-effects of eating hallucinogenic mushrooms, but undeniably something more alarming was now taking place. Mr. Burke was summoned and Ross was taken back to the family home.

Ross then left his job and was granted sickness benefits while he tried to pull himself together. He had abandoned the accounting course after only one year and had taken up agricultural studies instead. These he also dropped after one year and he headed for Brisbane, where he settled down to write a book of songs. It was about this time that he came to believe he was the inventor of rock and roll. There is some mention in medical notes of his having seen a psychiatrist in Brisbane, but no further details have been found.

Restless, and plagued by thoughts of Elysium Dream and their expected baby, he returned to Sydney to find that his daughter had been born on December 27, 1974. Elysium, however, refused to acknowledge him as the father and Ross suffered deep unhappiness for many years over his love for Elysium and his desire to be a father. His daughter's birth became hugely symbolic to him; he described it variously as "the invention of disco," the reason for the collapse of the Tasman Bridge (the scene of a deadly freighter collision on the island of Tasmania in 1975), and the cause of Cyclone Tracy, which had devastated the city of Darwin two days before her birth. He even apologized to some of his friends for having caused the cyclone.

The next two years are not well documented. We do know he took a trip to the Snowy Mountains in southwestern New South Wales with his friends in February 1975. Here they were raided by the police and charged with possession and use of Indian hemp, appearing in Cooma Court of Petty Sessions the next day. Ross was fined a total of $140. Soon after, he moved into a flat in Paddington, a Sydney suburb, with Baron Wasteland and, in November 1975, took a four-week trip to Bali with Uncle Cane Toad where they rode around on motorbikes, went sightseeing, smoked marijuana, and sampled the local mushrooms. In March 1976 he appeared in Central Petty Sessions and was fined $60 for failing to produce a railway ticket and for assaulting a ticket inspector. He then traveled to Melbourne where he spent several months, sick and penniless in a shabby flat.

Ross returned to the family home at the end of 1976 and attempted to settle down. His brothers were all doing well financially and his parents continued to make lucrative property investments. His father constantly urged him to get out and "make something of himself." Money, in fact, was very important to almost everyone in the Burke family except Ross. In our interviews one person commented that talk about money and investments was the one thing guaranteed to bring the family together. One brother was still an Air Force pilot, another was a mining engineer, and the third was doing well as an electrician—it is not surprising Ross found difficulty fitting in. He had little interest in money, material possessions, or clothes. Even when he did obtain work, as a clerk, he dropped all his unopened pay packets in his drawer and forgot about them. It was left to his mother, months later, to retrieve the money and open a bank account for him.

The job as clerk lasted three months. Ross then worked as a laborer in Ermington for two months before being layed off. It is unclear why his two jobs were short-lived, but his increasing mental instability may well have been a contributing factor.

Ross admitted himself to St. John of God Hospital at Richmond in August 1977. The hospital was originally a lovely old mansion built by Philip Charley in 1892. Much of its former glory remains and its magnificent setting on Richmond Hill, overlooking the Hawkesbury River and surrounding farmlands, made it an ideal place for him to regain tranquillity. He spent four months there as a voluntary patient in an effort to overcome his encroaching mental instability. Ross had come to believe that his mind was being read by ants which would inherit the earth, and was feeling unable to relate to anybody but his mother. He was painfully nervous with women because of his shyness. He said he "lived in a fantasy world" which he preferred to "real life."

Ross here met one of the psychiatrists he named Dr. Abraxas, who diagnosed him as a paranoid schizophrenic. Ross told him about his belief that he was the Antichrist and that he had wanted to "collapse the Roman Catholic Church" since about the age of five. At this stage he said his ambition was to be a farmer and he expressed a desire to join his uncle on his farm or to buy one of his own. He claimed his reason for taking drugs was to avoid going to war, but he also claimed that although his friends frequently injected drugs he was now content to use only hashish, which, however, he used heavily. Encouraged to take part in ward activities, he played squash, cricket, volleyball, and table tennis, took bus trips, and attended group therapy. Here he spoke about the guilt he felt for abandoning Elysium Dream when she was pregnant and for giving her LSD in the hope she would abort the child. He admitted to having no motivation to lead an industrious life and eventually realized that his plans to become a farmer had been based on the belief that he could spend most of his time "riding around on his motorbike and going swimming."

Ross was prescribed Stelazine, which was subsequently replaced by the major tranquilizer, Mellaril; then Modecate, another major tranquilizer. He was also given Cogentin to treat the motor side effects of the other drugs. Neulactil, which is often given for severe anxiety and tension states in psychotic patients, was prescribed to help him sleep, because of his severe restlessness. With the help of medication, counseling, and good professional care, Ross felt ready to face the world again in November 1977. He was discharged into the care of his family and was granted the invalid pension.

In January 1978 Ross was living in a flat at Bondi Beach with Baron Wasteland and Uncle Cane Toad, who was now heavily into amphetamines and working as a taxi driver in Sydney. It was during this year that Uncle Cane Toad was admitted to a psychiatric ward, suffering amphetamine psychosis. There is little documentation relating to Ross for the remainder of the year, although we do know he worked for about six months as a collator operator for a printing factory in Ryde, a suburb of Sydney. By this time, Ross had stopped taking his medication and was experiencing frequent delusions. He still believed himself to be, at one and the same time, the inventor of rock and roll, the Holy Ghost, and the Antichrist. He thought the "superpowers" had implanted a transmitter in one of his teeth, through which they relayed messages to him. He also "received" messages from television commentators and news readers. In November he sought a vasectomy, which was refused. It is not clear exactly why he sought this procedure, but perhaps it had some connection with his actions early the following year, 1979.

It was to be altogether an eventful year. Ross attempted to castrate himself on several occasions during his lifetime; one of these was in early 1979, when his mother found him in his bedroom, covered in blood, a razor in his hand. At about this time, Ross had begun to believe he was the new messiah and was seeking a disciple in one of his young nephews. Some of his family members were concerned about the radical change in his personality. He was moody and unpredictable and his behavior was often bizarre. One in-law told us:

> He frightened me in the way he was talking. . . . We were playing a lot of Beatles music and he was telling me his interpretations of their songs, that God was telling him the way his life should go, that he was a new Messiah . . . he really frightened me. He said if he could take away people's money he'd take away the power and then he'd lead them by listening to the songs because he got his messages from voices. . . . He was getting directions from God, particularly through Beatles music. . . . When I first met Ross he was great fun to be with, interesting, entertaining, attractive, he was just wonderful. The next time I saw him it was incredible. He was like an old, old man, very gloomy, very, very introverted, really very black.

Ross was admitted to St. John of God again in February 1979 at the age of twenty-five. On admission Ross stated he had stopped taking his medication nine months previously and admitted drinking heavily and smoking tobacco and marijuana. He spoke about his belief that he would "die in the desert" at about the age of thirty. His hospital records note that he was "extremely delusional" on admission and that he claimed to have gone there for "asylum, peace and serenity." Mellaril, Stelazine, and Cogentin were prescribed, but he was reluctant to accept them and discharged himself after only five days, against advice, refusing to take any medication with him. In July, in a desperate attempt to find a cure for her son's illness, Mrs. Burke took Ross to a naturopath, who believed schizophrenia to be a "toxic malabsorption state, secondary to food allergies." He prescribed multivitamins and a special diet, but (perhaps not surprisingly) to no effect.

Ross and his friends had been using hard drugs for some time by mid-1979. In the years since leaving school, Ross claimed to have used LSD, cocaine, amphetamines, and heroin, as well as the mushrooms and marijuana. To fuel their addiction, some of his friends planned an armed holdup to steal drugs from a local pharmacy. Ross did not wish to participate and tried, together with Uncle Cane Toad, to dissuade them. But the robbery took place, the drugs were brought back to Ross's flat, where they were used, and the following day the group was arrested. Ross was able to prove his innocence, but Uncle Cane Toad and the rest of his friends were jailed.

For reasons not exactly clear, Ross himself later decided to rob a bank. He certainly did not do it for the money. Ross himself stated that Brian Bury, a television personality, had sent him a "secret message" via the transmitter in his tooth ordering him to perform the holdup. His first official statement to the police says that he wished to "get his name in the paper to be a hero." He liked the idea of being a "twentieth-century Robin Hood." In his book he simply says he "decided to visit Wasteland in jail." Whatever the reason, on the morning of September 14, 1979, he took his brother's rifle from his parents' house, minus the bolt, which had been hidden elsewhere. He wrapped the rifle in a sarong and drove his mother's car to Kingsford. Before leaving, he had the foresight to alter the rear license plate with black marker pen. After parking at a bus stop, he entered the bank and ordered the tellers to fill his bag with $20 and $50 notes, instructing them to "forget about the ones and twos." As he emptied his drawer, one of the tellers tripped an alarm, which also activated the security camera.

Leaving the bank, Ross found himself face-to-face with a policeman, who had been alerted by a bank customer. Ross pointed the rifle at him and got back into his car. The policeman later testified in court that Ross "had a crazed look." Ross then drove around the streets of Kingsford and Randwick, throwing handfuls of money out the window as he went. Quite a few bystanders must have struck it lucky that day; of the $16,304 stolen, the bank eventually recovered only about $5,200. In fact, many people were observed leaving the scene in great haste, clutching wads of banknotes.

The subsequent police chase ended in a dead end at Randwick. Ross climbed from the car and walked toward the policeman, arms outstretched. Pointing his gun at him, the policeman ordered him to stop, but he kept walking. Under the impression that Ross intended to strike him, the policeman knocked him down with his pistol, handcuffed him, then brought him in. Ross's explanation for his actions was that he was attempting suicide; he was certain he would be shot if he kept walking toward the gun and intended no harm by his actions. Charged with robbery and assault of a bank officer, he was remanded in custody, bail being refused.

Ross was in custody in Long Bay jail for three months before his case came to trial. Two weeks after his arrest he was interviewed by the jail psychiatrist whom he informed, among other things, that he was God and "the center of the universe because I invented rock and roll." Ross claimed he was being influenced by the world because he was the "nucleus" of the world. He was certified mentally ill and unable to care for himself. One month after his arrest he struck a warden who had entered his cell to waken him, and was sentenced to sixty days for assault.

In the Sydney District Court, Ross pleaded guilty to the charge of robbery and assault of the bank officer, and was sentenced on December, 12, 1979, to four years. The sentence may seem harsh when one considers both his psychiatric condition and the fact that the boltless and unloaded rifle was obviously not meant to be fired. An unsympathetic judge, however, ensured Ross was to be locked away for at least two years. During sentencing, the judge acknowledged Ross's mental instability at the time of the offense but considered that the sentence was lenient. Psychiatric treatment was ordered. Ross's family, although distressed, was generally of the opinion that jail "wouldn't do him any harm" and would keep him safe.

The evening following sentencing, however, Ross attempted suicide by slashing the veins of his wrists and feet, inflicting ten lacerations. Threatening to kill his cellmate if he called for help, he remained upright for about an hour, walking around the cell while the blood poured out, then lay down on his bunk to die. His frightened cellmate banged on the door and Ross was taken away semiconscious to the prison hospital. He had lost a large volume of blood. His wounds were stitched and he was placed on an intravenous drip to replace lost fluids. The following day he removed the drip, deliberately tearing open the stitches, and walked around the room. He did this again in the afternoon, stating afterwards that he was "living in hell and wanted to die to go to heaven." Two weeks later, he forced open the partly healed cuts on his feet. The prison psychiatrist, on this occasion, confirmed the diagnosis of paranoid schizophrenia. Ross was still receiving "messages" via "the transmitter in his tooth" and claimed to be able to transmit messages all over the world. On February 4, 1980, his wounds at last healed, he was transferred to Morisset Prison Hospital, having been certified mentally ill (insane) by the prison psychiatrist.

Morisset is situated in beautiful bushland on the shores of Lake Macquarie, near Newcastle. However, Ross was undoubtedly unable to enjoy fully the natural serenity of this spot, housed as he was in the maximum-security section. The ward in which he served his time is now out of use but the bleak buildings still remain, surrounded by a high, crumbling brick wall.

Ross was first treated with Largactil (chlorpromazine), an antipsychotic drug, but showed little improvement and again contemplated suicide. An antidepressant (amitryptyline) was added to his medication and he then began to improve; by April 1980 he was certified no longer mentally ill but was continued on medication. His discharge summary of May 9 gives a principal diagnosis of schizophrenia: schizo-affective type, depressed phase. No doubt the slight change in form of schizophrenia reflects the prominent depressed mood state Ross was in at this stage.

Ross was returned to Long Bay jail and put to work in the prison library. He was also given a cell of his own. Medically, he was considered by the prison psychiatrist to be "in quite good remission" and he continued to take his medication regularly. By September of that year he was working in the laundry, where he remained for the rest of his term. By November 1980 the prison psychiatrist considered Ross to be completely clear of psychotic symptoms. His overall conduct during imprisonment was recorded as good and he was considered a "quiet but efficient worker" who gave no trouble. He attended Bible classes and prison fellowship and also became involved with GROW, a worldwide self-help group for people with mental illness that originated in Sydney in the late 1950s as an off-shoot of Alcoholics Anonymous. All these activities sustained him during his imprisonment.

Ross was released from jail on December 12, 1981, and began reporting to his female parole officer, named Surrender in his story. Ross's father had earlier written to the prison psychiatrist asking how best to help his son after his release. Mr. Burke was advised that Ross should receive continuing medical care and see a doctor as soon as possible for continuation of medication. Ross resumed living with his parents. Although his medical condition was considered stable upon his release, his friends report that his personality had changed: he was more aggressive and showed an uncharacteristically "brutal" streak. One friend described him as "a mess." Not long after his release, Ross discontinued his medication, claiming that it affected his memory, lowered his motivation, and prevented him from "gaining insight and resolving his personality problems." He again began a downward slide. He still tried, however, to understand his problem and bring about some improvement in his life. He attended weekly GROW meetings, enrolled in a counseling group, and became involved in volunteer work. He formed a casual relationship with a woman in the group.

Ross again planned to apply for a public service job in response to his father's continued urging. In February 1982 he sat for the state government clerks' selection exam and was successful in obtaining an interview, which took place the following month. His motivation for securing employment, however, began to diminish. He had started writing his book in jail and he continued with this for long periods, shut up in his bedroom. He was writing it, he said, specifically for Elysium Dream. His mother began typing the manuscript for him. By now, both parents were again concerned about his lack of initiative, his introspection, his unwillingness to take responsibility, and his poor self-image. They were also worried about his suicidal tendencies. Ross himself told Surrender that he would consider taking his medication again, as he had begun having some "grotesque" nightmares, but he does not appear to have followed this through. Ross began attending Mass daily and took to dressing all in white. He went for eight-kilometer walks, visited friends at Morisset, and read and wrote constantly. By keeping active, he was attempting to stave off the psychosis which was again threatening.

In early April 1982 his good friend Baron Wasteland died. Baron Wasteland had been arrested on a drug charge and was in poor physical condition with sores all over his body when Ross caught up with him. Ross had taken him to the hospital, where his condition had improved. Baron Wasteland had then discharged himself, taking with him his prescribed supply of drugs; he overdosed on these. Ross was deeply affected by his friend's death, feeling that he had failed in his efforts to help him.

By mid-April 1982 Ross was again in a bad way. He had stopped attending his GROW meetings, giggled often to himself, was experiencing frequent sexual delusions, and occasionally thought he was God. He believed that he was having a psychological war with the television and radio and was "stuck in their magnetic field" and that he was a prophet. Ross realized he needed to be rehospitalized, but when Surrender made arrangements at his request, he changed his mind. Ross had almost daily interviews with Surrender at this time, during which she tried to persuade him to resume his medication. He was reluctant to do so because of the side effects but eventually agreed to try taking his tablets again at a reduced dosage. For a week or so he was quite stable and seemed much happier, but he again began neglecting his medication.

At the end of April, Surrender went on extended leave and a male parole officer, N. W., took her place. This was a tremendous blow to Ross, who had become deeply fond of Surrender. He suddenly "disappeared" for a week, resurfacing to announce he had been walking through the bush near Dubbo for five days and five nights, intending to "fast to the death" and thus achieve a "glorious" end. This incident is interesting in view of his prediction in

1979 that he would die in the desert when he was thirty; he declared this had been a dress rehearsal for that event. On his first visit to N. W. after this incident, he accused his new parole officer of having murdered Surrender and barely restrained himself from attacking him violently with an ashtray. N. W. recalls subsequently urging Ross to admit himself to St. John of God, as his parole might otherwise have been revoked. Ross mentioned that he had been accepted for employment by the Taxation Department but had turned down the offer, feeling he could not cope with full-time employment.

Ross's condition continued to deteriorate badly. By the end of June 1982 he was, according to N. W., "in utter fantasy," claiming that spheres, "like a mass of bright light," had been rolling around in his head constantly since childhood, keeping him always active. Ross had another violent outburst when he assaulted his father during an argument (one of several such attacks) and abused his mother verbally. After attempting to knock his father on the head with a bottle, he took the family car and disappeared for two days. When he returned, his mother easily persuaded him to seek read-mission to St. John of God.

On this occasion, the staff found him extremely thought-disordered. He claimed he was the third messiah and could send telepathic messages to rock stars. He had forsworn the Catholic Church, taken up the Pentecostal faith, and linked himself some-how in his mind with Moses and Jesus, as well as God. Ross stayed at the hospital for three months on this occasion, while his condition was stabilized, attending group therapy, receiving counseling and attending the Mount Wilga Rehabilitation Centre for work training. For the first time, he was prescribed Serenace (the trade name for Haloperidol), a major tranquilizer, used in psychotic states for the control of aggression. He appears to have responded well to this medication and his records report he was more realistic and rational within a short time. His psychiatrist was quoted as say-ing that "he will never be anything but crazy but should improve better than this." It seems the improvement in Ross's condition was effected by the medication rather than any remission of his illness.

When Ross was discharged in late 1982, he decided to live at a halfway house instead of his parents' home. Relationships within the family were fragile and he was aware that his presence heightened tensions and often brought them to the breaking point. Over the next fifteen months he changed address four times, moving in and out of various halfway houses in the suburbs of Richmond and Petersham (thrown out of two because of his bad behavior), staying at his parents' on weekends and attending the Queen Elizabeth II Rehabilitation Centre for five months of that period. Ross also sat again for the public service exam, but this time was rejected, possibly on medical grounds. His poor job prospects, his poor financial situation, and the drowning suicide of a good friend from one of the halfway houses (Sneak in his story) threw him into deep depression. Finally his father suggested that Ross become a "permanent university student" so that he could "loaf with dignity and aplomb."

In February 1984 Ross enrolled at the University of New England, Armidale. His discharge notes from Queen Elizabeth II Rehabilitation Centre indicate that although he had been accepted at the university for a bachelor of arts degree, prognosis for success at university studies was "guarded." Ross took up residence at Wright College and enrolled in philosophy, psychology, and sociology in his first year. His choice of university may well have been influenced by his discovery that Elysium Dream and their daughter were now living at Glen Innes, near Armidale. Ross had written to Elysium Dream many times in the years since they had parted. She had earlier moved to Adelaide in order to break the connection, having no desire to continue or renew their acquaintance. But in 1984 their daughter was ten years old and Ross had predicted their paths would cross ten years after her birth. Some time that year he set out to visit them twice, taking his mother with him on one occasion. He located his daughter at school, arranged a meeting, and confronted Elysium as well. The meetings were not a success. Elysium was struck by the change in Ross; he had gained a great deal of weight and he spoke about wanting to die and about claiming his daughter as his. Elysium said:

He told me he would play this game while driving his car, a hit-and-miss game, weaving in and out of traffic, basically because he wanted to die. It was the lack of concept of the other people that would be involved with his death that I found quite shocking, and that was what decided me to keep away and not to introduce him to my daughter as her father. He was dangerous.

Frightened by his manner, she refused him any further access, and after the second visit Ross never saw his daughter again.

From the beginning of his first university year Ross began to attract attention. The college dean received complaints from students that Ross was causing arguments by claiming to be the inventor of rock and roll. The dean remembers him as "a striking individual with an imposing build and a substantial black beard" who became agitated when his claims were disputed. Ross tried to avoid confrontations with the other students but throughout his first year he continued to make contentious statements and behave provocatively toward students and staff. By the end of the year he had worn out his welcome at college and was asked to find other accommodation.

Ross was admitted to Armidale and New England Hospital on November 2, 1984, in a suicidal state, following reports that he had made suggestive remarks to domestic staff at the college and presented one of them with a gift of his underpants. He had passed his first-semester sociology exam but was in no condition to take his second-semester exams and applied to take these at a later date. Ross stayed in the hospital for two days, discharged himself, then was brought back again two days later, his condition having deteriorated. This time he stayed for three weeks while his medication was adjusted. He was represcribed Serenace, Largactil, Modecate, and Cogentin, as well as Tofranil for his depression. Frequently during his hospitalization he claimed that he wished to die, that he was telepathic, and that his head was "full of rock and roll people." By the time he was discharged, his condition had improved and stabilized and he was released on Modecate injections. He took up residence in the university flats. In January he passed psychology and sociology but failed his first-year philosophy unit.

Ross made some good friends during 1985, his second year at the university and the last year of his life. Notable among these were the Bangladeshi students with whom he shared his flat and the girl whom he named Star Ship (chapter 57). Ross enrolled in two psychology units as well as sociology and the first-year philosophy unit he had failed. Star Ship, a fellow psychology student, remembers him affectionately as:

> incredibly dishevelled-looking, flannelette shirts hanging out of trousers, a really messy sort of person on the outside and in some ways really messy inside . . . always making reference to a song or quoting Jim Morrison . . . a lot of really heavy Doors stuff . . . a very furrowed brow with glasses just sitting on his nose and always a very thoughtful "playing with the fairies at the bottom of the garden" look. . . . He didn't like the world much and would often talk about the darkness and the blackness and the hell he was going through.

Although Ross had told her he was schizophrenic, Star Ship was only twenty-two years old and inexperienced with such people. Nevertheless, she soothed him with endless cups of tea when he was agitated and listened while he talked and talked about his past, his love for Elysium Dream, his daughter, and how, unlike his brothers, he had never been able to live up to his father's expectations. Ross was drinking heavily and often indulged in binges in an attempt to escape his symptoms; at other times he would sit in his room for days playing loud rock music. On one occasion he swallowed a large quantity of antidepressants and ended up in a dazed and drugged state at the local police station. One of Ross's major frustrations at this time related to his sexual functioning. Although his drive was unimpaired the drugs severely impeded his performance. Star Ship remembers his depression and how he refused to take his medication regularly. Ross preferred to self-medicate with alcohol and marijuana.

Six months before he died, Ross travelled to Sydney during school vacation and booked himself into St. John of God hospital again, complaining of depression, insomnia, overweight, suicidal thoughts, and overindulgence in alcohol and cigarettes. He was drinking six schooners of beer, smoking sixty cigarettes per day, and weighed two hundred pounds, having gained nearly forty-five pounds since his 1982 admission. He had long talks with Dr. Abraxas, describing his childhood as "a cross between nightmare and beautiful." He remembered enjoying being alone to fantasize and mentioned, yet again, his disturbance at being made to repeat second grade at school. He claimed he ate hallucinogenic mushrooms "for expansion of awareness." This had been a common theme of the 1960s and 1970s, perhaps reinforced in Ross by his reading of such literature as Huxley's *The Doors of Perception.* His great desire, he said, was to be loved. His file notes that he seemed to have a good relationship with his three brothers, as well as his mother, although the relationship with his father was a little strained because of "differences in values."

Ross wanted his medication stabilized and some time out to rest and think and to try to improve his self-image. He told Abraxas that he intended to commit suicide in one year's time, when his book was finished, and that he preferred psychosis to normality, which was "boring." His medications at this time were the antidepressant Tryptanol and the antipsychotic Modecate. Ross left after two weeks, physically rested but little better mentally, and returned to college. It is clear from his hospital notes that he felt comfortable at St. John of God and regarded it as a refuge from the pressures of the world.

Ross's relationship with Star Ship petered out over the final six months of his life, although they remained friendly. He had always had difficulty attracting women and maintaining steady relationships, another source of his depression. He had become close to his Bangladeshi flatmates, but they were due to leave Australia at the end of the year. He informed close friends that he intended to finish his book, then end his life, but it is unlikely that they took him seriously. As it turned out, that is just what he did.

A few days before he died Ross traveled to Sydney for the weekend to visit his family. He gave no indication of what was on his mind, but on the day he left for Armidale he rose early, made his bed perfectly, and dressed in his best suit and tie. This was so uncharacteristic of Ross that his family joked about it at the time. A few days later, when they received news of his death, they realized this was how he had wanted his mother to remember him.

Ross returned to Armidale and sought out and talked with his friends during his last days, without revealing his intentions. On the evening of November 26, 1985, he had dinner with a flatmate, watched television, then went to his room to work on his book. He was heard typing until late in the night. Some time between 11:30 that evening and 9:30 the following night, Ross wrote several suicide notes, then swallowed a large quantity of drugs, "considerably greater than considered to be lethal," according to the subsequent coroner's report. He put on one of his favorite LPs, *Blues for Allah* by the Grateful Dead, then lay down to die. His completed manuscript lay beside him, and on the back of an envelope containing one of the suicide notes Ross had written his last words: "P.S. I'm sorry God."

It seems clear that once Ross had finished his book he considered his reason for living was at an end. His final attempt at suicide was carefully planned not to fail. With his mind subjected to the unceasing torment of schizophrenia, his life was, as he often pointed out, "a living hell." Ross is remembered by his family and friends with great love and affection. He will never be forgotten by all those who knew him because of the force, color, and depth of his personality. His friend Star Ship summed him up well when she told us:

> He'd never die. . . . Even though he's physically gone, he hasn't, because so much of him has stayed on with his book. He had a very strong physical presence, but his way of seeing things was really what Ross was about. . . . Once he'd written his book, that was it, he'd said everything, he'd explained everything and he knew that was the time. He just needed to be here to do what he wanted to do . . . to try to make sense of why it was he who went through that.

THE TRUTH EFFECT

ROSS DAVID BURKE

WARNING
This book is not to be read while listening to music.

WARNING
This book was written by a drug-induced alcoholic
psychopathic paranoid schizophrenic with manic depression,
a sleep disorder, claustrophobia, and he's mighty partial to sex,
and not only that he is not sure of the truth . . .

The schizophrenic is a soul not merely unregenerate, but desperately sick into the bargain. His sickness consists in the inability to take refuge from inner and outer reality (as the sane person habitually does) in the home-made universe of common sense—the strictly human world of useful notions, shared symbols and socially acceptable conventions. The schizophrenic is like a man permanently under the influence of mescaline, and therefore unable to shut off the experience of a reality which he is not holy enough to live with, which he cannot explain away because it is the most stubborn of primary facts, and which, because it never permits him to look at the world with merely human eyes, scares him into interpreting its unremitting strangeness, its burning intensity of significance, as the manifestations of human or even cosmic malevolence, calling for the most desperate counter-measures, from murderous violence at one end of the scale to catatonia, or psychological suicide, at the other. And once embarked upon the downward, the infernal road, one would never be able to stop.

ALDOUS HUXLEY, *The Doors of Perception*

1

The man who betrays himself is a dangerous man.   Sphere

Once upon a time, the story began with our hero, hereafter called Sphere, answering the unasked question. I wonder why I answer when the answer presents itself? I answer because I am a little-known secret that is soon to become a well-known secret. I answer because I am.

"But what *is*?" Baron Wasteland asked.

"I am the object of eternity," I replied. "I come from the testing ground."

"Winky wanky woo! Then what is the unasked question?"

"The unasked question has just been asked, so I will remain silent."

"That's heavy crap," said Wasteland.

Uncle Cane Toad leaned across the seat and jabbed me in the ribs.

"Philosophers are mad," he said.

Rainbow Moonfire whispered something to Wasteland.

Elysium just smiled.

Magic Star Flower frowned, but I laughed. Yeah, I laughed. I was out of control, lost in my world of confusion. I realized that something was going wrong with my reasoning. I was talking shit again. My thoughts jumped.[1]

Let me again introduce myself. I am Sphere, and this is the book of fear. It is a book of years. It is a book of power and here is its strength. It is about non-reality and reality and dreams and nature and truth.

I am not normal.

I am not a woman.

I am a man.

Yes I am.

I live in a psychiatric hospital,[2] so if you want the truth I will tell you lies. Society is out to kill me and already my thoughts have begun to hallucinate about this place. I am going to use you for my own monetary ends. Yes, I am going to confuse you about the truth of my fragile dream. My dream is going to take you to a delicate, sensitive world. In my psychosis I am going to take you on a little trip of confusion. A trip into insanity. I search for beauty. Beauty is the essence of everything.

I detached myself from the words my thoughts had constructed and traveled on, as I spun the magic mushroom. We were on our way to the local hotel to get the monetary system into our septic system. In other words, we were high out of our minds on hallucinogenic mushrooms and we were on our way to the pub to get drunk and forget our sexual problems. In Oz[3] it's a tradition of long standing to get drunk on icy-cold Aussie beer after a long, hot day. The clean, clear taste of malt and hops is a bottler of a way to end the boredom of a humid day.

"To the beer men!"

The kombi[4] was parked. My companions were Rainbow Moonfire, Magic Star Flower, Uncle Cane Toad, Baron Wasteland, and my woman, Elysium Dream. I am Sphere.

Baron carefully combed his hair, checked for his smokes and, when the whole ritual was completed, he opened the side door and we piled out. The group strolled to the beer garden at the back of the pub.

A cry went up. "Hey! If it isn't the drug fiends!"

"Hi kids," Moonfire replied.

I plopped into a vacant chair and ordered a middy of orange juice. The others ordered the same.

"How's it going, crew?" We looked up to find Bandit.

Elysium smiled and replied, "I'll be fighting fit when my biorhythms get their shit together. I read my tarot this morning and according to the cards I'll be dead in a week."

"She's got the same old psychotic shit," said Wasteland.

The trip came on me and I needed a beer to bring me down. I ordered one for the second shout. The wonder of the cosmos opened before me. The hotel, my second home, became a sight for weary eyes. I smiled and knew nothing except a kaleidoscope of ecstasy. I know all, I see all, I am all. I scratched my balls.

My consciousness retreated from the cosmic realization of beauty and I listened to the conversation. There was talk of starting a new rock band called The Sadists. I got the choice position of general freak who hung around on stage. I pictured my introduction: "Ladies and germs—here is no-good, layabout, burned-out mind-fuck Sphere." Too much clichéd shit, mate. The band has no talent, but they could do a few vulgar songs for the beer garden and drunken parties. Baron would sing "Good old fungus fanny, loved by few but fucked by many."

We downed another five schooners and the blue jokes began. Baron Wasteland started off:

"It was April first when a young father went to the hospital to see his newly born son. Standing outside the glass partition, the nurse pointed to his baby son. The nurse smiled as she lifted the baby from its cot. She then strolled over to the table and bounced the baby's head on the timber. The father was horror-struck and his hands went up to the window. The nurse smiled at him and started to swing the baby by holding it by its penis and scrotum. The father was pounding frantically at the glass partition by this time. The nurse let go of the baby and with a sickening thud the baby went careering into the wall. Blood and guts went everywhere. The father took a running jump at the glass partition. The nurse picked up the baby and tore its arms off as the father went hurtling through the glass. He was foaming at the mouth when he faced the nurse. She said, 'April fool, he was dead already.'"

"That's sick," Elysium shuddered.

Somebody suggested we go up to Kings Cross to see some blue movies. "I love it when those girls take off their clothes and gyrate their furry holes."

"Get real, Bandit!" Rainbow exploded.

"So you girls don't dig the Cross?" said Cane Toad. "Then how about we all go to the haunted house at Castle Hill?" It was agreed that the haunted house was in, and after another four schooners we got the fucked unit together and made our way to the cars. I had a discussion with other drunks to get the directions right till everything was organized. Putting the kombi into gear, we were hurled into the night.

Wasteland built up the suspense. "Tell them the story of the haunted house, Cane Toad."

"The haunted house, right," said Cane Toad. "I read this article on great Australian haunted houses in the newspaper. Years ago, when convicts built the house, one convict was flogged to death but before he died he cursed the guards and house. So the story goes that his spirit is sometimes seen walking and groaning in the grounds of the house with a bloodied whip in his hand, searching for his tormentors. Two owners of the house have committed suicide and the wife of one is rumored to be buried among the foundations. It's a crazy hell-house and that's its tragic story." Nobody doubted his words. I could almost feel the grins in the darkness.

"Everybody is going to need nerves of steel tonight, especially if you stay alone in the room of doom," Wasteland added. Goose pimples began to appear on exposed flesh. We loved it, especially Magic Star Flower, who was right into the trip.

We skidded to a halt and the house loomed dark and ominous by the deserted road, an evil mockery of death. Wasteland opened the side door and we piled out. Two other cars arrived and the headlights were turned off.

"Well, this is it," said Wasteland.

"Not much of a haunted house," Rainbow sneered.

"Bullshit," Wasteland replied. "Obviously you didn't listen to its evil reputation. Tell her again, Cane Toad."

"It's haunted all right, right down to its rotting foundations. God knows it's haunted."

"Are we going to wait out here all night or are we going inside?" Rainbow asked.

Climbing over the barbed wire fence, we entered the darkness. We lit matches and in the front room old decaying furniture and a crumbling fireplace were revealed. My mind began to swirl in the hallucinogenic trip and to whisper grisly tales. I gripped Elysium's trembling arm. Magic's teeth chattered in the silence of the night.

The rooms at the bottom of the house were explored until the ultimate terror had to be overcome: the journey to the upstairs rooms. We approached the spiral staircase and began the journey upwards. Each step was cautiously checked as the quivering assembly approached the top. Elysium squeezed my sweaty hand and whispered hoarsely, "The house is breathing." The house began to pulsate with life as she whispered again, "Get me out of here, Sphere."

"Keep your cool," I trembled in reply. I thought, *Jesus, this horrible house contains the essence of the Evil One.*

We continued our steady pace till we reached the top of the stairs. Marauders of time and space, we huddled in a group of dilated pupils.

"This is where the owner of the house hanged himself," Cane Toad whispered.

"What a joke, some haunted house!" Rainbow exclaimed.

Suddenly Elysium screamed. She screamed again as a shadow darted across the room. Drunks and trip-freaks panicked in confusion. Hair bristled on end. The initial fright faded. The freaks stood stone-still.

"Did you see that?" Elysium shrieked. "It was a ghost!"

"Ghosts, ghosts," Cane Toad agreed.

"I saw it and it was a rat," Wasteland explained.

"It was a frigging ghost!" I said.

"Let's go," Rainbow Moonfire pleaded.

"Yeah, let's go, this place is alive."

The troops hastily retreated down the creaking stairs, raced down the hall and sprinted out of the house.

Safely outside, Cane Toad shuddered. "What a mad, demented horror house." We scuttled into the kombi and with a screech of tires were hurled into the night. The kombi remained in silence.

"That rat freaked me out." Elysium smiled ruefully.

"You freaked us all out, you daffy dame."

"My eyes are still bugged out," said Magic Star.

"Every fool knows there are no ghosts, only psychos," Wasteland sniggered. "How about we go to the Cross?"

"No," the girls echoed.

"How about Luna Park then?" Wasteland suggested.

"Yeah, mate," Rainbow replied. "Let's get this trip on the road."

Wasteland blasted the horn, let go of the wheel and finally belched. "Here we go kids, into an acid haze . . . "

2

I don't even know myself. I change my mind so often.
Uncle Cane Toad

It was the early 1970s and I was doing the pub circuit, living with Elysium, while subsisting on my savings, when my attention was turned to the stones of Wisemans Ferry. I phoned up the old rascal, Cane Toad (he's senile but nefarious), and made a plan: Elysium, Cane Toad, and myself would go to Wisemans Ferry.

"But what about Wasteland, Magic Star Flower, and Rainbow Moonfire?"

"Forget them," I said.

We drove to the Ferry and all was as usual as the cassette played Captain Beefheart. We had expectations of good things to come. Past the police station on our right, past the school on our left, and on to our secret fields where heaven and hell waited.

At Wisemans Ferry we strolled in the paddock and began picking up mushrooms at random. Soon, the mushrooms flowed through our veins and on the return journey the trip was on us again.

"Could we stop off at the barber's at Castle Hill?" I asked. "I need to get a haircut. It's been three years since I last had a scrap with a barber and I want to get the edges trimmed. I'll be the sharpest-looking freak in town by tonight."

Feeling no ill effects, I took my place in the barber's chair and, while waiting and watching myself, the balls began to roll again.[5] *Your dreams drive you insane*, I thought. *Without your thoughts there would be sanity but there would be no consciousness, no soul. Maybe the missing link in man's ancestry was a madman. Maybe the dream parables are mathematically set to protect the next master symbol. A geometric progression.*

"What, who is saying this!?" The voice bounced out of my blood-shot eyes and was reflected in the mirror.

"You said something, sir?" the barber asked.

"No hopping hayseeds, not me mate. Easy around the edges sport." *Maybe after all is said and done, the dreams are a distraction not worth the pleasure or discomfort they afford. The voices of insanity. The identification of myself in the swirling clouds, water, sun, and lightning that has not found rest and it cries out to be heard, to be loved, to be made, and to be described.* I fell past the words into a deeper state.

The barber was cutting my hair and I began a conversation with him.

"I will tell you what to do, to think, to feel, to change, to reason and awaken. Happiness is better than pleasure, peace better than war, strength better than weakness, and sanity is better than insanity. Now I will tell you the truth, about me who catches the world and twists it around till I am too confused to perceive the truth. I am the bullshit substitute. I remember the past, I give double meaning, I am for the young and ignorant, I slander the truth, and there is no reason to experiment in your mind with my mistakes. I'm the hypocritical bastard." I stood up suddenly. The barber jumped and then stood still with his jaw hanging open. I yelled, "It's a fucking deathtrap!"

Balls of lightning appeared and disappeared. The adrenaline was building up. The barber and customers were freaking out. My mind was in a razzle-dazzle peak of a black and red swirling anxiety attack. Blinded by the puzzle, my body slumped down in the barber's chair. I was ashamed of imperfections in myself as the mirror went psychedelic. My reflections broke up into squares and my mind was disassembled, as I flew outward into the squares of my mind. In complete confusion I crumpled into the chair.[6]

The terrified shaking of the barber woke me up. "Is it over?" I mumbled.

"No, you were babbling and then you blacked out. Please stand by the window."

"Rightio, mate." Cane Toad and Elysium helped me to the window. The window had a crazy-square pattern.

"Drug addict!" a customer exclaimed.

I was too freaked out and exhausted to do anything except stay on my feet and gaze outside at the cool, calm park with its shady trees. It was a haven from insanity. Covered in sweat, I held on to myself till the peaking was over and with my eyes and tongue hanging out I was escorted back to the chair, where the barber continued to cut my hair. In a daze, I paid the cashier. I had come down as fast as I went up.

Once outside, Cane Toad, Elysium, and I chuckled. "Friend, you nearly got us put away," Cane Toad exploded. "Your little exhibition just about gave me a heart attack. I was ready for a blood-curdling yell, your body hurtling through the air, clutching at the barber's throat."

"I was worried about you," Elysium said.

"Mate," I gave an amused chuckle, "you missed the point. When I get stoned and confused and start babbling away, I black out in a past realization."

"That's heavy. I don't understand it but it sounds heavy," Cane Toad thought out loud.

"I'm very sensitive to the sunshine cosmic vibes. The barber's a case. I could pick up his karma and it was all bad. It was a case of sadism, if I know my waves. I didn't like the way he cut my hair. By the way, I meant what I said when I was in the chair. I don't think it's funny anymore. Mushrooms are killing me. People freak me out. People stare at me with telepathic eyeballs. Did you get a good look at his eyeballs? He was a gremlin, I'm sure. He had a screw loose. He lives in a dream, trying to erase his memory. He's as mad as a two-bob watch. Yeah, I think he was a case."

"More like a babbling idiot who talks too much," Cane Toad said.

Elysium smiled and said, "You can't stand eyes either, Sphere."

"Yeah," I replied. "They remind me of the balls."

"Balls?" Cane Toad asked.

Elysium and I remained silent and then I replied, "It's where I come from."

3

I'm a man. What are you?   Baron Wasteland

On the creaking wharf I had inconspicuously smoked a couple of joints of fine Aussie heads and I was at my peak, where my mood was as light as the autumn leaves that floated down to earth in the nearby park. Fish darted in the turbulent waters below me. The sea was dark green. Fresh, salty sea breezes blew around me and the harbor waves splashed on the calloused rocks, then rolled back along the rock of ages. The seagulls squawked while the people stared at the shifting horizon. The ferries came and went. How deep does my mind go when I'm stoned on your shores watching your ceaseless, restless rhythm. Oh lord, it's good to be here. It's good to be alive.

I was wrapped in my old yellow sweater, green sneakers, and blue jeans, fishing line held between my delicate fingers, the sun smiling down in morning glory. The raw prawns and sardines beside me filled the air with their particular tangy smell. Perched on the wharf, I dangled the line into the harbor salt. This blood-lusting angler had already notched up three sardines to his credit and was still angling for more. Tonight we would dine in style.

I sighed to myself and waited till the oil slick pranced away. "Here you go little fishes. Here, little fishes," I quietly called as the ravenous fish danced around the tantalizing bait and then disappeared into deeper and darker waters with maybe a bite-sized snippet of raw prawn for their trouble. The fish unknowingly danced with the dealer of death.

Restlessly, I stretched my creaking bones. Oh well, all good things come to an end. So it is with life. I threw the raw prawns and sardines into the harbor water and ambled back home thinking about the wanton cruelty in blood sports. I lived near the harbor now and, stoning along the road that led to my home, I had fleeting thoughts from the past.

Cane Toad, Wasteland, Elysium, Rainbow Moonfire, and Magic

Star Flower were there when I arrived home and they wanted to go to Wisemans Ferry for some mushrooms. I agreed. So we got our act together, hopped into the kombi and headed off to Krishna's colored-in paradise. We arrived at the Ferry late at night and before hitting the sack we had a few bongs of poor-quality weed and settled in for an uncomfortable night's sleep.

Soon day dawned. *Where the hell am I?* Smack parched lips, wet dry throat, and blink potato-spudded eyes. Wisemans Ferry. Teeth glittered in the morning light. I felt terrible. *All right, who stuffed the feathers up my nose?*

"Okay, Elysium, I'll get up and greet the welcoming day. A good day for a stone." With creaking bones, I pissed out the window.

We picked the mushrooms. A fine batch. We placed them in a blackened billy of water to boil, left them to draw for five minutes, and we had an excellent repast of mushroom tea.

A bunch of freaky-looking people arrived and we invited them to share our harvest. We exchanged greetings of Peace mate; You're cool; we're cool; Where did you get your sneakers from? They agreed with us that it was an excellent tea.

Being sociable, I lit up a couple of nuclears of good strong stoning weed and passed it around the gathered throng. It felt good to be stoned before the trip came on. A sense of alienation from all earthly gods surrounded us.

The dreams came and went. The trip is all in the imagination and this one came on slow, but it looked like it would continue on strong. Cane Toad was as white as a ghost, rocking to and fro on a gnarled gum tree log. I was sure he was going to fall into the fire. Watch it, digger. Several times he was about to fall but righted himself at the last second. I was getting ready to pass out when the world around me changed. Cane Toad's dog, Psychedelic Dog, had eaten the remnants of the stewed mushrooms and was running around chasing his tail. Soon he wobbled away and crashed on the bank of the river. The still of the trip descended. The stuff that crystal dreams are made of. This is heavy psychosis. This is happening now, mate. It's happening again.

The fire's fascinating warmth held its grip on my swirling mind. Wonderful changes of mood danced in the colors of the flames. I got up and walked away. The ceaseless fire had burned an illusion into my mind: *So this is tripping. Is it real or just a delusion? Am I caught in something beyond my control?* The trip's time bomb ticked away. I glanced at my watch, fascinated by my imagination. Lost in time, I breathed deeply and held the world still for a moment with no movement, just frozen time. The musicians were right when they sang that it is all too beautiful in this place of tranquillity. Wisemans Rock. The rainbow's end. God's playground in the light of the golden sun warming our innocent inner essences.

I turned around suddenly to see a freak hold up Psychedelic Dog, who gave a yelp of dismay and was thrown violently into the river. Instinctively, the dog seemed to know what to do. He swam for the shore, scrambled up the bank, shook himself dry, and collapsed into a blind stupor in the hot, glaring sun. That dog was really out of it, mate. He was really gone. Come to think of it, I was really gone, and the vibes that these freaks were giving off was affecting my internal combustion. They were real heavy mullets. Heavy with lead in their heads. Just keep them away from me. You big dickheads, don't take your aggression and conflict out on me, mates. I've got to be careful with whom I trip.

Snapping out of the dream, I watched the old farmhouse in the background, the bamboo patch to my right and trees and the Hawkesbury River before me. *This is the right perspective on this swaying environment,* I whispered to myself. *This could be heaven.* I watched and marveled at the intricate designs of nature. This miniature world at my feet was fascinating as I tripped off.

My crystal mind was fragile. After eons of evolution, my mind was locked in nature. It was ready to run in panic at the slightest pressure. I withdrew my mind. It was wonderful to belong to this earth's country. My mind snapped back to half-reality.

"Hey, Cane Toad, over here is a mystery, a true revelation of cosmic delight." He ambled over with a familiar, strange, tripped-out vacant look in his eyes. He squatted down beside me. "This is the trip's highlight. It is the wonder of nature. Look deeply into the grass at my feet and tell me what you see." I could hear his heart warming to nature's delight as he looked deeply into nature. Hypnotized, he stared for a second or two at mother earth and then he stood up with an enlightened gleam in his eyes.

"Well, what the blanky blue blazes did you see?"

"Dirt." He smiled. "Dirt with weeds growing out of it. It's all dirt." He started to dance. "Dirt, dirt, dirt," he sang and danced. Then, looking melancholy, he wandered away to be by himself.

I thought to myself, *Careful, don't interrupt this crackpot's trip. Show care, mate, give him plenty of space. It must be some strange force of the trip that's brought on premature senility. What a cracker! But I won't tell him that while he's tripping. I'll tell him later that he's a fruit.*

The dream came. I am the guardian of this shimmering country. It's a wonder to belong to nature. I yelled, "Get your arse over here, Cane Toad."

Uncle Cane Toad wandered back till he was an inch from my face and said, "I don't agree with your delusions."

"Hark, a voice," I yelled. "You say something, Cane Toad?"

"Yes, it's a revelation," he replied. "I've discovered the mystery of dirt." His eyeballs rolled as he reached down, dug his fingernails into the earth and scraped up a handful of dirt. He held the soil above his head where it shone on fire like an Olympic torch.

"God has discovered the secret of life." He lowered his hand and dropped the sparkling jewels on the ground. He turned to me and solemnly spoke. "Nature is dead."

It's alive, I revealed thoughtfully to myself.

Getting up, he wandered off.

"Get into your own trip, Uncle Cane Toad."

He turned and smiled. "Keep it cool, friend."

The trip flashed me again. I followed Elysium within the universe of another universe. She was sitting in the bamboo patch. I walked up to her and she smiled. Her face looked empty and blank. "Heaven," I said. "Heaven is the reason that we are here. We have a program. We have the programming of the universe in our bodies." We would follow till we reached the stars. The birth and life place of God.

"Don't interrupt me, Sphere," she replied. "I want to be by myself. I'm a woman, Sphere. I really am a woman. Leave me alone. You don't understand."

I shrugged the hair from my shoulders and walked away. I photographed the scene. Elysium and Uncle Cane Toad drifted from my mind.

I am God.

Cane Toad wandered over to comfort Magic Star Flower, who was huddled against a tree, shaking like a leaf. Elysium Dream started rocking her, while Uncle Cane Toad held her hand. Nightmare hell. She screamed.

I stared across the river towards the town, with supernatural serenity. I could understand the motives of my generation. In the future I would try all kinds of explanations to attempt to duplicate nature's harmony while trying to repair the deluded acid mind. Shaking my head, I thought, *Creeps and freaks. I've got to get out of this trip. It's too insane.* I washed my hands in the river to cleanse myself. *Find the impossible,* the mind said. *The testing ground.*

"Far out," Cane Toad said. "Look, Magic."

A freak was racing around, flapping his hands and arms. He shouted, "Look, I can fly. Look, I can fly." He raced past me and plunged into the river. Mate, I laughed. Magic closed her eyes and withdrew into Elysium.

I wandered over to the farmhouse and entered. Wasteland and Rainbow Moonfire were fucking on the floor. "Sorry, fellows," I muttered and wandered out.

In the acid mist you could make dreams and that is what is happening here in this heavy psychosis of racing thoughts, because across the river in the cliffs and rugged bush terrain was the past. Here was the ancestor of man that was once reptile. He lived there. The lizard had intelligence and could use it to survive. All the lizard wanted to do was eat and lie in the sun. He was poor but happy. He existed and multiplied and that is all he knew about the dream. He was dreamless.

Rock music was playing from the cassette. Magic Star Flower was still crying and sniffling. My feelings grew with the music and the weeping of Magic. I walked over to Cane Toad.

"Cane Toad, I've got to talk to someone. Do I look different to you?"

He replied, "A bit yellow around the gills, but basically you look all right. Break your trip if it's no good. Don't contemplate your noodle if it has no answers." Cane Toad paused. "I saw my death in nature, so I broke that trip."

I sat down and contemplated the noodle of a crazy swami. Dreams are real.

My thoughts caught hold of reality and I suddenly remembered that it was election day. Wandering in a dream, I teamed up the trip's dimension, and a journey of a thousand steps began with a sigh and a grasp of reality.

"Yoo-hoo, Toad, Magic, Elysium! I hate to bother you but we've got to elect the illustrious leaders of our homeland. Vote donkey, you swine. To the polling booths, men."

"Lead on, democratic one," Cane Toad replied. "We'd better tell Wasteland and Rainbow."

I yelled into the farmhouse, "Baron Wasteland and Rainbow! Get your shit together. We're going to the elections."

The troops ambled to the barbed wire fence. Elysium followed, holding Magic's hand. We climbed over the fence near the TRES-PASSERS WILL BE PROSECUTED sign and proceeded down the road to the township of Wisemans Ferry.

"See that cloud, trip-freak? It looks like thistledown floating in a blue ocean of swamp. Mate, I'm a poet," Baron Wasteland said. "No animals live up there except starlings and Boeing jets. It's a wonderful spiritual age we live in, Cane Toad."

"Hey gang," Rainbow Moonfire exclaimed, "let's see if we can make the papers by saying we were captured by a flying saucer."

"And blow our trip?" Wasteland said. "Not likely, girl."

"They'll institutionalize me again," I said.

"Why not astound the world by saying that we were held hostage by hairy gorilla men from outer space? Yeah, we'll all run into town."

"Not my happening, Rainbow. I know a bloke who saw a flying saucer, but he was just a nut."

"They'll lock us up, Rainbow."

"Let's talk rational," Magic Star Flower said. "The hippies are dead; forget them, you fools."

"It could have been a great freak-out."

I didn't know what they were talking about as I slipped in the gutter, stumbled, and got it together again.

"Are you all right, Sphere?" Elysium asked.

I was flipping out into a science-fiction nightmare. "Rainbow, did you say that we had been captured by an unidentified flying saucer?" I asked.

"No, mate."

Shit, the meaning of the universe lost.

Suddenly Elysium went off. "Let's kill some picnickers," she said. "Casually walk up to them and with a savage grin disembowel them."

"Heavy," said Moonfire. "Don't even think that. Play the game straight."

Civilization was coming down fast. See the sun, see the dream in nuclear orgasm. It's all peaking out by riding the bomb. I smiled and said, "Let's blow up the polling booths."

"No gelignite, mate."

"Let's piss in them, then."

"You and your dreams usually make no sense. You've got a disturbed head."

"Yeah, I'm just a crazy man, friends," I replied.

Cruising over the bridge, we traveled on. Suddenly Rainbow Moonfire was overcome by uncontrollable laughter. She was reading the plaque on the bridge.

"'This bridge was opened by the Governor of New South Wales,'" she said.

"No shit," Wasteland said.

"It goes nowhere," Magic said.

"Yeah."

Elysium began to laugh hysterically and soon it caught on. "Mates, you haven't got balanced minds either," I said. On to the elections we proceeded in our tripped-out way.

Silence.

"God is a woman," Elysium said.

"Cool down, Elysium. We're all insane."

The wonder of the world around us held me hypnotized. I found shapes alive in the trees; their wood spirits must exist in the mountains. Sacred fish must swim in the river. Uncle Cane Toad had a smirk across his face as he chuckled away to himself and hummed a song. I read his mind. He was engaged in a simple daydream that was then popular: he thought he was one of the Beatles.

We arrived at Wisemans Ferry Primary School and voted absentee with no ill results. No freak-outs, no trauma, no drama. A drop in the ocean for democracy. Once outside, we were again in the trip of dreams.

Time passed. We were back in the magic garden where there was a freak with a bamboo staff who thought he was Moses the lawgiver about to cross the Red Sea. Lost in our dreams, we sat exhausted around the fire as night fell. For hours we discussed slanderous innuendos and the derogatory comments of the trip. Magic told us about her bad trip. Elysium told the freaks to get fucked and split the scene, while I just smiled and thought what a glorious trip it was. Soon, exhausted by the conversation, we each slowly slipped away to the farmhouse to go to sleep.

Day dawned.

I thought, *Where the hell am I?* I smacked parched lips, wet a dry throat, and blinked potato-spudded eyes. Wisemans Ferry. Yawn and teeth glitter in the early morning light. I felt terrible. "All right, who smells bad? You Melbourne maggots stink." I caught a whiff of Elysium and nearly died.

"Elysium, did you bring my deodorant?"

"Hippies don't use deodorant," she replied.

Well, then I dragged her naked body out from under the blankets, swept her up into my arms, carried her out to the river and threw her in. I followed. "Now wash it out."

"You do it for me, Sphere."

"Okay, you multi-orgasmic creature!" Soon the whole crew were wildly masturbating in the river.

Then the elderly farming couple busted us.[7] Wasteland walked out of the river with an enormous erection, to be faced with a double-barreled shotgun pointed at his belly. He screamed, "Don't shoot it off!" and plunged back into the river. Six heads bobbed in the river.

"Get out!" the farmer ordered. His wife turned around to avoid our naked bodies. "Get dressed," he said. "I want a little talk with you. What in the blanky blue blazes are you doing here?"

"Who, me?" I stammered.

"Yeah, you."

"Why, I'm having an early morning swim. Nothing harmful, just cleansing water and fresh air."

"Bullshit," he said. "We're getting the police. You can do your explaining to them."

"Play it cool, friend, you don't want to do that. We're just passing through. Our kombi broke down and we had to stay the night here."

Uncle Cane Toad had a smirk on his face as he chuckled away to himself. He muttered under his breath, "My first bust, glory of glory, we'll make the papers."

"You warped bastard. Someone get the insect spray and blow this cat away! This is a job for Supergrovel. To the rescue, girls!" The girls wheedled, pleaded, and begged the farmers not to ruin their vaginal reputations and when Wasteland broke down into sobs, the farmers couldn't handle it.

"Okay, you can go. But don't come back—and first, give us your addresses." We gave false addresses, which is pretty slick for bail-jumpers. We got our gear and drove off into eternity. Definitely a good day's groveling.

"Home to the record machine, Wasteland, you sniveling sly bastard!"

4

I love to change my mind. You should try it.   Elysium Dream

I do it all the time. You should see my dreams.   Sphere

Days passed and it began again. The kombi, the cassette, Baron Wasteland at the wheel, destination Wisemans Ferry. The trees flashed past. The sun landed momentarily on me and then was gone, and then was here, and then was gone. Like the flickering of pictures, it was right for daydreaming and I swallowed the mushrooms as we drove. We stopped by the creek in the gorge and wandered from the kombi, singing softly.

I stared at the pool. I crouched over it, a rock, a god, a dream watching the swirling of waters on the smooth stones underneath.

The clean, clear, pale blue water surged through the rock-pool. Here was peace and quiet. Here was enough to wash a man's sins away. Here was the beginning of life where the vegetation could breathe the forest air. Here was a time without time. I had never felt this good as I watched and listened to the slowness that touched the world. The forest sentinels guarded this holy place. The intruder was not one. He came up to me talking of wisdom: *To have wisdom you must have a fool.* I escaped from the adrenaline surge. Could man be this disturbed? His inventions haunted me. There were no questions here. *Find a particular man and you could have all the answers that you desire, but not here . . .*

I staggered back to the kombi to escape the voice and while lighting a cigarette my mind and hand went numb as I blacked out in a psychotic attack. The cigarette dropped unnoticed onto a blanket, which caught fire. When I awoke there were tripped-out people running everywhere. *Where's it coming from? Is it a dream?* Suddenly I realized the blanket I was sitting on was smoldering. In a frenzy I staggered from the car.

> *Here is the hallucinogenic mushroom. Here is the black hole of the abyss. There lie your dreams. There lies your life. There lies paradise. There lie the mountains you traveled so far to see. There, over there, by the riverside.*

Staggering away from the kombi, I felt sickness well up in my head. Shock, fear hit me straight between the eyes. I thought I might vomit in horror: disease, infirmity, ages of suffering ending in the birth of violence. The black weight of adrenaline surge. I thought, *I'm freaking out.* The juxtaposition of the images of hate and death caused nausea. A billion cells scared. I stood up and blacked out. The bad trip.

It will soon be over. It's not real.

I got up.

It's only in your head.

I staggered back to the kombi, my body bathed in emotional sweat.

It's not real, nothing is real, real is real. It is not real.

Battling, I became a kaleidoscope and then abruptly I came down from the nightmare.

I thought to myself, *Bummer, another bad trip.* I was diseased, that was the only answer. Sick in the head. I couldn't handle the mushrooms, so maybe my salvation lay elsewhere. All things in the mind belonged to me. I had to get back to how it was before, but I had forgotten. The flames and the screaming. How did that melody go? My identity was drug oriented now. My mind accelerated with pictures that made earth strange. Life was too much. It was a contradiction. That was one explanation. This foreign insanity. Who is acid? What is the prime cause? More questions for the Elysium mind.

"Elysium," I called. "Who controls the extension of the central paradox of this kombi? Is it three-dimensional with theta emissions that lead to a multidirectional code and associated microcosms, or is color vision finally coming to town? Two plus two equals lies. A science-fiction nightmare being driven insane by a mind hysterical with the normal." I held on to the truth till, curled in a ball, sleep overwhelmed me. "A bad trip, mate, into infinity. Take it from me, eating mushrooms is the last resort."

Touching distracted as Elysium rocked me in her arms and told me, "It's all right . . . "

5

If you want to be beautiful, look into a mirror.

Rainbow Moonfire

Alone, the changeling twins drove to the Ferry, found some mushrooms, and then drove till they came to a hidden valley where they had once found bliss before, with its silent creek and bellbirds' song echoing in the space. It seemed that I had found us an ideal place to trip. We dropped the last of the mushrooms, sat on the Nepalese blanket and talked.

"Elysium, what's it like being a woman?" I asked.

"It's shit. I'll tell you, Sphere, because I love you. You understand and I trust you. You know that Magic is my cousin. We grew up together and in our adolescent years we loved each other's bodies. We're bisexual. I'm turned on by pictures of naked women. We love who we are and we are women. I want you to understand that. I'm not turned on by pictures of naked men. The mystery of women is that we do not need you. We love each other. I can get a man any time I desire. Men are sex deviants and psychos. So are women, but we know what mother nature is and we can live in harmony with the earth. Man dominates and tears up the earth. He changes it to his own desire and finally destroys everything. The trip of women is to find a man who will not rape and keep her image in fear but will look after her, know and accept her. We love to control foolish men. We're looking for mature, intelligent men in harmony with themselves. We want to be entertained and then loved and cared for. A woman's emotion has got it all over man's intelligence but unfortunately man does not like to lose, so he fights. He fights everything. He gets drunk and doesn't grow up. He's a fool. I'm a fool. I love you because you're shy and you still know the trip. You integrate my dream into your life. You make me laugh and forget my pain. I love you because you admit confusion about the drugs. If you never hurt me I will always love you.

"I answered your question, now answer mine. What's it like being a man? Do you really love?"

"Yes," I replied, "we do fall in love. Man is the biggest romantic in the world. But still, it's a bad trip if you don't follow the leader. People put you down if you're different. There are many sadists in this world and they'll tear you down if you don't stand up to them. You want to know the secret of man's love? He has to masturbate. Every four days his sperm matures and it has to be replaced. He can have crazy wet dreams, or masturbate, or love a woman. We're programmed for love. To me sex is love. It's one man's secret society.

"You know, I never knew that women have a clitoris and a G spot till you told me and then when I tried to find it you explained that the area around it is sensitive. You didn't laugh at me. Thank you. I'm sensitive all over. Just now I noticed that you're a very pretty woman but remember, *pretty* rhymes with *shitty*. You're a very shitty woman."

Elysium smiled. "It also rhymes with *witty*. There's no vaginal orgasm." I got out a deal and rolled a number. Elysium began to rattle on. She asked, "Do you want to know how I got the name Elysium Dream?"

"Okay," I said.

"Elysium is Greek for heaven. Anyway, the Aborigines believe there is a valley of heaven and dreams somewhere in Australia. You must get to it through a secret tunnel and you can go through the tunnel a million times and still never find the valley of creation, but if your mind is pure enough you can find an exit that leads to a garden in the valley. There is a crystal spring there with waters of illusions and if you drink the water you can read the minds of men. There is the dreaming tree with fruit that can change you back to a child and if you drink the dew on the petals of the dream flower, you can change sex and become a woman of wisdom with feeling that can create the life and death wish into becoming one dream. At the end of the valley is a land that exists outside of time where the flowering garden of life exists and there is the dream of God. A giant opal. The origin of heaven.

"The Aborigines believe that a black snake somehow found its way into the valley and fractured God's good dream and replaced it with his own nightmare and that is the reason the earth is a nightmare, except in the valley with its close proximity to the fractured opal. We live in the nightmare of God's dark sleep with the opal his mind of perfection.

"The valley of dreams exists in your own mind and it is the progression from a fractured opal. You create heaven in your own mind and can live in the serenity of your own creation. The dream flower doesn't exist except when it grows on the vagina of a woman. It is a journey to the cunt tree. My clitoris and your penis. The crystal spring is your urine, now polluted. The dreaming tree is your body and its fruit is your mind. The valley is between my breasts and I am a woman who wants what she can see and touch. I can ride you and be inside of you. I want to ride you as long as I can."

She reached down, her hand slid inside my jeans and she fondled my penis. "You see, you have something where I have nothing." She directed my hand inside her jeans to her vagina, which I stroked. "You see, I have nothing. I want to go sperming in you. I dig your penis and scrotum, Sphere."

Unzipping her fly, she took my hand and began to rub herself slowly with it. She unzipped my jeans and as I wriggled up her body she used my hand till we joined. The trip was on and I was Elysium, then I was myself, then I was Elysium Dream, then Sphere, then her life as a woman, then I grew into a baby, boy, man who felt that her love was mine. Her vagina, my penis was me, then I was her and then we reached union and love's biology flowered and blossomed into karmic endless dream in my body and mind that drifted and eddied into heavenly bliss in my aura of strange pleasure. Let it flow forever. We parted slowly, my glued penis slowly, sensitively coming out of her, with infinite maya in our minds and transcendental love for each other.

"Elysium, you possess what I don't possess. You said it before. Where I am hard you are soft and where I am gentle you are strong. We are love's union. We complement each other. We are the twin forces of creation. The fields of Elysium and the night-mares of creation. We're positive and negative force-fields which let us live energetically in this world of hell. Elysium Dream, I love your pain and I want to take away that pain."

Elysium spoke: "I had a baby when I was fifteen but it was adopted out. I had an orgasm when she was born. The father was your cousin and that is one of the reasons I love you. It was in the days when you could buy a matchbox of grass for five dollars. I'm quite crazy and I can talk the feathers off a parrot, but Sphere, you're a great wanker too. Anyway, I'm going to have a swim. Coming in?"

"No, I'll watch for sharks."

"Freaky."

The magic stillness came on and I was silent in the trip. I got up and watched her. She shouted to me, "I had my first orgasm when I was five years old. Beat that, wank!"

"No, I can't beat that, you bastard," I shouted back.

Her glistening body, taut and erect, tanned by the weather, stood naked and proud in the crystal flowing waters. She smiled as she remembered the past love given to her. Her lips slowly parted as she sighed, inhaled like a dog. She was an Alsatian. A big smile filled her lips as she lifted and tilted her head to the right. Her eyebrows were slightly raised in an enigmatic quirk. Clenching her fists, she placed them on her thigh.

"You know," I shouted, "I don't want to say it but you've got a beautifully shaped body. It's sexy, sex, sex." I could feel it reflected in her mind. Our eyes touched. I smiled and loved her. I was very happy. I waited on the beach, naked to the waist, with my feet in the sand. My old green jeans hid my nakedness. Looking at her from head to where her legs disappeared into flowing waters, I was amazed at her loveliness. Breasts of milk and honey. I kept my thoughts to myself: *You've got a beautiful vagina, Elysium, with soft fur. I'm a lecherous old fuddy-duddy and if the mountain won't come to Mohammed then the dreamer will go to the mountain.* I smiled and loved her. I was happy. I waded into the water. My toes gripped the smooth granite and the cold mountain air washed through my mind. I walked like a man. I loved like a man. I am a man. I reached her and looked down at her. I am her. I said nothing.

She said, "I'm getting cold."

I smiled while reaching down and slowly unzipping my fly, uncurling the monster. "Exercise more," I said.

It hung out. I held it in my hand. Shy, pale, slightly shriveled, and with its matted black hair, it had a hidden beauty. It had the lovely soft pink pastel color of recent erotic pleasure. My lovely, sensitive penis. The black snake.

Simultaneously we smiled. She shrugged her shoulders and we both started to giggle. Reaching out, I gently placed my hands on her shoulders to steady myself. Taking it as a cue, she reached out, put her hands on my waist, sank to her knees and put her mouth over my sleeping member. Her tongue flicked as she sucked up and down without biting. She gently chewed while moving backwards and forwards, stretching, enjoying and trying to give pleasure to me, getting pleasure herself. She had told me before that she wished she had a penis, her own penis to love, excite, and fondle. Secretly I wished that I had a clitoris on my penis head to really give me pleasure. We were both crazy. We looked so young and natural with clear skin and bright eyes, but appearances can be deceptive. We lusted after the flesh. We dug sexual abuse till it burned.

I sighed as my mind swirled in the mushroom trip. I was being aroused. The blood flooded my phallus and it jerked and began to swell and half-stand. Time for a screw. I gripped her under the arms and raised her up. The penis slipped out of her mouth. Letting go of her arms, my hands fell to her waist and she looked up, disappointed. "I love you," she said.

"You don't have to worship me. You're not my slave. Anyway, I don't dig being sucked off. Too many teeth marks. It's a great appetizer, though."

"I know," she said. "You've sunk your teeth into my clitoris on more than one occasion. Your cousin used to force me to suck him off," she said, "and swallow his semen too. I used to gag because of its terrible taste. He had a foreskin with a dry semen taste to it. God, it was awful."

"I'm not my cousin," I said.

She came in closer and wrapped her arms around me.

"I know where to put it," I smiled. "I want to be inside of you." Hugging each other, we laughed at the sky while she made an obscene gesture.

"Let's get out of here," I said. "Do you want to go home?"

"Yeah, I'm cold. Sure you don't want to fuck me again? I've got an itchy clitoris."

"No, don't talk like that. We're civilized creeps. I don't know where you got that from but I don't like a girl swearing. I don't dig it when we're tripping. Shit, we don't live in a garbage can."

Casually she took hold of my penis and led me from the water. Lifting her thighs high, she splashed out of the creek. I followed obediently behind as she gently squeezed and relaxed her grip. It looked as though, whether he liked it or not, this man was going to be milked. Collapsing on the sand, she spread her legs. Hoo, boy! You ever seen anything like that? My mouth just watered at the prospect.

"Do you mind if I lick you out?" I asked.

She nodded. I dropped to my knees, wrapped my hands around her thighs, and buried my nose in her thatch. Opening her outer lips, I began to move inside and outside of her and before you could say "she washed herself" I had an eager and waiting erection. Slowly I moved to the top of her slit as my tongue sought her clitoris. Like a cat at a dish of milk, my tongue slid in and out. She moaned and moved. Nothing but two bloody animals, but she's my kind of woman. She knows what she is. She's not afraid to play with herself. I like to play with her tender red steak surrounded with moist hair.

I let go of her steak as it got too damp and, rising, I unbuttoned my jeans, which slid around my ankles. Placing my hands on either side of her, I crawled up her body. Kissing her mouth, I reached down and grabbed my member, directing it in the general area. She was wet and large and I slid right in. I let the fact that I was deep inside her seep into my brain. Slowly at first we moved. We moved in and out and up and down. She wrapped her legs around me. She clutched my buttocks as we both tried to quench our appetites. She moaned. A little slower, and I started to slow down and stop. I was worn out.

I stopped. "I'm sorry," I said.

"You should have kept your mind on sex," she said. "Anyway, tripping usually cuts down the sex drive."

I lay on top of her, rivulets of water and sweat flowing between her breasts. She caressed my back and tenderly played with my spine. I rolled off her and lay beside her on the sand while she masturbated, her eyes on my penis, and soon she moaned in orgasmic shudders.

Satisfied, quiet and fulfilled, we rose to our feet. Tenderly, she took hold of my penis and, starting from the base, she squeezed and pulled the skin till a teardrop of semen was expelled from the tube. She dabbed her finger in it. It stretched like elastic and snapped. Bending down, she washed her finger in the stream. Walking further out into the stream, she stood half-submerged in the water. Using both hands, she cleaned out her vagina. I stood, hypnotized, on the beach, watching her, proud to be a witness to the sight. Turning away, I pulled up my pants.

"Come on, sexpot. It's time to go. The mushrooms are not potent. I usually can't stand being touched while tripping."

We walked side by side back along the creek. I was dreaming of what the future would hold for me and this woman. We knew each other, we lived together, we loved together, and we were having a good time together. I hadn't been this happy in a long time. We had plenty of destiny. If we played our cards right, we could reach the stars in this beautiful generation and never come down in a million years of rolling eternity.

A million years passed and the trip was on:

> *Then the Lord God said to the snake: "You will be punished for this; you alone of all the animals must bear this curse: From now on you will crawl on your belly and you will have to eat dust as long as you live.*
>
> *I will make you and the woman hate each other; her offspring and yours will always be enemies. Her offspring will crush your head and you will bite their heels."*
>
> *. . . Then the Lord God said: "Now the man has become like one of us and he has knowledge of what is good and what is bad. He must not be allowed to take fruit from the tree that gives life, eat it and live forever."*
>
> *So the Lord God sent him out of the Garden of Eden and made him cultivate the soil from which he had been formed.*
>
> *Then at the east side of the garden, he put four living creatures and a flaming sword, which turned in all directions. This was to keep anyone from coming near the tree that gives life.*

GENESIS 3:14–24.

6

The battle between life and death has been fought since the beginning of creation.   **Baron Wasteland**

Rising from the dead, I checked out the scene. I got out my disguise. I would wear my red Superman suit today. The rains had fallen with the night. The day was alive with sunshine, fresh air, and the whistling of birds. The sky was a serene blue with white wool clouds in a feather-spring breeze. It was a day to sit in the sun and listen to the music of bygone times. It was another splendid day in the great dream. It was a day when we would again go and search for the goldtop mushrooms that grow in the fields near Wisemans Ferry. The Buddha would point his silent, contemplative way. The villages of Christ were on a further horizon. Socialist politics ruled civilization throughout Australia.

I sat on the front seat with Uncle Cane Toad driving us along at a sedate speed. Baron Wasteland reclined on the back seat with Elysium Dream and Rainbow Moonfire. Five longhairs out to enjoy the country and sunshine. The crystal sweat on my hand glistened in the warm sun as I passed the joint to Uncle Cane Toad, who took the number and kept on driving. I loved being in the car listening to the cassette as my mind wandered on in a golden age. You won't laugh if I tell you how childish I am? I was dreaming that I was a great rock musician, creating images to the music, playing with them for a while and then moving on to another mind-game that my thoughts developed into a different realm. It is a childish game, but my other self was on stage. I am Sphere.

Staring ahead at the glazed bitumen road, my internal emotions had been building up for some time. I slowly released the plug and then all of a sudden I let it whoosh out. The car was filled with shuddering vibrations, complete with pungent odors.

"Oh God!" Elysium said as she frantically wound down the window. "Mate, you're crude, rude, and undesirable. A veritable fucked-out head. Was that necessary?"

With a smirk across my face and showing the faded fangs, I said, "I don't want to feel uncomfortable, mate. I just want to be who I am. Let me be who I am. Maybe I should have sucked it up, but I didn't."

Silence.

Elysium said, "*I* am who *I* am. I've got my likes and dislikes, and that is how it is. I'm not a fascist who gasses people and subjects others to antisocial behavior. Control is the word for today."

"You're a pig," Moonfire said.

"Yeah, I'm sorry. It's just that I want to be as natural as possible. I've always been an animal and it's hard to change my philosophy."

Baron Wasteland said, "Suck it up, Sphere."

Frank Zappa and the Mothers of Invention played from the cassette. I was distracted and then mesmerized by the music as my feelings went higher and crashed into a swirling dream. Raising my voice above the noise of melodious insanity, I said, "I dig Frank Zappa's time signatures, mate. He's a man seeking perfection in imperfection. I especially dig his psychedelic blues. I admire Frank because he changes so much. He sees right through civilization's hypocrisy; he's got the craziest band of plastic chrome-haters the world has ever spawned and his music shows up the blatant contradictions of society. It's brilliant. He's a genius. He's an insane megalomaniac who's not afraid to say, "'Hey look, I'm different and I don't dig your shit.'"

"Maybe he'll destroy us all."

"He doesn't smoke dope and he's dead against it because it makes him lose control. He's actually a conformist making us all into little Frank dolls."

"We all conform, mate," said Wasteland. "We're a school of fish changing directions uniformly with the currents of time. Zappa is one of the cosmic fishermen and we're caught in his net. Jesus, Einstein, Darwin, Zappa, et cetera, will get us all yet. You're in my cosmic time net sucking up to the universal wheel. I dig saying farout fuck things like that!"

"Maybe together they will destroy us all?"

"We're never free of the past."

"Good hash," Elysium said.

Rainbow smiled. "Yes, my good fellows, it dements the imagination and drives the dreams wild."

"Is it our good karma coming back on us?"

Silence.

Cane Toad changed down gears as we arrived at the hairpin bends of Wisemans Ferry. The car sped past the police station and the old church hall and came to rest on the ferry ramp on the banks of the Hawkesbury River. The river is wide and muddy with a slow movement that carries it past the town of Wisemans Ferry, which lives in its own river valley, flanked by sandstone cliffs and rugged bush countryside. The town has a hotel with its own ghost, a wooden church hall, a milk bar–general store, a police station, a garage, and a few houses and cottages for the local denizens. It is a meeting place and branching place for roads and rivers that go and flow to even quieter towns. We watched the farmers as we inspected their rich paddocks, cursed the water-skiers on the river for the confounded noise, and shook our fists at the Sunday-bloody-drivers who were taking in this quiet location and this bright dew-spangled morning. Surrounded by bush, orchards, and cattle, we sat in silence and observed the scene. A place between places with no industry—just its good soil and picnic areas. Wisemans Ferry, set in the Australian countryside, is a special place for me and after I make peace with my age I will return to live there and live a good life with my eternal god by being a natural man. Someday, if the cards are willing, I will be a farmer. A cosmic farmer of the hallucinogenic mushroom.

The Devil will be proud of my illusions because, as he knows, in the fertile fields where the cattle graze grow the magic mushrooms. There are two varieties nurtured by the cattle dung. There is the goldtop mushroom that looks like an ordinary mushroom except for its shiny gold skin, while the other variety is fragile, with a long thin stalk. The goldtops and blue moonies. The magic mushrooms. The gates of eternity. Some say that if you break the stalk of the mushroom you can tell its psilocybin potency by the richness of the blue oozing juice. We began using them early in the 1970s, finding ourselves, after a very long, institutional journey through the school system, in the diverse society of Australia. The wonder contained within the mushrooms took over and we went for our lives. The concussion had begun.

Hallucinogenic mushrooms can make you very quiet and attuned to life as the psilocybin—the hallucinogenic substance in the mushroom—stops the thought processes and heightens your feelings; but if anything upsets you, a struggling mind emerges with runaway, confused nightmare-thinking which automatically reacts to the root of the problem and if it can't relate, it breaks down into delusions: fear, anxiety, confusion, and, ultimately, insanity, where the mind tries to adjust by inventing its own solutions, where it hopes to escape the pain. The bad-tripper lives in his own head and therefore mind-fucks everyone else. The poor fool can't see the truth and that's a bad psychological trip. He should externalize and freak everybody else out. You've got to be careful who you trip with.

"What are you thinking?" Elysium asked.

"Most probably bullshit," Wasteland remarked.

"I was thinking that the vast majority don't buy the trip. Most people are opinionated bigots who can only observe their own private ego environment. They don't realize that they condemn themselves with their own backbiting gossip. They are self-centered, ignorant pigs fighting for their own slice of the pie."

"We only criticize what we don't like in ourselves," Elysium replied.

"Yeah, we only see our own minds. I'm an opinionated pig, fighting for a slice of the pie, trying to get you to take my side in the war of intellect. It's a battle of twits. You agree that we'll be playing that greed game forever. If only you could read my mind, you'd find out what a shithead I really am. I'm straight with you four, though. I am who I am. I speak from my heart with no forked tongue, but others play me for a fool because I believe in the life wish."

"That's original," said Elysium.

"We're a little band trying to find our own identity in a land that still believes in playing football, golf, cricket, and surfing. We were raised on competition and we need the exercise."

"We're a band of fools trying to outdo each other."

"Is there any solution?"

"I don't know."

"Give up football."

"I'd like to give up going insane, because I don't know the rules anymore. Society has sent me insane and you, my friends, have made me afraid to be myself."

"We're a band of backbiters."

"You have to backbite, otherwise people get out of control."

"Yeah."

"I want to get out of this trip, but I've gone too far."

"I hope you four make it when I kill myself, because I'm not responsible. We're all on our own when the trip comes on."

"The four of us have felt more pain than most other people. They say we've got no brains, but I know we've only got pain."

"If I wasn't hurt so badly I wouldn't be here. With all our far-out talk, we're the garbage of society."

"We're the ones who didn't make it and that's why we get along so well and why we will most likely die together. We're on a downhill trip and nobody is going to save us. Deep inside we want to die."

"You may want to die, but I don't. I'm just enjoying myself, mate."

"Me, I'm going to raise a tribe of kids."

"Fucking breeder."

"It's not the breeders, mate, but capitalists who hoard wealth."

Elysium tickled my neck and said, "How about a baby, kid?"

"I think we're fools pretending to enjoy life."

As the ferry approached from the opposite shore, I cured some hash and sprinkled the warm crumbling Afghani onto tobacco held in a Tally-ho paper. Mixing it up, I rolled it nice, being sure not to roll it too tight or too loose. I lit it up and breathed in the sweet-smelling smoke, then handed it to Cane Toad. We drove on to the ferry, ignoring the NO SMOKING sign. We were not particularly antisocial, just a wee bit stoned and didn't know where we were. I got out of the car and strolled on the deck of the ferry. The old familiar ferry chugged under my feet and the fresh air was invigorating. I could almost live in the wind like a willy wagtail. I was afraid of the people on the ferry and didn't want to be engaged in a conversation on another plane, a different level from the one that was going on inside. I always lived inside and it was crazy but that is how I felt, afraid. I got back inside the car and felt secure as we approached the shore.

We left the ferry at the other side of the river and drove along the battered sandstone road that ended at our familiar paddock. We were in luck—as I looked over the fence I saw a bunch of gold-tops just waiting for us. We carefully hopped the fence near the TRESPASSERS WILL BE PROSECUTED sign and, taking it slow, walked towards the cow dung and magic mushrooms. Carefully we nipped the mushrooms out of the cattle dung and they were in our possession. A rich harvest. We climbed back over the fence and divided the mushrooms up on the back seat of the car. Cane Toad turned the car around and drove towards town. I switched on the cassette and, tapping my toes nervously, I stared at my mushrooms as the scenery went rushing past. I picked up a potent-looking goldtop and contemplated the situation.

There was a certain revulsion at eating raw mushrooms, as each was carefully and fearfully devoured. There was a certain awe of the trip. We were isolated in the hum of the car. I studied the mushroom for a moment and then started to chew the goldtop; it tasted like an ordinary, edible mushroom. My thoughts drifted into the music within the cabin of the automobile. The delicate symbol of life now flowed in my veins. We were still stoned from the hash as we drove back on to the ferry. I alighted from the car and my long hair blew across my face into my mouth. God, I felt good, never let it be over. I felt peace in this place, let me exist in these moments forever. My hair streamed outwards in the breeze. I shook my head and my red Superman cape, which I wore on special occasions when away from civilization, twisted about me. Then it was over. The love of my life was captured by my imagination and then was lost.

I got back inside the car and we drove down the iron ramp on to concrete and then the asphalt road. Past the church and police station. (Lord, I remember the day Wasteland stalled his kombi in front of the police station.) I broke into a cold sweat until the danger had passed. We reached the milk bar. Cane Toad and Wasteland were hungry and it was time, according to them, for a snack attack. I waited in the car, anticipating the approaching trip.

Big greasy hamburgers and imitation-chocolate milkshakes approached the car. Baron Wasteland then went for a couple of cans of beer while Uncle Cane Toad began to munch and gurgle his mid-morning breakfast. Baron Wasteland, an alcoholic since he was fifteen, presently returned with his mid-morning relaxants, his beer belly and shoulder-length hair bouncing as he sprinted the last few yards to the car. Now I won't say Baron Wasteland is fat, but he is chubby compared to the rest of us. He wasn't impressed by the new generation, as he had been influenced by his World War Two digger father in a country town where the only excitement was drinking and knocking up the local girls.

Cane Toad was the real philosopher amongst us, Wasteland the introverted cynic, and I was a little of both: philosopher and cynic, a masturbator extraordinaire. Elysium was a barbarian and Rainbow a half Aboriginal who wanted to destroy herself. We all had long hair and thought ourselves a freaky-looking bunch. The car was turned around to the accompaniment of the Velvet Underground on the cassette.

The mushrooms came on as we drove through the bush reserve between Wisemans Ferry and Sydney and replaced the hashish-stone with crystal vision. The world became diamond clear as trees melted and visions appeared. The colors of the bush were deeper and richer and we once more had the understanding of children. Our purpose in life was expanded and it was good to be alive in shimmering magic. Squirming, glowing sparks danced in the light and our feeling rose and fell on the beach of reasons.

Closing my eyes to contemplate the situation, I saw the universe as black as night with shimmering stars of golden and silver light. The yellow of the sun turned black and red in flickering rays on the void of my mind. The music was clear and the daylight beautiful. I looked out of the glass window and dreamt the road and farms into my head. Suddenly out of nowhere there was a country hayseed with cowshit between his toes selling pumpkins by the side of the road. He was holding a pumpkin up as we streamed past. He had a euphoric grin on his face stretching from ear to ear. What a grinning mouth; the great pumpkin reigns again! In my mind there were colorful flashbacks, visions, heavy sweat, and the car was rocked by insane laughter.

"Mate, this is too much."

"You know, guys, I've been thinking ahead. If I count on picking strawberries for some bread I can get another deal of hash."

"Why do you need another deal?" Wasteland asked. "The free mushroom is at your command. Get mushroom madness and trip on to a far-out path."

"Get real, you fascist! But you might be right, I can't deny the logic."

Cane Toad yelled out, "Superman, hash, smash, we're going to crash! We're all going to die. We're in a time vortex. Hold on tight till we escape its gravity fields. Take the controls, Sphere."

I reached over and took the wheel, steering the hurtling car down the road, as Cane Toad held his hands over his eyes. The car swerved violently.

"Keep it cool, brother!" Elysium yelled.

I thought I'd better bring Cane Toad down. "Let's talk about strawberry picking. I want to go strawberry picking with you and Wasteland next week before the season's end." The statement echoed in my head and I thought, *What an idiotic thing to say.*

Cane Toad took the wheel again, muttering. Danger passed.

"There is nothing to talk about since I last went picking with you," said Wasteland. "You dragged me out of bed at four o'clock to break my back picking the little bastards. Hard labor is not my thing, mate."

"Everything's okay," Cane Toad said. "Passing asteroids now."

"Shit, those are houses, mate. Get your shit together," Rainbow said.

"I could find happiness picking the little red devils."

"Get off the strawberries. You've got a phallic fixation."

"Cane Toad's about to cream us! Get real, you freaks!" Elysium panicked.

Cane Toad spoke. "There was something that I forgot."

"Forget the strawberries, mate," Wasteland muttered. "You drive, Sphere."

"It was something vitally important and it was critical to the survival of mankind as we know it. Our future is in crisis. How's this for being profound? 'The world is a turd and we are its arsehole.' You drive, Sphere."

"That's a shit revelation. I can make up a better revelation than that. How about this: 'There are reasons why we are here.' Now that is profound."

"Why are we here?" Wasteland asked.

"To live out the story that each of us invents."

"We're here to fuck the women," Cane Toad said.

"Fuck off, kid," Elysium replied. "You're out of it."

"Shit," Rainbow said, "you're all too profound."

Cane Toad stuck his head out the window and said, "Mate, this is great. I see death in the clouds and she is beautiful!" The car wandered to the other side of the road on a collision course with another car. I reached over, grabbed the wheel, and jerked us back to the right side of the road as a blaring horn careered past.

"You're in a crazed-out pickle, you know that, Cane Toad? Sphere, you drive."

"Pickle? Careful, I'm driving and tripping. What do you mean anyway? What's this pickle? I'm just digging the trip."

"You're tripping out. It means nothing. Your truth is lies and your lies are negative."

"That means nothing," he replied. "You're not driving. You're too fucked."

"We're all tripping out, mate. Stop the car."

Cane Toad screamed, "Let me out!" and as I struggled to bring him back through the door and steer the car at the same time the auto slowed to a crawl and stalled. "Ran over a hitchhiker. Damn fuckwit's own fault," he explained.

With that, the violence of the trip ended and we were back in the dream.

There were suburban houses by the side of the road by this time and sometimes eye-spinning pretty girls to stop time and stare at. Inside the car we listened to the music and dreamt in time to the song the musicians wove. Cane Toad concentrated on the road, but I was a million miles off the planet. Venus, Uranus, Mars to the asylum because we're on them all.

"You're going good, Cane Toad, but you didn't give way to that car," Wasteland sighed.

"Bummer," Cane Toad muttered.

"You know," I said, "I was once driving along with a mushroom maniac and he thought the road was an artery and we were blood corpuscles. We were driving out of Galston Gorge at five miles an hour with a hundred cars trailing behind blasting their horns. He must have had high blood pressure. I remember looking down that precipice and saying to myself, *God, this is it. My number's up.* Driving out on that crazy road. The driver just kept babbling away about blood corpuscles and arteries. I couldn't shut him up and all he could say was "Dig the artery, man, it's all red." I was covered in sweat and ready to plummet over the edge.

"Good thing is that when *you* lose control, Cane Toad, you only laugh hysterically and let go of the steering wheel a couple of times. You don't drive me insane. It's predictable. Some people are just cool, you know that, Cane Toad? Sometimes it's just too much sweat when I see what's happening around me, and when my head explodes and the world is swept by World War Three I can't handle it. You can drive through a dream and back again. You're a good mate to keep me alive. I can't drive for two bob. You know I crashed the family car twice before they took my license away? I once crashed into the garage. Dream and reality are sometimes too much for me. What was I talking about?"

"Blood corpuscles," said Wasteland.

"Yeah, that trip keeps coming back on me."

"Yeah, people get preconceived ideas of trips," Rainbow said.

"I rehearse them beforehand. I get this flash of a leather-bound book of trips hurtling towards me. I see my trips with my mind. Getting back to the point. How can you drive one of these monstrous machines while tripping? You wheel and deal along the road quite nonchalantly."

"You get into it, mate. There's nothing to it but enjoyment. You know what I mean?"

"Yeah," I said, as a series of symbols, crossroads, and hysteria flashed past. Instinctively I reached for the door to dive out, but I had been here before.

Don't grab the wheel. Stop the car, let me out. If I'm like this, Cane Toad must be just as bad.

My eyeballs were hanging out of their sockets. *Relax,* I thought to myself. *Cane Toad's got good insanity. He's not dreaming. He's got contact with reality. We'll get there. Just sweat it out, mate.*

The car careered down the road and an instant later we arrived home. We walked up the back stairs into the living room to crash and listen to music. We leaned back and let the trip take hold.

My evaluations and judgments of the world were only glances at the truth. So much of it wrong. I lost control of the adjustments. I had to make the river, the girl, the village and sandstone cliffs of Wisemans Ferry and not be confined by four walls. There was heartbreak at a road that goes nowhere. A machine, money, security, a wife, and children were lost to me. My heart went to the country. My mind slipped with the trip.

He died in the dream and no one could tell me why he died. He just died. In that moment the man withered like an old tree and settled down into death. What was death he didn't know. He was tired and worn-out. His discoveries in life meant little to him now. A hollow drum, his pleasures receded into the twilight night that was with him. He welcomed her touch as the last flicker of thoughts played in his mind and he died.

He awoke to find himself alone looking over the holy city that God had built. A beautiful holy city. The gentle mind of God played with his hair. He was naked, at peace, how a man should be, and his mind held contentment. There was no more death, no more suffering, no more mistakes, no more enduring the pain. There was no more waiting. He walked towards the gatehouse. The man smiled at his approach.

"May the lull be with you," he said. "Wisdom, honor, glory, strength, praise, and peace be with you. Welcome to the world of God. Eternity has begun. You are the chosen." Everlasting truth and perpetual beauty. The world of clouds that stretched to infinity. Heaven. I had passed the test of righteousness.

"Can you tell me why I am here?"

"You are here because life grew from death. This is your reward, your destiny, your home. You are uncertain although you will not admit it. You have come from the abyss, the universe, hell. Earth's instincts still cling to you. You wonder if good can come from earth, from ignorance, from rotting vegetable matter, but there was something good there. You once loved a woman and that is your salvation. That woman is here to love you."

"I am sorry, I have felt against heaven. Can I see the real Elysium Dream?"

"Your adjustment is not complete. Wait a moment longer."

I waited a moment and my reverie broke as Elysium opened the door. I raised my head. I had been slipping into a dream. "Anyone for a cup of tea or coffee?" she asked. The others replied and I asked for tea. The mild shock brought me to realize my mistake. Inside of me the talking started again.

"You didn't die, did you?"

"No, it was just a daydream."

"Is any of what you say true, or are you just a pathological liar? These are strong terms, but your feelings have been altered. They have been deceived. You will never find an answer or find rest believing in infantile dreams. You will come close to the secret of the universe, but by the buzz of the cigarette you will be denied. You have come across the first steps of insanity. You will hurt yourself again and again. This is the curse of man. Your life is a contradiction and this is the earth's explanation. Do you understand now how the distortion, violence, and disconnection of your own mind make you greater than you are?"

"No, I do not understand any of this."

"No one who is rejected understands. That is the price of life that reality has chosen. We will not hurt you, because that was never our intention, but you have hurt us, so there is separation to protect the kingdom of heaven from your voice and the chemicals you use."

I awoke a third time and found myself in a sort of secret time temple. I had been altered more than I knew. The daydream parable was lost as all thoughts are lost.

I sipped the hot tea Elysium had placed in my hand. I was apprehensive as I listened to the music. Lately it had been the same monotonous story. The trip going out of control at the conclusion. I wondered if there was something wrong with me. I couldn't see my real self. I made no sense. Elysium Dream could tell me. She could see me. I was becoming more afraid of people. Silence greeted me. The record had finished. The dreams passed.

The sun was setting. I got up and stretched. I wandered outside to see the sunset. The sun cast long shadows on the stones at my feet. I walked and wandered erratically on the sometimes overgrown footpath. A straight line didn't seem to matter. Casting my mind ahead to my parents' home: the Sunday dinner was being prepared. My father would be drinking red wine and my brothers would be watching television. It had been a good Sunday. The fever was still in the evening as the song of the trip brightened the air.

Slamming the screen door, I stuck my head into the dream and then went quietly into the living room. God turned the music machine on to the channel that played urban rock. Not my taste. Superman must live on in Metropolis. The country is my life, contrasted to modern city slickers in concrete echo chambers. They most probably never dug the earth as I knew it. Their trip was indoors, enclosed in commercialism.

"Dinner's ready," Elysium Dream called. The stereo was playing as I sat down at the table. A hamburger and chips lay before me.

"Hoe into it. It's good tucker," Rainbow said.

"No, I'm not hungry. Excuse me."

I made a pot of tea with vacant thoughts in the dream kitchen. I retired to the living room and put on an LP and went straight into a plastic concert. Lighting up a cigarette, I stared at the oil painting on the wall. The ever-expanding Australian economy most probably subdivided it and built houses and roads all over it. That is what happened to our farm. The past is over as civilization expands and expands. I mustn't feel sorry for myself.

In a daydream I consciously remembered the experiences of youth on the farm. It was something that I hadn't done in a long time. Memory analysis consisted of a duck pond, a long-ago broken-down chicken yard, the pepperina tree, and a sunken well. A poor farm in rolling hills with two cows and an abandoned orchard. Colorful impressions came and went in the closing darkness. This had all been replaced by a redbrick house in suburbia, but life satisfied me for one reason or another.

Sphere, you've built a grass fort and your imaginary foe will be attacking you at any minute. One more rock fight and you'll get a thrashing. Wild colonial boy, feed the chickens. You're a charmer, you delight me, son, with your innocent smile and wide brown eyes. Do you know that your mother still loves you, even if you fight in a psychological war? Little Sphere, you're into mischief and filthy from playing in the creek. So Mrs. Green's ram bunted you. Cheer up and have some bread and Vegemite. What are you doing under the veranda in your new cowboy vest? Coo, coo, coo, friends of adventure, money is beer labels. We'll get some tar from the road and patch up our corrugated-tin canoes. The cows are being milked. The butter churn is being cleaned and I'm planting peas in the vegetable patch this spring. Playing in the paspalum grass where the geese lay their eggs. The fence post where you stuck a Wanted poster for yourself. Selling rhubarb that you grew in the garden by the side of the road. All lost, all gone, all remembered. Sphere, your mother is still calling your name . . .

The record had finished. "Elysium, I'm going out to make a phone call." I walked on outside. Where are we going? *It's where we've been before,* my thoughts replied. *Elysium Dream, I want to be alive because then I can love you. I want to go home. It's been a long, strange trip.*

I found the phone booth. "Hello, psychiatric hospital? It's Sphere. I've taken a strange trip."

7

The dream is over, Mama, and the nightmare has begun.

Sphere

They took me away and locked me up in a psychiatric hospital.[8] There were weird people with no brains wearing purple helmets, tranquilized zombies and raving heroin and drug cases, and I was back home again with my nurses and my Abraxas.[9] Dr. Abraxas was good and evil, sadist and masochist, my mentor. He was full of knowledge which he never shared and he took my thoughts and labeled me in a self-fulfilling prophecy.

I didn't know what was wrong. I just couldn't handle it. I was afraid that they would find out my secret and Abraxas was always listening and asking his questions. He gave no replies; he always asked and never gave. So I ate some datura to make me forget and tripped out in the psychiatric hospital. I lay naked outside all night and when I walked in naked to breakfast some nurses locked me in the shower. I don't know. I want no inhibitions. I don't want to be hanged or locked up.

I talked Abraxas into taking some patients on an outing to a nudist beach to release our inhibitions. I dropped some datura and was freaked out on the beach. Some patients had erections and one girl started masturbating in the water. I just dug it on the beach and contemplated a thatch. It was a cosmic curve of a furry blighter. I just wanted to get into it, so I talked to her while she watched the juice slowly ooze out of my potent bean. She just watched it and didn't take her eyes off it. She watched and I was cool and used my imagination. God, I wanted to touch myself but I was cool and it just oozed out and I was cool and I was hot but I kept my composure and oozed on the beach like a blue-ringed octopus.

A month later I was released with a rap on the knuckles and some tranquilizers. I was glad to be out. Psychiatric houses are such bummers.

8

We talk through our music.   Uncle Cane Toad

The trendy duplex welcomed Elysium Dream and me as we blundered in blindly, stoned to the eyeballs: a degenerate Commonwealth clerk with hair three-quarters of the way down his back and an unemployed dental assistant with beautiful firm breasts, but remember: *dental* rhymes with *mental*. "Freak" was written all over us. It was the age of LSD and the psychedelic flower-power scene of the big smoke merged with our innocent, childish ways. Simply, we liked tripping to the colored neon lights of the city and being astounded by glass and concrete skyscrapers. Music became our addiction, while conversation became another dimension. We walked in and out of a dream. The synthetic drug turned normal people into mysterious atomic scientists experimenting in the half-real state of continual trip. A bit of this hashish and a bit of that tripping weed, laced with acid, can blow your mind into beautiful oblivion.

We played dream-games in cannabis psychosis with the mind inundated by Aussie tripping grass and it seemed that everything was going our way. The sun and money and peace caught the sparkling light and I stashed it in my brain. The acid was strong and the grass was vital. My destiny was beautiful.

The paranoia in the city was a natural condition. Nothing was really happening. The changeling twins were lost in a gigantic city, observing the people while never being observed. We walked crowded streets stoned, with the beautiful and ugly people surrounding us. We were in the river that flowed while the wind flowered in our hair and blew our minds into blossomed gardens of cosmic supermarkets. Our minds exploded as we selected groceries into an insane trolley that darted in all directions. Shopping the harvest of creation, we smiled at each other and knew.

On this particular day, we wandered into the living room and found Baron Wasteland, Rainbow Moonfire, Uncle Cane Toad, and Magic Star Flower sitting around twiddling their thumbs as Clapton played from the stereo. There was a depressing atmosphere to the place. Could it be that World War Three had started? The world hadn't been destroyed. I took a chair and anticipated the worst. The day was alive with monoxide air and radio fallout.

"Well, chaps, what's the problem?" I asked.

"Well, if it isn't the psychedelic kids," Uncle Cane Toad said. "Have a good outing?"

"Yeah, we dug it. We've each got a pizza tonight."

"Did you smoke the last of the weed?" Baron Wasteland asked.

"We did," Elysium replied, "but no worries, we've got a crop."

"Not anymore," Rainbow replied. "We've got depression, bad vibes, and noxious karma."

"Do tell," I said.

"Our plantation got busted. We're flat broke."

"You mean to say our crop is no more?"

"That's the story, kids," Wasteland said. "The cops are watching it now to pounce on anyone who approaches it. We can't even get a leaf. The dream is over."

"Have they been around?"

"We didn't get busted. The police haven't been around here."

"Have we any hash?" I asked.

"No," Star Flower replied.

"Can we rip a cheroot from anyone?"

"There is no green anywhere, mate. Some cretins, who shall remain nameless, smoked the last of the weed before they went shopping," said Wasteland. "Get real, you fascists, we'll be going to the Santana concert straight."

"We didn't know the plantation would be busted, mate. It's not our fault. Weed contains vitamins and minerals that are essential for good health. We needed to build up our strength for the shopping. Anyway, I'm stoned," I beamed. "So you won't make the great dream today. That's okay. Combined with sex, marijuana turns grown men into raving lunatics. You don't want to be transformed into monsters, do you? Man is afraid of love, truth, and peace, but digs incest. Smile men, we didn't get busted. Elysium and I have just saved you from your addiction."

"You bastards," Wasteland sneered, "I can't even make sense from you."

Silence, as more seminal fluid is manufactured.

Wasteland sang, "I didn't get a screw in '62."

Rainbow said, "I can't handle boredom."

Then Magic Star Flower started to drivel on: "When man replaces his toys of inebriation with crafts of knowledge, that's the day I'm waiting for. Drugs are not for the sensitive. The more sensitive you are, the higher you go and the further you crash. Turn all the children into veggie freaks, eating soya beans and drinking pure orange juice. Let's go straight."

Wasteland retorted, "What are you babbling about? Nobody here is all aglow about life. It could have been different."

"I'm sick of arguments," she replied. "Can we agree on that?"

"I agree to disagree," Wasteland said. "God will explain everything one day. He just needs time to work it out."

"It's a spaced-out world and we can enjoy it," I said.

"That's crazy philosophy," Magic said. "No wonder I'm half-mad. I'll get a new trip and you, Cane Toad, my love, will straighten out."

"Never," Toad replied. "Love came to me too late. I need to screw around. People who screw around and go through the trip are more mature. I'll take eagles[10] till someone loves me. Then the trip will end. Acid contains a nightmare which I want to control. Sphere and Wasteland are like me. Nobody gave a damn about us. We'll always be looked upon as freaks because we know pain and confusion. They know the psychological war."

"We love you guys," said Elysium.

"You only love us because we screwed around before we met you. The three of us worked it out," Cane Toad replied. "You made us grovel in the dirt for so long till it was too late and then you saw that it was too late so you sugared us. We've got the bread and we've got the trip."

"Will you save me, Elysium?" I asked. "I'm a sex maniac, an immature bastard."

"Not me. You're just a weirdo freak."

"I see what you mean, Cane Toad," I replied. "They're into their own ego trip."

"Yeah, nothing but status seekers," Wasteland muttered.

"Gravy train," Rainbow said. "We can get executives for lovers."

"Go ahead. Sphere, Wasteland, and I were going to commit suicide before you came along. All we love is our pitiful selves. You know how vulnerable we are. We destroy you and you destroy us. Our dreams have merged. I should forget the past, but I can't forget the dirt laid on us."

"This is a heavy conversation," Elysium muttered. "Let's change the subject. You blokes just can't handle being straight."

"Yeah, we can't handle being straight," said Wasteland. "We always take more of the trip than you girls and you are finding out you can't live by our rules. At school, we lived by your rules but now our game is a little rougher and crueller."

"We don't need your shit," said Elysium.

"Get fucked, you runts," I sneered.

We all stared at each other with black hearts and cold eyes. "I'm sorry," Elysium apologized. "I know what you went through, Sphere. You're the boss."

"Yeah, you know what I went through and you understood. Life is meaningless. No children, Elysium, and that is all I ask. I can't escape my mind. I thought acid would make me into a genius but it just drove me crazy. When life has been a nightmare, hemp projects the inner insecurities. I know I'll be locked in a mental institution again. My life wish is flickering. The trip has a steel grip on me. I'd like you to get out of here before it's too late. I do love you, Elysium. I don't want you to die or be driven insane because of me. I was destroyed because of women and do you think you can heal the nightmare? I'm sorry."

"Shush, Sphere. I'm with you. I was destroyed by man and then you came along and made me live again. We won't hurt each other, just fade away together."

"Yeah, let's dig it," I said. "Let's plant an Indian hemp plant and watch it grow. Work is the salvation of mankind. You're not insane. We've just got to watch out for our hatred. Most people see a grand future. Let's join their trip."

"All right, none of us is insane," Wasteland said.

"We're just going a little loopy," Rainbow said.

"Shit, you're fucking insane, Sphere!" Wasteland yelled. "You bastard, nobody wears a woollen Superman suit in summer."

"Me? What about Cane Toad?" I replied. "He wears a crash helmet and leathers while driving."

"I'm going outside," Magic interrupted. "I can't stand this cynicism. You're just loud, foul-mouthed animals."

"Have a beer," Cane Toad said.

"Thanks, I need it," Rainbow replied. "The next person who swears has to pay each of us a dollar. Is it a deal?"

"Okay, it's a deal. No more swearing."

"Let's go see Mind God and Flame Garden," Elysium said.

"All right, forget the beer," Magic replied.

So we got our act together. Cane Toad put his crash helmet on and we drove down the road to Mind's house. We trooped in. "Howdy Mind, mate. Have you got any weed?"

"Me? You're the ones with the grass," Mind replied.

"Our crop got busted," Wasteland explained.

"Bummer. I was looking forward to some cheap grass. How did it happen?"

"We don't know," Wasteland said. "Someone must have found it and reported it to the police."

"Bummer."

"Yeah, it's a bad trip. We loved those marijuana plants. The cops took away our dream."

"Bummer. Yeah."

"We've still got our freedom."

"Yeah, it's still a bummer," Mind God replied.

"I'm angry, really angry," Baron Wasteland said, "and a philosophical attitude is all shit. My feelings are warped. The state had no right to ban our hooch. It's a fucked picture."

"You owe us each two dollars for the bad language you just used!" Magic exclaimed. Wasteland shelled out the smackers.

"Get into panty sniffing," Elysium said. "It can get you high."

"Damn deviants," Wasteland sighed.

"Learn from Tom Foolery," I said.

"My man, you've got bad ideas," Wasteland replied. "Let's get Elysium to give us a strip show. Come on, baby, shake it."

"No thanks, mate," she replied. "If it moves, laugh at it, and if it's dead, it's even funnier."

"Let's get out of this depression," Rainbow said. "The bust hit us harder than we realize." She suddenly jumped up on the table, undid her jeans, and slid them down with her panties. She started to rub herself.

I told the assembly that Elysium didn't like my penis.

"Yeah," she replied. "It's an ugly monster. It's just that I've seen it too many times."

"Let's create a new generation," Magic exclaimed.

"Switch up the record machine," Cane Toad yelled. "Let's just don't get depressed."

At that moment Flame Garden walked in with some Indian hemp. So we got stoned and forgot our miseries. The rugged indoor types. Cane Toad tipped his coffee onto the table and watched the configurations. I fell forward and rested my head on the table. The coffee dripped to the floor and Baron Wasteland started to laugh.

"Get me out of this, mate. I promise to give my penis to science and liberate myself. Anything you want. Do you love my scrotum, Elysium?" I asked. She said nothing.

Baron Wasteland said, "I dig older women because they are real and have something to say."

Elysium said, "I dig older men because they take the time to turn me on."

I said, "I like women my own age because they're not into bullshit, only equality."

"Shell out a dollar to each of us," Magic said. Everybody laughed as the merry men got stoned again. I retreated from the conversation and began to talk to myself and Elysium.

9

History is the tower of fables.   Magic Star Flower

God, I've got to go to work. Struggle out of bed and light a cigarette. Get dressed, catch the ferry, walk the streets into the arcade and up the elevator. The eyelids are prised open with the help of a Camel plain cigarette and the office is off and racing. The weekend fiasco fades into obscurity as I shuffle scattered papers, smile at the girls in the typing pool, and answer the telephone.

"Hello, Sphere here, is there anyone there?" Very wired and strung-out. The voice on the phone replies as I fly into the working week. I brush my hair out of my mouth and face my career.[11] One lunatic careering across the universe.

In my dream I keep it straight. Keep going, kid, because you have only seven hours and fifty-six minutes to go. Yeah, I keep it up. Oh dear, I've got an erection from the titillations of the girls in the typing pool across the aisle. Very uncomfortable but predictable. I get one every day at this time. Blue knickers today. Hee-hee! Very stylish.

Rearrange my attire and get the books. Answer the query and hang up the phone and wait for the next. So my job goes all day long with a buzz in my ear and an answer on my lips. The public service is such a bummer. Work, the curse of mankind.

Elysium would visit me some days and we'd play tennis after work. She became my woman for some strange reason. She digs strange blokes because she's pretty strange herself. Looking like she had just been resurrected from the earth, she was peachy pale like a marijuana plant, her energy revitalized, her mind knife sharp. She was every woman but was nowhere. She lived in her own circle. The wind circle that she could summon about herself that excluded the sexless. Coming out into the open, she would say: "How is it going with the girls?" and I would make the usual reply in the words she had used before: "The ones who talk about it the most do it the least." We'd then fall into a dream and go and play tennis. We both knew that soon we would be arguing and sharing our addiction on the grass while the world threatened to exterminate our existence. She would curse it for both of us, for its cold lack of feeling. The planet never cared for us. It just let us live on its cold revolving rock while I believed our innocence would save us from the pain that huddled in life. We were ready to fight against death's completion. Fighting against that dead rock with a cry of love. The pain which is life's companion would say its piece and the dead rock would watch as life shouted and devoured itself. Crazy Elysium and her mission man were fighting for survival.

Recently the earth had made me afraid. I couldn't tell Elysium I was afraid of her and afraid for her. She had eyes and to talk about my defect in character would have dispelled the illusion, but I chose to hide because I was afraid.

We played our tennis and went home while in my imagination I anticipated Elysium's questions. I have an explanation for everything, even the differences found in men and women. Later that night, entwined together, I said, "Sex is boring. Let's save it up and really explode. Let's do something kinky. How about you get dressed up as my mother and look in my bottom. Can you wipe my bottom?"

"You weirdo freak," she replied. "You've had your fun, so just warm me up and we'll ride into the night." She hopped on top for the choice orgasm position. After riding for a while I turned her over and finished my orgasm off. Later she said, "Sphere, I'm leaving you. I can't stand this life. I need my time and space."

"We've gone too far to stop now," I said.

She replied, "I can stop and I have to stop and I want to stop."

She left me for three weeks and while she was away I realized that I really loved her. I knew it was better this way. A schizophrenic is hard to live with and I was glad and hoped she would find happiness and give up the drugs. But her new life wasn't how she pictured it and next thing she was back. Time passed as once again we fell into the complacency of a monotonous life.

I hit the hot spot and once more we rode. As I went down for a growl I discovered the difference between me and Elysium was that she internalized more while I externalized more. Obviously we had solved our compatibility problem. I just fell in love faster than her. Most men do, I suppose. I love you, Elysium, I really do. You're every woman and my special lady, honey.

10

I'm in search of reality.   Elysium Dream

"Why do you want to be a drug addict?" I asked.

"I was right against drugs in my younger days," said Elysium. "I was taught that drugs destroy your life, but when I tried them and didn't die I caught on to the trip. Maybe I've got a secret death wish."

"We're both in a psychedelic straitjacket. Hallucinations inspire and scare hell out of me. I want to go into clearer and higher visions. I want to discover something that will make me famous. I want to spin you out in the fields of Elysium. I want to give you magic."

"You'll never discover anything or any great answers. It's all been said and done before."

"I'm sure acid holds a great secret. If only I could discover its power. I want to write a book about it. The power of the dream. My quest to be someone is driving me up the wall. I can't get to sleep at night unless I'm completely out of it."

"I love you, Sphere," she said. "It's getting late. Good night. Your daydreams are your creativity." Ten minutes later, after several restless turns, I got up and went to the refrigerator for a feed. I ferreted out a cucumber and some garlic bread and ate at the kitchen table until the death blues vanished. I finally fell asleep, slumped on the table.

Day dawned on a beautiful world. The sun said 6:45. Roll away the stone and rise from the dead. I lit up a joint in the bathtub as Van Morrison crazed out from the cassette. Walked naked to the living room with a reefer of fragrant sticky Aussie heads, and a glass of milk and a banana. Mood happy. I took an agreeable look down the road past lovers lane and, feeling like a child, I stuck my head out the window and yelled: "Marijuana!"

"Hey, pleb!" I was called a pleb by the alderman next door as he raked the leaves on his lawn and I didn't even know what it meant. Bloody marvelous, an innocent child of autumn. I retreated from a certain bust and decided not to disturb the peace of the morning. Choosing a fine-looking head, I systematically broke and crumbled the fragrant mass of leaves, flowers, and stem into the evening newspaper. Crazy. I mulled the weed a second time and sticking two Tally-ho papers together I sprinkled the green evenly along the hollow. Another lovely added to my morning repertoire. More lovely dreams of life.

Whacko-the-dillyo! This is the life. I laughed. This stone has no beginning and no end. I'll be insane forever. After a crazy flashback I recovered my composure. Time to get back to Buttercup.

I walked into the room and yelled: "Rise and shine, crazy legs!" She groaned and rolled over. She was cool but this was for her own good. This was the way to get her out of bed. "Wake up, tulip, like it's a stoning day." I flashed a stupid smile and said, "Don't you want to hop out of bed, touch and twiddle your tootsie toes, and get stoned, bumpkins?"

"Get lost, creep."

I felt real enthusiasm. I felt the life force of the morning. A great inspiration: I'd wake up the rest of the neighborhood with Wildman Fisher. Baron liked his music loud and his hair long. I retired to the living room, turned the volume control up full, and spun the disc. Wah-wah echoed down the hall.

There were shrieks of agony, running feet and gnashing teeth. I thought they were going to string me up. No sense of cool or camaraderie. *An Evening with Wildman Fisher* is a great way to start the day. I had better remember not to play Janis Joplin and maybe for future reference I should put on a cloak of depression and steal around the house with silent goodness and sweetness—but that wasn't my bright-eyed, bushy-tailed scene. Morning is the best part of the day. "Get up, you little fart-arsed slut, Elysium."

Saturday morning, so I rolled a couple more nuclears, put a record on, and wandered out to the porch and, cripes, the alderman from next door approached, shaking his fist at me. These busy days are going to destroy me. Back inside, I lit incense, sprayed underarm deodorant around the room, and covered the smoking dope on the table with a newspaper. Now get in contact, he's coming up the stairs and soon he'll be at the door.

Knock knock.

I'd face the insane blighter alone with my marijuana delusions. I knew he hated me. I'm a paranoid bastard. Maybe if I lie on the floor he might think we're not at home. Get off the floor, you fool. I sprang to my feet and chuckled.

Knock knock.

You're overreacting, kid. It's not the law.

Knock knock.

I opened the door and slowly said hello, chuckled a chuckle and rolled my eyes.

"Mr. Sphere," he sternly replied. "I could hear that rock and roll garbage halfway down the street."

"We like music nice and soft, sir. We're into nature's harmony," I replied.

"Not good enough," he said. "I'm going to phone the police. And, kid, put some clothes on before they arrive." And with that he turned and stormed off.

Shit a turnip, he meant it! The coppers are going to arrive and bust the lot of us. Make your play quick, kid. I slammed the door and like greased lightning I flew across the room into the bedroom and got dressed. My hands shook as I did up my shirt. I began to hyperventilate. I felt sick. No time for being sick, first clean up the living room. I quickly cleaned up the situation and had another legitimate excuse for another number. The danger had passed, and with my memory gone, I lit up a reefer and started talking to myself. Drawing in some smoke I started coughing and reached for the water glass as my lungs were giving out on me.

I remembered the day we moved in and the alderman wanted to get acquainted. I had just finished my morning marijuana when, surprise of surprises, there was the alderman from next door with his wife and a fruitcake. At the first knock the pipes were hidden away behind the rubber plant and the coffee table was covered with the evening newspaper. I sprayed the room with deodorant and answered the door. The alderman explained that he was the welcoming committee for the neighborhood. We sat down for a pleasant chat. They talked about local politics. They told me how the previous tenants had turned over a bunsen burner while making LSD and burned the top section of the house.

"You're not into drugs?" he asked.

"No," I said, "we're nice people." I then noticed Baron Wasteland's sign on the wall, which the alderman was reading: THE SADISTS, A HERO AND HEROIN BAND. There was a prolonged silence.

Then the alderman said, "I've got to go and clean up my backyard, so hooroo."

I said, "Yeah, fuck off."

The alderman didn't take to me after that and he used to watch me on the porch. Sometimes we'd open the windows and let the marijuana smoke blow down the road and over his backyard and he was just waiting to bust us. Captain Beyond played from the stereo. I took another draw of Indian hemp and got down to some serious delirium tremens. Imagine, he might retaliate tomorrow morning with a tape recording of Frank Sinatra. How boring. I finished the reefer and waited for the police.

Knock knock.

The police arrived with the alderman. He wasn't lying. Instantly, I broke into a sweat while my mind became a kaleidoscope and my legs gave out from under me. I took a sip of tea and nearly heaved up. The deal of grass was stashed in my underpants. Well, this is it, lad, there is going to be a showdown. I walked in soggy shoes to the door.

"Hello, sir," I said, "won't you come in? Lovely day."

"I've received a complaint, shit-freak," the copper growled, "that you smoke Indian hemp and have wild orgies here."

"Not us, sir," I replied. "We're just normal working men and women."

"Well, I'll have to search the place," he growled again. "I've got a search warrant in my pocket."

"Can I see it now, sir?"

"No," he growled.

His partner pushed past me and began to ransack the living room. He then went into the bedroom and freaked the others out. The poor devils weren't expecting a copper at nine in the morning. The alderman just smiled in the background.

After turning the place upside down and emptying the corn-flakes packet, they were satisfied there were no drugs. "I'll give you some advice," the copper growled. "Don't use drugs."

"Rightio, sir," I muttered. The other five huddled around me, wrapped in blankets and sheets.

"See you, sir," Wasteland added, as he closed the door.

Cane Toad walked across the room into the wall. Rainbow fell over her blanket while I sat down on the lounge and hugged myself. Insane again. I've got to get out of this dream. One day, cobber, I hope it will end. I hope so, because I've got an ulcer and nervous tension and I've just got to get out of this weird reality.

11

So you love and trust women. You know, man, we're just as deviant as you are.   Rainbow Moonfire

Our man arrived back with some black triangles. I sucked and swallowed: no taste and no immediate effect. The insanity would arrive later. Timing it right, the LSD special came on strong and overtook the confusion of marijuana and gave us greater awareness without the rabble of words messing and echoing in our heads. Suddenly, we became a future race of men and women having nothing but our genuine intellect. It was a time when reality and unreality changed places and somewhere in the cosmos a dream was unfolding. With a savage grin I broke into the conversation.

"Does this dish look like a mandala to you?"

"What's a mandala?"

"It's a circle that represents the universe. Completeness."

"I'd rather eat off it," Wasteland said.

"No, you missed the point. It's just a mandala, something interesting, a circle. Religions are becoming my hobby."

Wasteland picked up the mandala. "Are these hieroglyphics significant?"

"No, mate," I replied, "they're just cracks in the plate."

"What about this piece of potato and tomato sauce stain?" Wasteland asked.

"Get real, Wasteland!" I shrieked.

My introduction to the circle had not gone favorably and I couldn't handle it anymore. My nerves began to crack as I remembered the bad karma I'd just given.

"Where did you find out about mandalas?" Wasteland asked. "Because there is a Mandala Theatre at Taylor Square."

"It was in a book about Jung, the psychiatrist."

"You don't oughta read that garbage, mate," Wasteland said. "The less one knows about mandalas the better, I say. Hear no evil, see no evil, and speak no shit."

Uncle Cane Toad said, "Monkey see, monkey do." So monkey impersonations caught on and it was feeding time at the zoo. I couldn't communicate and went down in a barrel of fear. Phony hippies playing pretend.

"You're reading too many books," Wasteland finally said.

"I read them on the way to work," I replied.

"Work stinks," Wasteland replied.

"Yeah, I see your point. I stink." My whole personality crumbled and, feeling like a fool and going red, I got out of the conversation. Everybody should have a hobby, I thought. You should immerse yourself in all aspects and leave no stone unturned. Wasteland's hobby was tripping. I went inside to my own world, which was under destruction. The words around me meant nothing. I tried to voice my thoughts but they were laughing uncontrollably. I had been distracted by my thoughts and missed the hysteria. I retreated to isolation and didn't want to interrupt the union. It was easier to think about the morality play. I turned my eyes inward, faded out, wobbled on the edge of memory and returned, following the music and conversation to the end, for they were my friends. I was attuned to humanity, with a solitary state of being. The fields wavered and mankind wavered with me. The waves of color flooded my vision. The earth stopped and the earth and mind fused and it was then that I belonged to mother nature. The mandala caught my attention as it shimmered on the table. It was indescribable foolishness but I belonged here in the dream's eternity. The water in the glass on the table was my element, while a spirit deep inside of me wavered hopelessly and helplessly as it wanted to pronounce me but a half-strangled laugh died when another wave of color flooded the room.

The others talked on. What were they saying? I had been drifting off by myself because of the interesting listening of my silver mind. My idiosyncratic shyness could not dominate the conversation so, in fear, it lay dormant. I thought that I had better not say anything anymore. You know the fear of sitting around a table and not knowing what is being said? I needed to get away for some silence. I got up and moved away from the chatter and stared at the chessboard. It was an infinite, indescribable, wonderful game. I externalized.

"Wasteland, do you want a game of chess?"

"Yeah, mate," he replied.

Caught in my own trip, I felt like a genius with slow deliberate moves that dismissed and grasped objects and people. I saw it all in a huge dream. I was attuned, then distracted, then followed chess paths to their ultimate conclusion. There was a particular immensity and then small objects would flow through my mind. Giant visual configurations and then the insignificant parts that man dismisses because of their size. I made my final move. Time had passed. I had swept the board clear in four straight moves. This is it, kid, you've done it, broken the intelligence barrier, discovered the ultimate reality of mind expansion. Pictures in my mind of pure

reason. The ideas behind man's evolutionary mind. The philosophical, psychological game in the twentieth century. A time to change
eternity. Direct contact with the great dream.

The psychology of life's game lay before me. Failure, then cor-
rection to eliminate the pain. Success, then happiness. Life is a
game of vision and action, thought and reaction to the movement
of the dream. Life is a game of war and conquest, of struggle and
fruition of thought's emotions and dreams of purpose and creation.
An eternal triangular spherical square that exists, changes, and van-
ishes. The greatest game on earth is the dream of Sphere. The
game of love and hate that represents all life from the sea to land,
from space to time, from matter to intelligence. The meaning of
yourself. A spiritual, tranquil game of the kingdom in heaven. In
reality a game of pain and aggression, then pleasure, then respect.
Lost in the now, I spiraled out into the madness of perfect silence
and drifted into the future of now and knew that I will have to tell
you all I know.

Silence.

A feeling flashed and I said, "Greatness."

Do anything on the board and it has meaning and is meaningless. It's a slow, steady, balanced walk through personal symbols.
The words and the dreams of knowledge confuse the real object.
The real object is outside while the light is gathering strength. It
flickers until it is released in a blinding flash of illumination. An
infinite description of feelings. An infinite infinite. A separation of
the mind that dreams of life and the physical body that is the real.
The mind drifts further and further away till it is lost over the horizon of time. Time is one and is round, sucking us into a vortex of
infinite eternity, making us one in our own destiny. The universe is
infinite. Acid is here. The thoughts that take us on a journey to paradise or its opposite. The random game satisfying the countermove
and automatically traveling on to a new existence. The mathematically intelligent constructions of the principles of life that fights for
its survival and in the futile, infinite struggle reality is achieved
where everything is infinite. The beginning and the end of the
dream of evolutionary conclusions. Now the void is full of a game
of knowledge where the infinite creates infinite. I know that this is
the end of the acid revelation, where I have to become everything.

I finished the game and changed to watch and listen to my thoughts that had become mine. The culmination of rock and roll dwelt in the air. A wave of music pounded the shore. I was buffeted by the sound and a patch of my life flamed before my eyes. It went away as I cradled Elysium Dream.

"Dream, I know your dream and game," I whispered.

She whispered back, "I want a baby. We are one."

Time passed. The strychnine gave me cramps in my stomach and the heavy acid music of Jefferson Starship was screaming feedback.[12]

In the gray morning, when the sun came up, I made love to my girl with a hundred tons of TNT in my dream. The words of Jim Morrison flowed in my head: "Ghosts crowd the young child's fragile eggshell mind."

She said, "I want to be pregnant." I knew that, because she had just told me. Pregnant with acid child. She had the acid child inside of her now. They will find me. The three of us were at the dawn of creation of the universe.

> *God walked towards her. Sphere came down and screwed her good till the mind of the newly realized was blown back to the beginning of the orgasm. I kept coming after ejaculation into pain. The pain of rape came again and again. I screwed my face into an ugly mask and kept coming in pain. Pain, pain, and more pain as I went to the center of my brain, going back into the turmoil, but the balls had gone so I created a cue ball, the discus, and hurled it out of the game to disperse the spheres and complete the ritual. My ritual of soul sacrifice of the beginning of the nightmare. Mind suicide to eradicate every memory of my mind's birth. I blacked out in the orgasm's pain and fell out of her, as the discus went flying into space.[13]*

We all died and I woke up on the floor, I walked towards the dream of the rock and roll psychedelic era. I am not a star. Elysium Dream had bought life and I had tried to suffocate the dream. I had really screwed Elysium. She was dry and just lay there. I was the father, God, the Beatles and Elvis. I was rock and roll's acid rock and now in 1974 I had created disco in my dream. In my nightmare dream of rock and roll. My baby. I remembered the horror of my nightmare that I called dream. God, I'm back there again in the seduction theory. My rebirth.

I thought you understood, Elysium. I wanted to die and live in the same instant. I told you I was tortured and raped as a baby. I now know who I am. It is lost but it will be won for the inventor of rock and roll. The balls are rolling again. I have hurled a discus into infinity. I am a sorcerer. I will not tell the truth. This is the birth of disco and madness.

12

Every person needs a map to see where they are going and that map is in the flashbacks.   Rainbow Moonfire

Elysium Dream was tripping and she was pregnant. I'd have a nervous breakdown if she continued. What is happening to me? A child ripped into the infinite. A mutation. Stop everything. What is happening in this place? Has everybody gone insane? Does anybody know reality?

I tripped all day Saturday and Sunday and went to work in the city on Monday, suffering from a wired mind. There were flashbacks and I wondered if this was really happening to me. I didn't know. Maybe it was all in my imagination. If she was pregnant, that meant I had actually become God. I was mad, I knew that now. This was not a healthy environment in which to raise a child. The only experience I had had as a father was in raising an Indian hemp plant. It was no doubt the best weed I'd ever tasted but still no credentials for fatherhood. I laughed again. I'd fucked it up.

Elysium, you're beautiful, and I love you more than ever, but isn't it time we said goodbye? I couldn't handle a baby crawling under my feet, bawling at daybreak and vomiting on my Levis. I couldn't live that lifestyle. I want the best for my baby and you

know where I come from. We had it worked out that this world would destroy itself.

On the Easter weekend we went away for a holiday in the Blue Mountains and at Wisemans Ferry. I couldn't stand the confusion for much longer. We were two eccentrics in the same house, ready to freak out. At Wisemans Ferry, as usual, the mushrooms were growing in the valleys. I went searching for some answers and I thought the mushrooms would make everything clear. I needed some answers.

I ate some mushrooms and crashed out in the back of the van. Elysium had not taken any mushrooms and it was good my little girl junkie was straight. I ripped off my mask and thought in a clear dream. *I like this tripping with you, Elysium, and you having our child. It's love's potential to fulfill itself. I have given you the blueprints of myself; I can purchase the food to make you and our undeveloped child grow.* Higher and higher we climbed as we drove further away from Wisemans Ferry to the mountains. *Elysium, you look so right.* I could see why I loved this woman's eternity. Why I loved her heaven and earth. I had made a decision. I would have to let her escape the insanity trap. *I am no good,* the mind said. *I will never be good. I have come too far but my woman and child will survive.* The voice said that she is to become the mother of eternity. She needs the natural wind to caress her body. She is now responsible for a child. She cannot stay with me because if she does, we'll all fall to earth like the autumn leaves. She will never be alone again. She has created herself. With our fears we would both fall to the ground. She has loved somebody else and she has become a link in eternity. My songs are broken. I cannot save her. I lay buried in the van as the thoughts came back at me. I had clear dreams and screams of the discus in eternity.

I said, "I can't fucking stand you!"

She just cried and said, "Why don't you talk to me?"

Once upon a time you were so fine in faded-earth jeans and I can still see you now stuck in the mud while searching for mushrooms. I feel the nervous breakdown building up. Mr. Fool, where do we belong with our idiotic games? The last hallucinogenic scene of grotesque mind-games of a lifestyle that had been whipped into eternity. The dream said that the child and Elysium must go into exile. We had to split and let the songs roll.

I woke up wired and burned-out. There was no home for me. No freedom. I ran off into my own enchanted space and made a vow to return when I could accept the truth. In the castles of evil, through the palaces of good, I searched for myself. In the lands of the earth my mind pictures came and went. My thoughts telling me to kill myself or find my way back home. Petty criticisms dominated my mind. The fetus was driving me crazy. A mutated self, tortured by its mother and father. There was love and marijuana stems and seeds scattered on the coffee table. The game was over and here I was, torn between fear and madness. Surrounded by walls, I was alone with my secret.[14]

The inventor of rock and roll fell into the well of drugs with his life shattering before him. I couldn't stop. I couldn't sleep. I couldn't hate. I bashed my fists against the wall. I knew the answers, but nothing obeyed. Nothing believed me anymore. My body and mind were dying and in their death throes were following the paths to insanity. The drugs were clenched in my moist palms and I would not let go of the monkey trap. I didn't want to know the truth and secret of the universe. I didn't want to play anymore.

She left me to start a new life, making me sad. Elysium was going to live with a warlock in a witches' coven. Totally insane, the sorcerer was sure she was going to crucify him. I knew the warlock would rape my baby, but I had lost it.

At our last meeting, Elysium said, "I'm sorry," and I said, "It doesn't matter."

After she left, I sat in the room while the record player sang Ten Years After's "Cricklewood Green." The feverish nightmare from my childhood was regurgitated. The last cry of a baby before he is hurled into hell. My birth that was forgotten is once more relived. I thought that all children go through hell.

This must be the worst trip I have ever taken.[15] I don't know what to do and if I keep it quiet they won't know I am insane. The inventor of rock and roll.

Later that night I needed the love Elysium had given to me. In my bitterness and hatred I could do without her, so my hands found the part of me and the rhythm of my past life. Masturbation. It's all right, infinite's son, as the seeds burst out and landed on my belly. I got a deal of grass from the drawer and walked into the living room. I was ridiculed by society. I was overreacting and the weed tripped me out. I kicked the coffee table. Again I will take the mushrooms. Never again will they laugh at me. Taunted and haunted, my thoughts began to run. Get out, stay inside, smoke marijuana, create a vacuum and erase your mind. I thought fast.

The group was talking and laughing about me behind my back.[16] It's a heavy game. The voices continued without interruption in my infantile daydream. I wanted to be loved. The dream of rock and roll. I filled in the emptiness of my mind by picking up pieces of scattered conversation. They thought I was an idiot, a goose, a clown, and they would talk this way until they drove me from the group, and then make snide comments behind my back. They were all looking at me. I felt heat, pain, fear, and shame. They were all looking at me. I had to face the tension of the great dream. I was hated. I am the inventor of rock and roll. I am not a star but a discus, a sorcerer.

I'm going crazy. I'll have another joint and I'll be right, mate, but I think all the time on hooch. It's all about me in symbols and illusions. It makes my emotions warped. More and more, over and over, they're looking at me. Leave me alone, mate, and don't hassle me about the past. Ghosts everywhere.

My elevated mood was alternating from depression to manic high. I hated myself and this tore me apart. Vanished, gone from existence, the trip took hold and the loser sat in the chair that he couldn't understand. The lifeless branches reaching for the sky, only to die half-completing the ritual of a feared god. A senseless and forsaken business. Just building a civilization to rape a civilization.

Have another beer, mate, and if you can't drink them, leave them. If you can't leave them, drink them.

I swayed at the urinal, looking down at my feet, which were out of focus and swayed and moved. I was fucking off across the sky. I was rotten drunk and full of pity for myself. It's a contemptible world. *I'll follow you, Elysium.* I'm not a leader of men or women.

I was stoned and drunk again and had taken two macro-dots. I could drink to my heart's content and feel nothing except the refreshing taste of alcohol. I was strong and there was no fear here. I could face the world with confidence—and where are the old evil spirits now? I have defeated them and nothing is beyond my capabilities. I talked and laughed. The world was to be enjoyed and every shift of reality brought happiness. Here was my art form. A demanding mind with the substance of spiraling smoke that coiled around the shades of existence. How long does the alternate reality exist before it is replaced by the children's story? Hours go by before the electric current is barbed and meshed into circuits that leave the victim in a crusty shell of secret irrational forces.

I walked into the static of the night. Elysium was with me and we connected well. Our waves were synchronized. We talked and walked till we reached our destination, so I touched her cheek and started to laugh. The dream faded and I walked on alone. I would be forever alone, but we are never alone with our thoughts. The phantom of the half-dream walked on in his sweaty nightmare of rock and roll.

I sat in the pub reading faces, talking and listening to myself. An imaginary Elysium sat beside me. My hand reached out to her. I thought that the pain could not handle itself, so it created life to escape itself. Reality has no emotion, only painful movement. Pain is the creator of the universe.

I got up and ambled to the bar. Beer is the greatest little calmer in the world. I threaded my way back to the table. The conversation in my head hadn't left me.

People are mad. They created their god of no pain. Love is the greatest hallucination of all and they imagine that it is so precious. Yeah, it will most likely save us from our own pain. The creation of love is so beautiful. Love from pain and pain from love. Love, the antidepressant.

I was in the black hotel that served glasses of pain, surrounded by devils and angels. It was time to go home. The chance to go to a home because, my Elysium, you're coming with me. After ten insane years, you will bring acid child back to me. We are mind to mind. I was going to die but now I am going to live. They will not destroy my world before the completion of my plan. I will destroy myself with the hallucinogenic mushrooms and come back at the end the same as the beginning. We'll all come through the music of Sphere. I do love you, Elysium Dream. Pain is the secret of the universe, love's power is secondary. I guess I take second.

13

Insult people by playing the "I am better than you" game.
Magic Star Flower

The worlds of Cane Toad, Rainbow, Magic, and Wasteland were left behind and, in my conflict, I left acid child and Elysium waiting at the altar of God. I had to hurt her. I, myself, waited at the altar to sacrifice the Great Australian Dream. I adjusted the cruel dream to the point where I could understand it. The levels were right. I tuned the fields till the image was right and I was standing in the golden realm. Then I walked into the religious imagination and felt myself one with the dream field where the sirens of promised pleasure with firm, soft bellies and beautiful fur waited for me, but now the fields had been raped by their own ideology. Blood on my hands as my erotic monster danced naked in the flesh and blood.

The dream pictures continued with a woman slowly undressing until I saw her breasts and swollen brown nipples. The slow-motion pictures continued and gradually moved down her moving, curving body to her vagina, where I became her clitoris and God. I am God in miniature. I cannot be trapped in pain on this planet for infinity.

The woman is looking into your mind and she wants to sexually play with you and you want her to but you are so sensitive and vulnerable. She plays with you until you hurt and then she laughs at you. She hurts you and forces pain into your hidden secret fears. Her mind is twisted. Her clitoris is twisted, her labia majora blown out. She sticks things into herself as she wildly masturbates, her id demented, as she rubs, loves, hates, and fears herself. Nature is deformed until a glistening ejaculating vagina is her only brain. The pleasure shouts obscenities and desires in a fur-covered pain. I scream. I hate our minds that have been melded. Mother nature destroying herself.

The pictures flash across my mind till the feeling comes and the semen gushes, explodes, and shoots out along the tunnel, from the half-erect penis. I wake to the sound but I know what is happening so I let it continue. Still, the ejaculation squirts and spurts till it is finished. Sex is man's love and love is man's desire.

Breathing deeply, I rise from the bed, remove my underpants and wipe the semen from my stomach, penis, and pubic hairs, then discard the underpants on the floor. I hate wet dreams and should masturbate. The tension is too much for me. Masturbation is the chore of the great dream. It is what separates us from the animals.

The sickness ends and the day begins. The manic cycle is completed. Programmed in trauma to repeat the cycle of remembrance and never understanding the cycle of man, the ritual of a loving, sexual being, the ritual of man.

14

I'm going to kick that Devil up the arse.   Baron Wasteland

A stoned week later, after rolling out of the abyss: getting out the strikers I struck up a number with Wasteland and Cane Toad. "I'm going to quit my job," I said, "and split the dream. I'm going to write rock and roll songs. I'm going to write the Great Australian Dream song about my life."

"So you're going to write some babble about your life," Wasteland said, as he took the joint and drew it in. "A dirty poet. You're going to tell the world who you are. They don't need your lies, mate."

"Yeah, I'm going to write it all down," I replied. "All my daydreams."

"Where will you go?" Cane Toad asked amiably as he received the joint.

"I've got a hundred revelations rocking in my head and I want to escape the madness. There's too much conflict here, so I'll go to Queensland to prepare for the birth of acid child. You know I'm insane. The balls are rolling again. It's coming back. Does it sound like I'm talking shit?"

"It sounds like you're in psychosis," Wasteland said, as he received the joint. "Why don't you get back with Elysium? You can play with her meat and still write your poetry. We can help you raise your junkie child. *Our* junkie child. We can dig the trip. Get real again. Wombat like that is hard to find and, anyway, she needs someone to support her."

"I'm out of it, mate," I replied. "I don't want to burn Elysium again. The astrologers of Zoroaster[17] say that the baby will be born on the longest day.[18] The baby is the birth of disco as I was the birth of rock and roll. When your trip ends and comes back on itself you will understand. If you're ever a father you might know as I know. I can see the future. I'm a prophet, a telepath, the next evolutionary messiah of earth. Acid child has the oracle and I'm waiting for my reflection from that oracle. She stands opposite me on the longest day."

"You're insane," Cane Toad said. "You destroyed something beautiful."

"We'll be waiting for you to return," Wasteland said. "This society runs on verbal diarrhea and we have a billion verses of poetry that nobody wants to read. It's an ego trip. Elysium gives birth to a baby and you give birth to a book of shit. Not only do women go leapy when they get pregnant but fathers do too. You can be what you want to be and do what you want to do, but remember Elysium Dream, because you've hurt her. Don't leave the dream, mate."

"You don't understand, mate, like I understand. It's the birth of disco. There are three insanities and I have begun my second one. The baby will be deformed or Elysium will have a miscarriage. You know that she now takes amphetamines?"

"Why don't you help her, then?" Cane Toad asked.

"She's gone," I said. "I tried to create God. I tried to create another Jesus Christ with the hallucinogenic chemicals, but it was just an instant of madness when the acid was talking. This is the last age and I was desperate to save everything I loved. I love her. I hate her. I have changed minds with her. This is the only world I've ever known and god, I don't want to destroy it. I have daydreams."

"In this life, some people get all the marbles and others get just a few but lose them in the game of life," Cane Toad drawled as he mulled another joint.

"You're playing with your mind. You're making wild statements," Wasteland said.

"I am mad. You would be too if you received the revelations in my head."

"You're mad," Wasteland said. "We're all wacko in this place. 'Some people do it, some see right through it, some wear pajamas if only they knew it.'"

"Don't quote Crapper to me, mate," I said. "I've got my own Crapper quote: 'You've got to get into it before you get out of it because if you never get out of it you'll never get into it, and if you never get into it you'll never get out of it.'"

"Write a book of poetry then. Nobody will read it. Your mouth is your religion. You put your faith in a hole like that?"

"I'll trade a book for a baby any day," Cane Toad said.

"It's my trip," I replied.

"We're trip-freaks, mate, we understand. Getting down to the nitty-gritty, we don't want a baby in this dream. It's a dead-end bummer," Cane Toad said. "Wasteland just got an attack of the morals."

"You understand, Cane Toad," I said, "but I don't. The balls are rolling again. I'll still have to destroy my mind or they'll find me. I have to be ready and I'm not ready now. This is the last psychological war. The Australian nuclear family is not my trip. Nobody is going to destroy my acid dream child. No woman will send me to war."

I crossed the room and looked into the mirror and thought, *Whoever knows the rules can play the game. Whoever knows the fear words can control who listens.* Still, I know that nobody controls the universe. In the end, it comes and goes and we're going back to where it comes from. Now it is coming back on me as five years ago it was the culmination of acid rock and now I have become disco. I am Sphere again and I know that pain is the ultimate power. I rolled into the bachelor's life because I fought for Elysium. My strained temper nearly exploded because of my pride. What's the use? Men have fought for women since the beginning of creation. I feel the pain, the hurt, the anger of the fool who loves her. I fight against everybody, even myself. I resent a woman who sends me out to fight for her. No one is spared in the destruction around me.

15

It's a good life if you don't weaken.   Magic Star Flower

The heroin–water–vinegar solution was sucked up through the cigarette filter. A few impurities remained on the spoon. When I tapped the side of the syringe, a few bubbles rose to the top. A bubble of liquid from the needle tip told me all was ready. Taking the belt and wrapping it around my left arm, I started to pump vigorously. The vein stood out on the arm. I had good veins. Pulling the belt tightly with my mouth and with the syringe in my right hand, I inserted the needle. Darn, I had missed the vein. Pulling the needle out, I tried again. I needed a new needle. This one was getting old. Grimacing with the belt in my mouth, I inserted the needle; jacking back-blood rushed into the syringe. Down went the plunger. It was a good charge; blood and heroin rushed into my brain.

Instant karma.

The rush was over and I staggered about the room and was quietly stoned. From the stereo, "Gimme Shelter" played.

16

You're insane with your friends to keep your sanity.
Rainbow Moonfire

Elysium Dream was free, so I escaped to Queensland to search for hallucinogenic mushrooms. I found a field and dropped some, but they were watery and not potent. Taking a few to the hotel, I made a foul-tasting brew of mushroom extract.

After a nap, I went fishing for catfish in the Brisbane River. I caught a mother of a trout and took it to the hotel to cook it up. It was a slimy foot-long slug with whiskers and it freaked a few people out when I told them it was my dinner. I thought I was a great angler but then I found out I couldn't eat it, so I never went fishing again.

I became affiliated with the official hippie movement and possessed a freak-out card. I would go through dreams of adventure, boredom, and bourbon. I walked into the toilet, dropped my strides, and did a psychedelic grunt. Got to crap sometimes. Excuse me, you perverts.

December 22, 1974. I left Queensland, my book of songs completed. The inventor of rock and roll had to live his own life and write his own songs.

> *Then the voice that I heard speaking from heaven spoke to me again: "Go and take the open book which is in the hand of the angel standing on the sea and on the land."*
>
> *I went up to the angel and asked him to give me the book. He said to me: "Take it and eat it; it will turn sour in your stomach but in your mouth it will be as sweet as honey."*
>
> *I took the book from the hand and ate it and it tasted as sweet as honey in my mouth. But after I swallowed it, it turned sour in my stomach.*
>
> *Then I was told (Revelations) about the babble of Sphere.[19]*

Children grow to adults, failure leads to failure, victory proceeds to victory. The genetically powerful kill the weak. My mind, crippled by the power, understood that I had to face the real world and my revenge was the book of Sphere. You may know what I mean as I hurl the image into your face. Sphere, the common theme is rolling. He is being captured by remembering the pain. His form has been melded by the great experiment of the testing ground.

17

There is more scratch in delusion.   **Sphere**

I lit up a special reefer and handed Wasteland my book of imagery songs. He quietly read them as he smoked on the reefer.

"So these are your poems," he said. "I'll tell you straight. They're shit, mate, just like all the other beautiful artistic people. Sorry, Sphere, but they are *poor.* Those poems are the biggest load of aggrandized garbage I've read since I read another budding penis poet's attempt at being noticed. More artistic, grotesque madness. You even had the gall to put my name on one of them. It's an ego trip of an academic orgasm. Winky wanky woo. You think the women are going to notice you?"

"You're sure?" I asked.

"It's all the same," he replied. "Poets identify with their own thoughts and think they are magical. They think insanity is beautiful. Mate, don't fall into the same trap."

"Maybe you're right," I said. "Maybe it is garbage. It's not alive. My baby's alive but my words aren't. I'd like to make my words cry, talk, sing, and dream—you're sure my words are dead?"

"Yeah, mate," Wasteland replied. "I could do better, but most poets are pompous wankers who believe the world revolves around their beautiful words. It just revolves around their turds. They think they are so important. It's because they are the beautiful generation of piss. They piss it out of themselves in never-ending streams of bile. They're full of their own conceited ego-piss. They're so shockingly beautiful. They forget that others have got to listen to their bleeding hearts of aesthetic drivel going on and on. You could work a lifetime on a single poem and that poem says who you really are. Babies fill in the monotony of life. All you needed to do was make one poem and you know that poem is your child. She'll talk soon, she grows and she loves. She's a work of art, but poems are the capitalist assassination of personality. Your child is beauty and she will recreate beauty for eternity. Think of her guts. They're more fragile and peaceful than any prestigious garbage. Reflect on her and you will find all the fulfillment and acceptance that you need. Your job is to support her, but you don't give a damn."

"You don't understand a psychological war. This fanatical religious world needs to get on to a positive trip. I want good dreams."

"Psychological war, psychological shit," Wasteland said. "Tear it all down and then you want . . . "

Silence.

"You didn't finish off the sentence," I said.

"You know yourself better than anyone else."

"You sure?"

"You're an idiot if you don't know yourself," Wasteland sneered. "We always know ourselves better than anyone else does."

"Yes, that's true."

"Well, what do you want?" Wasteland asked.

"I want Elysium Dream to be safe," I replied. "I want them to find me. I created rock and roll. I'm the inventor of rock and roll."

"You're the inventor of shit, mate," Wasteland retorted. "Here's some advice, Sphere. You're shut in a room and all you have to do is open the door. You think the door is locked but it isn't. You just haven't the brains to open the door and to see people how they really are. You can't even see yourself in the mirror. You don't want to look. You want to hide away in your own little world that you created. If you're the inventor of rock and roll, why hasn't someone recorded these thoughts?"

"The songs aren't about my painful visions," I replied.

"Is love a painful vision?" he asked.

"No, but sex is. Rock and roll is not about love, but sex, anyway.

Everybody has different personality traits. We're not all the same. We say the same thing in different ways at different times. The musicians believe in the same music that I believe in."

"Yeah. Good luck with your madness." And he got to his feet and walked away.

18

If you don't know yourself, who can you know?
Baron Wasteland

Sphere, the sorcerer of the asylum, gazed at Wasteland, the night-mare child, and Rainbow Moonfire. They had inflicted pain on him and so he would give them pain in return. Sphere, the sorcerer of the asylum, gazed at Uncle Cane Toad, the crystal mind, and Magic Star Flower, in a beautiful vision. They had given him peace, so he would give them all the peace and love he possessed. The love/peace/hate battled around the source of power that biology had intricately constructed in his veins. His heroes in his brain knew of peace and war. He had come from Valhalla and nobody knew the Sphere child flew at night to the darkness of fright. He flew around the electric wires of anxiety. He flew the wavelength of lukewarm sweat. Nobody knew Sphere and he knew himself as the sorcerer of the asylum. This was his dream. The alter ego that remembered the derogatory comments and slanderous innuendos which had surrounded him and tormented him in the trip. Again his violence emerged and merged with Elysium Dream, his love. This is his book.

"Elysium Dream," he whispers in his sleep.
Blood, everywhere blood. He again calls. The night is soft in the disco dream of Sphere, Wasteland's constructive criticism left far behind. The lights are turned on as the picture music dances in the mind of Sphere. The scenes change. We return to the great orgasm of mother god in the big bang. We are in the clitoris—

*G spot–scrotum–phallic stage now and soon we will metamor-
phose into the great orgasm dream. A sloppy, stinking death is
just a thought away. We will enter into her vagina and find her
ovum. What was conceived in orgasm goes back to organism
with no beginning or end or organization.*

*How did we come about? The void made us under pressure.
The void couldn't exist in isolation, so two opposite charges met
and conceived the Sphere. The Sphere had matter and consciousness, the opposite of the void, and in the organization the void
had given birth to the mother natural god. She was serene and
peaceful, living in the Sphere, and was one with the Sphere. She
controlled the Sphere and the Sphere controlled her and they
both lived in the magnetic fields of Elysium. They were the first
of the peace gods.*

*The void gave violent birth to the opposite, Sphere the sor-
cerer of the asylum, and death invaded Elysium. The peace was
shattered and scattered throughout the voids. The dream gods
watched themselves tortured, killed, and scattered across the
universe and in this world they still search for the dream children to come through the music into the great orgasm of creation.*

"Hey Sphere, we continue to procreate after we're dead," says
Wasteland.

"Yeah, I know, mate," I reply.

"I think I'll masturbate now, like I always do."

I slowly awoke from the dream. *It's morning time, Mama, and the
fairytale is gone.* My feet and brow were bathed in sweat. The elves
who visit the shoeman visit me. Gremlins infest my mind. At least I
was on the veranda, my favorite place to sleep. Roll out of bed
before it's too late and take the bedsheets with me.

I rose to my palms and did the Australian crawl to the kitchen.
Getting to my feet, I opened the refrigerator. They'd taken all the
beer, the inconsiderate sods, and it's always the elves who take the
beer, the filthy philistines. When did I deserve this? I've got to live
in this flea palace of faded chairs, second-hand fridge, and frayed
carpet that matches my perplexed personality. Growl into some

watermelon and milk, scratch my scalp till the white, itchy dandruff flakes fall down and leave me. Dandruff—I wonder if you can sell it as good-quality bacteria? Why not inject some? You have gone leapy, kid. Why be institutionalized like the rest of the dropouts? Get the watermelon and cigarettes into you and then some cold pizza and milk. Then afterwards some music to soothe the wild beast and curl up on the lounge with the stereo playing rock music that echoes in the skull. The last thoughts I remembered were wily gremlins singing while other morbid creatures played their instruments in the heavy-eyed darkness: *When did I deserve this?* And the dream's mistakes, guilt and insanity, came back on me and tripped me off.

I awoke. I walked to the corner shop and chatted with the proprietor. Then I was sitting on the veranda, stoning, eating a peppermint heart with cars flashing past and the sun a golden orb that bathed the landscape in sunshine. The people walked past. I thought to myself, *Am I a mindless fool? My life is a fragment, a disconnected dream that has no continuity. I am so tired of senselessness. I am tired of the music that my feelings sing, the dream music.*

19

Never reveal your weakest spot, because that's the part the dogs will attack.   Uncle Cane Toad

I admitted myself to the psychiatric hospital, found my room, unpacked, and waited to see Abraxas. The nurse entered the room and told me Abraxas was waiting. The nightmare had begun, but I knew how to handle Abraxas. How to lie. How to act normally. I could tell the difference between you and me.

The sign on the door said *Dr. I. M. Abraxas.* I knocked and a voice behind the door said "Enter." Dr. Abraxas was seated in a leather chair behind a mahogany desk. I sat down and waited as he shuffled papers and made notations with a pen. He looked up and asked, "Well, how is it going, Sphere?"

"Fine," I said.

"I want to know your history," he said. "Can you tell me about your life up until about ten years of age?"

"I don't remember much up to about three years of age, but my mother has given me some facts. I was sexually molested at eight months when I was left with a baby-sitter. I was poisoned by Folidol, a nerve poison, at sixteen months of age, was unconscious for three days and contracted pneumonia from the mucus trapped in my lungs. I stayed in the hospital for about a month."[20]

"Did your mother ever describe what sort of baby you were?" Abraxas asked.

"I was a very good baby and never cried, very placid, and was described by a relative, a nun, as the best baby she had ever known. I loved to wake in the morning and when I woke I didn't cry but would coo and sing. There is a story my mother loves to tell about when a cow began to chew the mosquito netting of my bassinet and I began to cry. Nobody could believe the baby was crying and they came running from all directions. The only other incident which has been told to me is that when I was born the umbilical cord was wrapped around my neck and except for the quick actions of the doctor I would have died."

"What about this sexual molesting story?"

"I was left with a baby-sitter and when my parents returned I was screaming. My mother said that I was never the same after that. I would wake up in the night and would be screaming. I screamed for a whole week and was a completely changed baby. She never left any of us kids with a baby-sitter after that."

"And what do you remember of this time?"

"I remember being crushed by a billion tons of force and then the balls began to roll through my mind. It was like living in a bowling alley. I knew nothing but balls and then one night the last ball rolled into its ordered place and I could see the spheres stretching for eternity. All the balls that had rolled in my mind were there and then I awoke and told my mother that the dream was over. I don't know if I thought it or actually told her but I knew that the dream was over. I then discovered the magical place of the earth. I have not told the story of the balls till now but I always remembered."

"I want to try an experiment. Go back into the pain," Abraxas said.

I went back into the pain.

Everything went dark and the child was suffocating in a swirling nightmare abyss of inflated black pain. I sweated and swirled in the nightmare of an infinitely small spark floating in a vast spiraling darkness. The screaming came down and crashed into the center of my brain. The beginning of memory sees a baby with useless hands trying desperately to push the blackness off his body. Bombing my mind into infinity with implosions of destruction. There were shadowy loud ghostly noises from another gloomy slum room. They were violent, threatening, haunting, and fighting in the moonlit night. Frightening him into and out of sleep with crazy gray dreams. He wandered into his brain. Who are you? Who do you hate? Who are you, screaming banshees? Quickly the depression swallowed me into the gulf of weightless, universal motion of heated black vastness. Pain, they call me Sphere. The balls are rolling. Insane, they know I'm Sphere, who has given birth to the dream of insanity. Imprinted with a symbol that I carried as a child in a black-and-white vision. The symbol is broken imagery. It was the birth of shock and roll. The symbol I chose is the death of truth. The white sphere has given meaning to me by the gods. I existed. The symbol was created for me. It was the stone on which a new name was written.

The name is Sphere.

I twisted in the chair as the psychotic attack subsided and my eyes cleared the tears. Abraxas noted the psychotic attack but sat motionless.

"The baby-sitter was a woman?" he asked.

"Yes," I replied.

"Go on," Abraxas said.

"My mother found no marks on my body so she assumed that I had been molested."

"No marks?"

"No, no marks," I replied.

"Tell me about the rest of your life up until ten."

"I went to school. I repeated second class but I got the religion prize next year. The sisters thought I was retarded, autistic, or both, or just another crazy. There were sixty to eighty kids in one class, so about twenty of us repeated second class. After school, I used to dream in an old caved-in water tank about a girl. I was very disturbed at the time and couldn't understand that I was a second-class citizen. When I was seven [in 1960] I predicted the Cuban crisis and the assassination of President Kennedy. Perhaps it was happening at the time, so I would just dream in my bomb shelter about the children in my class. I hated to go home because the old house was falling down and we didn't have a happy family life, with my mother accusing my father of being an alcoholic and, anyway, I rarely saw my father, as he didn't like being at home. I lived my own life up until ten with nobody telling me what to do. I did my own thing and everybody else did their thing." I stared at Abraxas. "Mother Superior sent me out to find the Kingdom of Heaven but she didn't realize that it's a metaphor." I laughed.

"Tell me about your school days."

"You understand that the nightmare had ended?" I said. "The phony priestesses of God knew a juvenile delinquent. They beat me every Friday with their stiff, dry cane, and their final psychological torture was to make me repeat second class. I would steal money from my parents' room and they thought it was a ghost but it was only my shadow as I slipped in and out of poverty. In my own mind I became the Holy Ghost in second class, and I knew that I could destroy those Catholic lesbians, but something inside of me told me to forget the sexually sadistic nuns and concentrate on the great dream. You see, I loved to dream and I loved a little girl, but nobody knew my mind. The love of a small girl made me dream."

"Do you think you are crazy?" Abraxas asked.

"Do I hear voices and see hallucinations?" I asked.

"Yes," he replied.

"I talk to myself, if that's what you mean. I hear my own thoughts."

"But do you hear people talking to you in your mind?"

"No, I'm not crazy."

"Do you see hallucinations?"

"Sometimes I talk to my Elysium Dream. She left me some time ago but I still talk to her. It's just daydreaming."

"Do you still use drugs?" he asked.

"Yes."

"What sorts of drugs?" he asked.

"Most sorts," I replied. "Anything I can get my hands on."

"You've used heroin, LSD, amphetamines, and barbiturates, et cetera?" he asked.

"Yes."

Abraxas then replied, after a moment's silence, "You know that you will have to give up the use of unprescribed drugs because they will make you psychotic? If you give up drugs all your nightmares will disappear."

We danced around the truth. I told some lies to build up my reputation as Abraxas looked up the report of my intelligence and inkblot tests. You know, I had kept seeing vaginas in the inkblots, so after a while I stopped mentioning them. I saw four of the mothers and discovered years later that if you don't see vaginas or a channel and you're a male you are lying. Mixed with a couple of penises, bats, butterflies, and satanic castles, I slipped through his psychotic clutches.

Abraxas finally spoke. "You gave some strange answers in your inkblot test, but there was no hesitation and that is good. You have a little over average intelligence. Don't worry about yourself and get off the drugs, take the tranquilizers, and you will have a fine life. By the way, Modecate is a sex stimulant, so don't worry about that."[21]

Then Abraxas asked me to free-associate. To talk and ramble about the present.

"Doc," I replied, "once upon a time there was a farm that grew hallucinogenic mushrooms. We were out of high school and thought that we knew it all. We discovered a world which had the clarity of dreams. We lived in beauty in this idyllic way till our trips went too far. I persisted with my escape from the idyll; I discovered the wonder that is nature. The world opened up its secrets and I journeyed till I found the truth. By this time, the veneer was cracking and so was my mind. I spent my days smoking and selling

Indian hemp and other days I bought bottles of bourbon and beer and passed each day in intoxication, but I was not always this disillusioned. In fact, I had an optimism, but that was my downfall—and childishness."

"You have friends, then?" Abraxas asked.

"I have very few friends. My idea of excitement was not a trip of training with the local Aussie Rules team. I knew I was unstable and my woman, Elysium Dream, tried to help me, but she didn't realize we were both lost trip-freaks. I was straight, mostly, with my friends. Baron Wasteland, Uncle Cane Toad, Rainbow Moonfire, and Magic Star Flower are wild people. I'm hip, they're cool. There are still some cool trip-freaks left in the world. We all suffered brain damage. Psilocybin is worse than acid. We've all suffered withdrawals from the needle and we live in a sadomasochistic delusion. I pray for deliverance from my nightmares because my life has become too ugly. Sometimes my inspirations are thrown to the wind and I can feel the cold nightmare as it awakens my fantasies. I possess the wisdom of nature as concrete reality. My problem is hidden by my mind, a sensitive mind that can't take the reality of life."

"Tell me about your friends," Abraxas asked.

"Elysium Dream is named after heaven," I replied. "She was my girlfriend. We used to trip, shit, and live together. She is small and freaky and psychedelic. She knows things that I don't know and she always tells the truth about herself and me. Her father died when she was twelve and her mother worries about her hanging out with a long-haired fuckwit. She loves screwing. She's freaked out of it most of the time and sometimes babbles on and on on acid when she doesn't realize it. She is very vulnerable and sensitive and that is why I love her.

"Next is Uncle Cane Toad. We've hitchhiked around the state and he's given it all he can, but lately he hasn't been around. He thinks I've gone too crazy and with his long hair and beard he gets along with his own philosophy, that a man's mind is his own business. If he isn't peacefully stoned playing rock and roll, he's out pushing a taxi earning his daily bread. He staggers around, refills his coffee cup, and hardly says a word. He listens a lot, injects heaps of Ritalin, and I'm sure he's made off with the dream. He's sane, not like me. His father died when he was nine. He didn't emerge from pain; it came much later. His intelligence is greater and quieter than mine and he could tell some good yarns if telling stories was his strong point. He has strength and peaceful intentions. That is who he is, you know, during the trip, the soft parade.[22]

"Baron Wasteland is the nuclear war child and is another mate. He is a born realist. He is Cane Toad's cousin and was born in a country town in Queensland. His father is an alcoholic and fought in the war like my father. He fell in love with Rainbow Moonfire, a half Aboriginal girl, but his parents didn't like the arrangement so they both left Queensland and came to Sydney to live. He is a good bloke. He speaks his mind. He uses drugs and is the coolest one of us all. I dig him and that is all he is.

"Rainbow Moonfire is half Aboriginal. She's a rebel. Her disbanded tribe was looked after by the whites and where she comes from her tribe was quite respected. She follows Wasteland. Her father was white but left her mother when she was young. She has two other sisters. She's terrific-looking and would do anything for Wasteland. She believes in Aboriginal rights but doesn't mention it very often. She is caught in a psychological war which she and Wasteland fight with all their might. I like her.

"Magic Star Flower is the last of our group and is Cane Toad's girlfriend. She is weird, but we all dig her. She gets into different trips like Buddhism, I Ching, tarot, astrology, palmistry, and things like that. She is always trying to give up cigarettes. She tries to get Cane Toad and the rest of us to go straight but she can't even straighten out herself. She's the baby of the group. I don't know much about her past except she's a Catholic like the rest of us. She is mixed-up and cool and digs Yoko Ono and that is who she is.

"We're all mixed-up and we all see ghosts. We're a very humble and nonviolent group who live together in the great dream. We all believe in the magic of the dream."

"Right!" said Abraxas. "I'm prescribing Stelazine and Modecate injections. I'll get the nurse to give you a shot now. You know the routine."[23]

"Yeah." Tranquilized again.

I shook hands with the doctor with my usual clammy hands, and went to the nurses station to get my tranquilizers. At least he didn't tell me that I'm a morally depraved cat molester. I'm as normal as Sigmund Freud and his sex-starved crew. I'll tell it to you straight. My future is warped into a sex trap. I'd rather be a philosopher, but I'm a hedonist. I'd rather be a psychologist, but I'm a playboy. I'm a devotee of the deviate. Man, I've got a pornographic mind with X-rated vision. I guess I can't fool you now.

The Modecate calmed me down. My ideas made me feel peaceful again. My mind was now taut and resilient. My spirit felt completion when my mind was cleared. A rewarding, simple life of controlled insights. My insights alternated between lies and truth, blasphemy and praise, pleasure and pain, good and evil. The truth is matter-of-fact, concise, lacking the embellishments of a psychic paradise. The truth involves the health of the body which, in turn, affects the ideas in the mind. Hey, God. I called him a manufactured invention of my mind so that I could escape to the world of a child and never grow up. God seems to have no basis in reality. Is the truth man's mind in this religious trip? I had felt the spirit of God with my mind. Had I set up a paradox? Had I grasped an answer that my mind deemed real but in actuality was the cunning of the hunter that wrestled with the frailty of death? The return to the child. I had been caught in a trap for sure. I lit another cigarette, had another drink of coffee and thought about the problem. There was no answer except faith, and faith caught the child. The innocent believed in the controlling maze-masters.

I had been daydreaming in the glass corridors, remembering the old days when we were children and we had games to play—the uncertainty in an uncertain mind. The trail we follow is littered with debris. I chose my steps cautiously. Drugs can maim and kill a man and even cigarettes can make you physically inactive. My future wavered to Sydney, the city I love. Another future projection occurred in my hallucinogenic mind: the hippie communes of Nimbin. My pseudo-psychic-psychedelic powers adjusted to the pleasure of a mind which had invented a heaven on earth. My mysticism has led you to believe in me. The wavering walls contained my enthusiasm and saved me. The simple elation of a rubber ball bouncing between the sensitive son and the lover of my acid child caught in the reality–unreality syndrome.

I would enjoy myself for a few days and smoke cigarettes and drink coffee till it came out of my ears. I would take the tranquilizers until I was out of pain and come back to my troubles at a later date. I would read in the library and find new things to occupy the space in my mind. The struggle for reality was getting tedious. I am not one dream but a thousand fragmented nightmares. I was again the lost, a teacher of bad habits, but humanity had not done much better than myself.

I would fool Abraxas. My thoughts were continually interrupting me. I saw hallucinations and I must be sensible if I was ever to be released from here. I still stuttered with uncertainty. My secrets worked havoc on my thought processes. I was an uncertain individual with a good chance of living my life in a psychiatric hospital.

I quietly drank ginger beer on the bench. I knew I had lost Elysium's love. She would not come into my wandering and searching. She could be here sharing my conversation and body but she had gone another way. She must hate me for who I am.

The universal sunset came down and was as black as the trip. Oblivion came into being as the last sunrays died. Two opposite forces pulling me apart. I wondered if she would ever come back to me. Each day I talked to her, called her name in despair, and waited for her to come through the door. I am a man who wants the best illusion for my woman and child and waits for the right moment to come through the music. Heaven and hell are with us now.

I had blood on my hands as I raised the child. It was a dream I had. I had taken some barbiturates and had fallen asleep in the sun. I was traveling to the mountains with Elysium. We had an accident and she fell out of the car. When I lifted her body it had become a baby. Blood was dripping through my hands.

I was afraid of that dream, but things will work out in the end. *Elysium, I won't hurt you. I have crossed body and spirit with you before we parted. Our destiny intersects in ten years' time when our baby is grown. We will be together in ten years. It is your trip, Elysium, to have the baby and bring it to me. We have joined illusions, my little trip-freak Elysium. If you never find heaven in this world, you will never find it anywhere else. This is our haven from the abyss.*

20

Sphere is as leapy as a cane toad.   **Rainbow Moonfire**

A month of group therapy, and once again I was out on the streets.

"Hey, mate, Wasteland, mix some sweat!" We shook hands.

"Hop in, Sphere," Wasteland said. "You're going home on the range where the baked potatoes roam." We climbed into the kombi. "How's the psychiatric hospital?"

"A bummer," I replied.

"Yeah, it's a schizo's trip."

"How're Cane Toad, Rainbow, and Magic?" I asked.

"Out of it, as usual. Magic's into Christianity. She believes Jesus Christ is going to come back and heal Cane Toad. She's really freaked Cane Toad out, but we handle her. Rainbow has started hawking her body at the Cross and she's getting plenty of scratch."

"Do you mean she's getting plenty of clams by using her bearded clam?"

"You guessed it."

"Far out! What else is happening?"

"We're all going on a magical mystery tour of the Snowy Mountains. Dig to come?"

"Yeah, I can dig the trip."

"We'll be leaving tomorrow," said Wasteland. "We were just waiting for you to get out of the funny farm to join in our greed game."

"I'm still into the great dream," I replied.

"Rainbow and I are into the game. We've become Marxists!" Wasteland retorted. We drove for a while in silence.

"Here, light up this joint," Wasteland said.

"Thanks," I said.

Wasteland had heard news of Elysium. She had left the witches' coven and gone to the country to live in a commune. We had a daughter, born on December 27—two days after Darwin had been destroyed by Cyclone Tracy. Perhaps the dream was over. We would be going in opposite directions. She stood naked before my eyes. I shook off the vision. *You'll be all right, Elysium. I love you, but I can't follow you. I am the inventor of rock and roll.*

"Here we are," said Wasteland. He parked the kombi on the street and we wandered up the stairs of delusion to home sweet home, where a civilized creep could sip tea while listening to West Coast psychedelic music. It had been a year noted for hysteria, paranoia, and madness.

As soon as I sat down, Magic began to explain that Jesus had literally endorsed homosexuality in the Bible by saying love your fellow man. He had also justified fornication by saying love your neighbor.

"Yeah, Jesus is cool," Cane Toad said.

Magic replied, "He's more than cool, he's enlightened. Why else did he hang around with twelve apostles and Mary Magdalene, and save her from being stoned? He can save you from being stoned, too. There is no giving or taking in a marriage in heaven."

Cane Toad broke in. "Magic, enough's enough. Nobody believes your homosexual trinity concept. We know who we love."

"Your dick doesn't," she replied. "It doesn't give a damn who stimulates it."

"Yeah, we know, Magic," Cane Toad said, "but keep it in the closet. We know who we love, so put the round peg in the round hole. I can't get into a man because my mind won't let me get it up."

"Let's change the conversation," Rainbow said. "I want to tell Sphere about the greed game. We've worked out a new philosophy, mate. We're not into any idealistic ideology now. Marx and money are the answer. We're getting into smack's mentality and we've got a welcome-home hit for you."

"Far out!" I answered.

"Get out the syringes, Baron, and give the lad a taste," Rainbow ordered.

Wasteland got out the fit, mixed up a charge, and I had a fine shot of white powder. Everyone then followed suit. The stereo played Company Caine's *A Product of Broken Reality* as the needle slid into veins and drew its crimson music.

"We're into a revolutionary game," Rainbow explained. "We're not going to be the workers of the capitalist swine and let them exploit us anymore. We're going to exploit them."

"I'm into a biological evolutionary dream. I'm on my way to heaven," I protested.

"We don't dig dreams!" Rainbow retorted. "We want reality, and scag is the ultimate reality. The poppy of knowledge. The real opiate of the people. We don't settle for second-best, mate, but go straight for the jugular."

"It's another trap," I persisted. "Grass is where it's at because she is mother god."

"Rainbow and I are going on," Wasteland replied. "Scag is the best drug there is."

Cane Toad disagreed. "Speed is where it's at. Speeding at night in my taxi to the neon lights is fantastic. I've got my own philosophy and it's joined with Magic's theology. I think I talk for both of us when I say we're into the science of orbital theory. Is the universe sane or insane? Physics and astronomy is where we're at."

"Get real, Cane Toad!" Wasteland exploded. "You're just a capitalist slave! Don't you realize it all flows up through the economy to the top two percent, who are the controlling capitalist slave masters?"

"Get real yourself!" Cane Toad retorted angrily. "Science is beautiful. We want nothing but our theories and concepts to explain to this ship of fools the reason why we exist. You don't want the truth, but filthy lucre!"

The group sat in silence as Magic changed the record to John Lennon's *Imagine*.

"Come on," Magic said. "Let's not fight."

"Okay, brothers," Rainbow replied. "Let's keep our shit to ourselves and share the trips. Baron is going out to score some acid, so if you want a trip give us three dollars and he'll score for us." We rummaged in our pockets and shelled out the shekels. "We'll go to the airport and watch the last flight from Sydney," Rainbow suggested.

"Okay," we agreed.

Wasteland soon returned with orange wedges and we headed off to the airport to rap in the lounges and watch ourselves in the mirrors in the toilets which reflected our images a thousand times on opposite sides of the wall. I looked terrible, with blemishes and horrible eyes. We then went outside to the observation deck to watch through the telescope as the last jet left.

Another trip passed us by and soon my jaw and teeth were like chalk and I had cramps in my stomach. I dug my wired mind as I babbled beautiful thoughts to myself. I was glad I had nobody to touch me. I was alone in my strung-out dream and knew we would be awake all night.

My face rum-red, later that night we celebrated with aluminum friends in the disco, as the sadists guzzled beer freely, while nihilistic philosophy was discussed. Baron blew us away when he told how Rainbow and he had put his sperm under a microscope.

Our beer-drinking needed a calming influence, like a mushroom, ham, salami, oyster, onion, and ground beef pizza. Baron drove the gang to Papa Giuseppe's Pizza Parlour. Five drunken louts braved the highway that night, and when motion ceased, the tripped-out drunks fell out of the kombi to lean against a shop window and a road sign in crumbling succession. The band was pointed across the street to the pizza parlor. We looked like the last surviving disco left in town, as we staggered across that devilishly tricky highway. I hunchbacked it into the joint and was very repulsive. The clientele seemed to notice us. The scene was augmented by Uncle Cane Toad heaving up on the counter. It was the funniest thing that happened all night. Mate, it stank.

He kept apologizing to Papa Giuseppe, saying that all he wanted to do was give a good belch. We got the poor blighter back to the car, with the psychedelic chunder cascading every now and then out of his mouth. The smell of vomit was too much for my digestive system. *Belch.* I threw up all over myself. It's nice to have a smoke, a trip, and a drink on a Saturday night.

We went home to watch the late, late movie on TV. The earth had been conquered by the deviants from outer space. The mad fools. The catastrophe was vague as I dropped a can of beer onto the frayed carpet and gripped the chair in tripped-out concussion. I yelled, "You senseless psychological killers!" as I dived behind the chair. I raised my head from behind the chair when the tension became too great. Some deviants whizzed across the screen in space city. I crumbled to the floor and closed my eyes and let the world drift in dizzying vertigo. All the vision I possessed dissipated, with no reason, in a blackout. "Let me die, let me die!" I called.

"Get that ruddy dog Sphere to bed!" Rainbow shouted.

I smiled. It's so nice to be loved. I staggered against walls, and Baron Wasteland, to finally crash in my bed and black out completely. My last thought was that I invented the flower generation at puberty.

21

If you can talk about it, you can laugh about it.
Uncle Cane Toad

Late the next day, the motorbikes were turned out and the kombi loaded with freaks for a trip to everywhere. The colorful entourage set off and soon the kombi was left far behind as I rode pillion on a BMW and, although I was not an ordinary pillion passenger, the cool wind cleared my mind from the trip the night before. I was astride the bike, facing the opposite direction to the way we were traveling. It was my now-famous backward pillion stunt. Out of Sydney we raced as I stared, stoned and mesmerized, at the back wheel turning round and round.

The bikes raced forward, crept up to cars, dropped down behind, and then pounced forward past the "red line" sailing out and around, the gears snapping up and down till the steady ton was achieved.[24] I was a child of the wind, leaning around corners to where bike and man became one on the white-lined highway of eternity.

We turned into the mountain picnic area and every man, woman, and child packed up and left as the roaring bikes churned up the grass. The informality of the gang was not appreciated. Soon steaks sizzled on the barbecue plate as the long-haired, bearded barbarians drank beer, esky-cool.

Two of our company had not taken a bend and soon news arrived that they had crashed into another picnic area. More hairy drunks arrived, with filthy swearing and dented front forks. We crossed ourselves. Mother Mary have mercy. More than one bike rider has been carried away to the morgue on a jinxed bike. After afternoon beer, we drove into the sun, reaching an all-time low on blood pressure in the greed game.

The rings of the kombi were worn away and it burned oil like it was going out of existence. Every now and then we'd stop to get old sump oil from a service station to fill our depleted sump. On one stage of the trip the occupants of the kombi were nearly gassed to death and, except for the timely demise of the kombi, they would have crashed. They came rolling out of the kombi, coughing and laughing, high out of their minds on oil fumes.

Cane Toad, Baron Wasteland, and Rainbow fixed the kombi, while I told wild and amazing stories to little Neurone, one of the freaks' children. Wasteland would get Neurone to rip off potato chips from the garage while Cane Toad photographed him in the act. We were a screwed-up bunch of fools.

Two days later, the last of the gang struggled into Thredbo Village in the Snowy Mountains. The next morning we were all busted, with 112 marijuana plants which were growing on the balcony of our friends' flat. Police came charging in, asking questions, searching and accusing. No chances for anyone with long, matted hair who refused to answer questions.

The girls got off with sympathy, while I got a smoking and possession charge. The coppers had to lie to convict us. Cane Toad got busted with a seed and a roach. The coppers said I held a deal of grass and therefore I was in possession, even if it was only for five seconds. In court they lied that I had confessed to smoking a joint the night before. In Australia you're guilty till you prove your innocence. It's just part of the game. I lie too. Baron Wasteland got charged with having unprescribed pills. The rest of the freaks got various charges. We all got freaked out by a spider in the cell, which we promptly squashed and, with the help of friends in the village, we were bailed out of jail some hours later, with little reminder of our incarceration except a squeezed-out spider kaleidoscoped on the cold cement floor.

In the village, little Neurone was crawling all over the mountain, biting tourists for scratch, and Rainbow wanted to organize orgies. But I got depressed and so, when the kombi broke down for good, I hitched back to Sydney. There was too much action these days and I needed peace and quiet, so I rolled myself a joint and started to vegetate and carry out the next part of my plan to integrate the Bible into my life.

The dream had come true in Genesis as cocaine became a fugitive east of Eden. I was there at the creation of the universe. I was there in the Bible. This is the last generation. I was sent to save the world. In the world where I play my games and dream my dreams, there is the confusion that man represents. A world that doesn't know. A world built on the experience of a thousand generations of struggling, frail humanity, and the Bible represents its ignorance. The Bible is antiquated. The Bible, the world, and I all have something in common. Nobody knows in this world. It's a world searching for its own identity and destiny. Maybe the truth is that we have to find out the secrets of the universe. My truth is the babble of Sphere. I have three brothers and we are the Four Horsemen of the Apocalypse. I am a truth-giving spirit. I am a man who has felt more pain than anyone on earth. My sex is amplified. My sex is the dream of life that we all share. My conviction is for all of our thoughts to be free.

"Bullshit," Wasteland says.

22

Sex is learned the same as most things. That and intelligence separate us from the animals.   Magic Star Flower

We went into the nightmare then and we rode her for five years, and for five years I almost never talked. We had reached the smack days and we were addicted. Cane Toad, the acid freak, was dealing acid, clear, light white lightning, orange barrels, cap rolls of one thousand trips for $300. Baron Wasteland was dealing smack, white powder, gray rocks, pink rocks, while I sold ounces of buddha and hash. Rainbow hawked her body and Magic babbled on insanely. It was a stoned life, locked in an inner-city apartment at Kings Cross. The five of us would sit around for weeks and play Five Hundred, waiting for buyers to arrive. Freaks would walk in and out and rap about insanity while I'd rock my head and think that this was not real. The karmic waves predicted that we were headed for a fall and I was getting further and further into it.

Wasteland asked, "Why don't you visit Elysium in the commune?"

"I'm a messiah," I replied.

Rainbow lit up another trumpet and passed it around, while Magic mixed up a charge. I'd win the card game, as I had marked the cards while we took turns at changing records. We had card psychosis, TV psychosis, music psychosis and, generally, psychosis psychosis.

We had become a group of geriatric cases, with yellow eyes from the hepatitis we'd all caught. We all read. Baron Wasteland read science fiction, Rainbow read Mills & Boon romance, Magic read the Bible again and again, concentrating on Genesis and Revelations, Cane Toad read science books, while I read on sorcery, because I was the inventor of disco. We would sit around and read to the music, passing a joint and occasionally congregating in the kitchen for a charge. Basically, we couldn't stand each other and avoided conversation because we had said it all before. Nobody wanted to say anything. Nobody wanted to do anything. Nobody wanted to exist.

I was tripping, as I read the latest book of sorcery by Castaneda.[25] I stuck a patch over one eye and stared at the orange lamp shade for half an hour, to mesmerize myself with spirit power. Then, with undaunted confidence, I strode outside to do battle with the forces of the night.[26] It was stone cold, with the music of Pink Floyd playing from a flat in the background. The night was alive with power and, no doubt, a coven of witches was nearby, dancing naked around a cauldron of boiling mushroom brew, howling up a willy-willy, preparing for the orgy to follow. A dog's howl pierced the night. My stored knowledge reacted automatically: *The sign that a sorcerer is near.* I'll go back inside and have another joint with Cane Toad and a belt of bourbon. Too freaky. Little did the others know that I was a sorcerer on acid. I had entered the world of the hidden magic arts. My eyeballs held the source of power. All the people who read this book are under my control. My cruel, razzle-dazzle eyes held black secrets and secret designs. I could read thoughts and control others with my telepathic mind. Love had once been my power but now pain was my glory. Magic had told me how Jesus had accumulated pain and that was his power and with my pain I could rule the world. I went back inside.

The scene changed, and that night, while accumulating pain, I took a series of cold showers on acid and came down with bronchitis and then pneumonia. My reckless lifestyle had made every winter a cold and flu misery but now, sweating to death on a fever, I'd cough up blood and sticky mucus. I'd cough up nightmares during the day in a fever of living hell.

The five bacteria came into the room and Magic spoke: "We've brought an astrologer to heal you, Sphere."

Leaning over me, the astrologer spoke star signs and the ascent of the moon. He looked up his chart of numerology, checked my palm, and placed a flower on my chest. He then smiled and said, "Death is just a moment away. Be quiet, all."

I smiled a weak smile and fell back on my pillow. "You bastards!" I yelled. "Get this clown out of here!" I was thankful he wasn't into acupuncture, or I'd find myself with a needle protruding from my lung.

Rainbow smiled and said, "Take this tab of acid and call us if you need anything else." I swallowed the acid and went into my delirium. After an hour I did feel much better as psychedelic colors dashed up the wall and the music took on special meaning. Soon, I was wired again and went to Satan's hell. A bad trip began as hallucinations flooded my eyes. Monsters and satanic devils pranced naked around me as they swore obscenities into my delirious mind. "Let me die, just let me die," I whispered to myself.

The fever was collected, arranged, and conglomerated into fever-pitch delirium and during the trip brain pictures, agitated by hell, were wired into a rock and roll experience. Jimi Hendrix came back from the dead and entertained my mind with his electric guitar. The creatures from outer space arrived and landed on my nose. I'll rise and make the universe out of cigarette smoke and then blow it away. The Beatles appeared in the dream and played the Last Post. It was a freakish time, with burning creatures running up the wall and swirling ghosts flying through the air.

Soon it was over and I walked out of the room into fresh air, to blow a joint. I know exactly what they mean now, man. I see ghosts all the time, flashing across the sky. It's way out, the way they organize it. Instantaneous, like a shot of heroin. Treasures, like the wind, stored and hidden by the men of knowledge and love, and callously disregarded by others in their search for pleasure.

The torture of earth can sometimes be unbearable. This is one of the most sadistic planets in the cosmos. The earth holds gold and jewels and the humans fight over them. We are always controlled to fit into the scheme of things. The trick is to know when you have had enough and then be content with moderation. The noble puzzler beams from head to toe with his workingman's philosophy. Peace, my friends.

After the fever I was stoned, starved, and sorcerered away with periodic flashes of reality. Sydney, the home of meat pies and Vegemite, basked in the sunny weather. I hated the people of the city because they were sick. The body that I lived in now needed fattening up—and did the pig eat! Where there was a shadow of a man who, only days previously, had been racked by fever and starvation, a new and wondrous transformation took place and my cheeks began to glow with blossoming richness. It was pure paradise, with a carafe of wine, sitting on my favorite chair on the back porch, listening to the illumination. Why leave Eden for reckless adventuring? It's all in your mind, kid. I'll be a lowly marijuana smoker until the end.

Wasteland came outside and sat beside me. "Always trying to find an answer within yourself," he said. "The answer lies outside. People like poverty because it gives them a chance to dwell on themselves and not the beautiful things around us. Confirmed introverts."

I sat, took a sip of wine, and thought about it. I shrugged. "Yeah, you're right. Where are we in the scheme of things?"

"We're here," he replied.

"Shucks, you're profound." I smiled back at him.

"We're all profound, mate," Wasteland said, as he smirked a

toothy grin and helped himself to my wine. "Invented any good rock and roll lately?"

23

Happiness is where you find it.   Uncle Cane Toad

In Kings Cross, with marijuana growing in the garden, I listened to the same record a thousand times and drank vast quantities of tea. Then I scored a job as a drug courier, so Uncle Cane Toad and I went to Bali to find the fabled Mountains of Madness, where there were rumored to be cheap weed and good women.

Arriving in Bali, we wanted to get stuck into the local customs as soon as possible, so we dropped twenty small mushrooms and spent a good day tripping on the beach and in the afternoon we went for a pleasant tripped-out ride on motorbikes on Balinese roads.

That afternoon, I bought myself a woman from the beach. We stretched out in the time garden as my awareness expanded itself and noticed a thicket of bushes and a grove of coconut trees. Confusion flooded my imagination as I spoke to her: "I'll tell you what to do. Build my ego," I said, "and I will give you anything you want. I want you to tell me everything that you love about me. I want you to build a man, because that is what love does. It takes away fear and gives strength." I rose on my elbow as the arena fluctuated with a soft, breezy ecstasy. Washed by the dream, she said, "Yes, I love you. I won't hurt you with my insecurities. Will you build me too, and tell me who I am?"

"Your mirror is at your command," I whispered.

The dream shimmered and vanished. I played in her mind on the bed in our stone home on the street that led to the holy city. I observed the colorful procession that wound its way through our bodies and lives and in her dream we laughed and swirled in the love, lovely, love. "I'm sorry if I hurt the women's race," I said. "I was a man who didn't understand your feelings. In the completion of the union of male and female," I told her, "beauty and ugliness walk hand in hand. There is no beauty or ugliness in love's attraction, only joined illusions. I'll build and give you a temple of divine delight. I love you and love completes a journey from me to you. Watch it grow and construct something beautiful in its bravery."

After lovemaking, I played the guitar and had universal knowledge in the tranquil paradise of heaven. I had opened another door to the other side of perception.[27] I am.

The following week, I decided to do something I hadn't done in some time and that was to take a full trip by myself. Rising early, I gathered twenty-three small mushrooms and ate them. The trip came on as I was drinking tea on the veranda. I sat and pondered, tapped my feet and, deciding on a change, I smoked some opium and then went for a ride to the local beach, where nothing was happening. My boredom was replaced when I lost the key to the motorbike in the beach sand. I walked home and on the way I had a beautiful vision. I had just passed some coconut groves and was thinking of the life hereafter, when a woman in a flowing white robe, whose face shone like the moon, came running towards me. The backdrop of coconut trees and village huts was ideal. She came halfway across the field and vanished in a drifting mist of hallucination. It was my Elysium Dream.

That night, after twilight, a tropical storm lit the darkness with flashes of lightning. Man at the dawn of creation, with the rain washing him clean. I believed that my dream had, like a magician, conjured up a raging holocaust. I had mixed my dream and drugs with religion and created heaven. I saw my girl ride the storm in her robes of white. She was suspended in the air and her voice was thunder and her eyes lightning, turning the night into day. It was the most brilliant hallucination I had ever constructed.

I stared, mesmerized, at her in the sky till the thunder and lightning abated and the night was filled with the sound of steady, soaking rain. Strung-out, I listened to my mind as it babbled on and on. I had on my mind a psychic soap opera, so I changed the channel to a psychotic nature series and it was fantastic again.

I spent the next wired day stoning on the veranda, but the world looked out of whack. It seemed to shimmer in yellow. There was something strange about the surroundings. I thought it must be the buddha grass I had smoked. Cane Toad wandered out of the bungalow and plonked himself down on the cane chair. Out of the blue I said, "Today I make the papers with the naked truth. I created heaven last night and today the populace will find out the truth about me. I'm a sorcerer and we will live in lightning flashes forever."

"Footrot, mate," he replied. "When are you going to talk straight?"

"I'm seriously thinking of storming through the town as naked as a Melbourne maggot. I'll terrify the ones who think there is something to hide and liberate the freedom thinkers. I'll shake the place up and then rinse it out. It will be just like washing the skidmarks from my underpants."

"Go ahead, Swamp Fox," he replied.

"My new name is Bent Nail. This will go down as my latest exploit. A great caper. A law for eternity."

Cane Toad replied, "Your childish mind will get you into trouble. Remember that we're here on business."

"Who cares about business?" I replied. "Remember the time we went to the Springbok football match and I hurled eggs at random into the spectators? That was a great day against apartheid but, as the nude rider of truth, the population will be integrated into my dream. I show all. My naturalism is truly great. Bent Nail has taken over. Heaven exists." (Little did Cane Toad know what the bent-nail effect is, and I was not going to tell him.)[28] I raised a cry of glory against the cleanskins. "To glory! Down, my faithful worshipper, Cane Toad. The stoned ranger rides again!" I took off my shirt and sarong and the beast hung down.

"Showing off the bum rocks today?" Cane Toad said.

"Yeah," I replied. I let out a crow caw and kickstarted the bike. I could almost feel the stares, whistles, claps, and cheers as, spinning dust and gravel, I stormed off to glory. On reaching the front gate, I met a couple of Australian nurses. I jumped off the bike and started jumping up and down and yelling. Then I threw a browneye.

They went running off into the day, yelling, "Madman, a madman is loose!" I jumped back on the bike and threw a U-turn. Cane Toad was there, waiting on the veranda.

"Couldn't hack it, Jumping Jack Flash?" he said.

"Freaked a few girls out," I said.

"Not my thing, mate," Cane Toad replied. "By the way, cover that monster."

"Oh, yeah."

"Why don't you go and visit the nurses?" he asked.

"They'll know I'm stoned again and give me a lecture on the merits of going straight. Anyway, I just freaked them out," I smirked.

"They'll get over it," he said.

"But will I?"

"How can they resist you? Show your impish smile. The famous Sphere grin. Exploit their sympathy. A degenerate always deserves sympathy."

"Thanks, mate."

"Go on, Bent Nail." He smiled provocatively.

"It's Sphere again. I just put on that mask. I don't have the effect."

24

Have you ever noticed an ant that has been stepped on and doesn't die but wanders around in total confusion?
Magic Star Flower

The next day followed the next, with me sitting on the veranda realizing how heaven should be. I picked up a kilo of smack, taped it to the inside of my thigh, and went flying home to physical decline in Australia, after a mighty fine holiday for a deviant and degenerate swine.

I dropped the smack off at Mr. Guzzler Sane's house, after taxing it a couple of grams. Mr. Sane sat me down and told me the ropes of the business.[29]

I sweated.

"If you break our rules, we will break your back," he said.

I sat, listened, and sweated some more. Guzzler was a large grower and importer of dope and he had decided I was to be his protégé. To start off, he took me into the organization. He started to teach me psychology, philosophy, and sociology. He had gone to university and so he had a few textbooks which he recommended I read. I was straight off the street and knew nothing about the psychology and philosophy of big business. He began to educate me. He took me into his confidence, while I did the books.

Taking me aside one day, he said, "We're all a little bit touched by madness, but the real people don't see themselves as different. Because a man is old, it does not make him knowledgeable. Aristotle, Plato, Newton, Marx, Christ, Einstein, Buddha were all insane. They had their own private hell that they went through, but the thing that made them different is they played at the god game and won. They simply thought they knew the truth. They were the first, and so staked out their immortality. They should have taken the money but they went for fame. Money, power, glory, and fame are the four idols that we all strive for, but don't fool yourself. Ideals and idols are for fools. We all need a taste of these things, but none of us can live on them. I use these things to get the things I really want and, my friend, that is a taste of the good life.

"A purpose in life, and the answer to the questions of life, are for the talkers. Don't try to be an individual. History is full of their efforts. Then what does it all mean? I'll tell you. It's a story to go to sleep by. Never destroy yourself and never play people's god games. Enjoy yourself in a quiet, easy manner.

"When I was young, I discovered the truth of the universe, but I was high on my back on petrol fumes and my truth was meaningless. We're all insane when we think. Insanity is many thoughts or words. They represent the universe. I use my hands to shape my reality. I know I only talk about my perception. I am everything that I thought you were. We're all trapped in our own body and mind. You must know there is no immortality, only stories to go to sleep by. Who gives a damn? Dig it. We're all shits.

"Don't be a fantasy person, because we all need to talk about reality. Don't be mechanical, because emotion is energy. You can get something out of garbage. Always have the patience to listen and learn. Even the fools who babble on and on have something to say. Care about people and worry about them, because they are your greatest asset. The rule is, never boast about your conquests but use your conquests to give you the confidence to exist in silence.

"I'll tell you about the hello effect. We get our impressions by what others tell us about people. We believe other people and not our instincts. This is the hello effect. Always choose your friends by what you know about them and use your own judgment to understand people. I know that you have a good perspective. We all see the same person differently. Play to win and if you lose, don't drag your friends into your misfortune. We're on our own and, win or lose, it's how you enjoy the game. Always play to improve, and if you improve you will have good stories with which to amuse your friends."

He placed his hands behind his back and paced off, leaving me standing in the garden. He had once said to me that learning is innate. We all want to learn, but it is a hard lesson to learn, that all our ideals can be converted into money.

Most people just go for fame, but that is only another idol.

25

When in hell, do as the Devil does.   Sphere

Wasteland's words: "Your mind is the room. Find the key and you can escape; otherwise the room will overwhelm you and you will be lost in the insanity of the cosmic room."

This is where it all happened. The cosmic room. This is my room. The ultimate in luxury. This is it. The place where it happened. The vibes fill the air, mate. They are all around us. The vibes' colors really shimmer off the walls. Those waves are really fantastic and they bounce and echo all over the place. The cosmic room. The old cosmic room with its clean bed and sheets, its sunshine and cask of red wine shimmering in the warm sunlight. A casket of red starlight, and a loaded syringe.

This is where it happened, mate. I lost contact with reality and went insane. Elysium Dream was in my mind then. She was there in spirit. She filled the cosmic air room. That red wine was good. It was from Guzzler Sane's private cellar. He knew I was ripping it off and I picked the place clean. Years of wine collecting down the drain. My drain that went straight to my brain. He didn't care, because he knew that wine collecting was a status sham. Years of wine collecting went into my insane brain.

The room was clean in a compact, leafy house of wide open spaces. There was plenty of room to breathe the perfumed garden. A white woollen carpet, curtains of white and desk of mahogany. The housekeeper was there with peanut cookies, roast lamb, and baked potatoes nearly every night. It was streamlined treatment. It was beautiful, mate. Privacy in every corner. Leisure at every turn of the hand. Life with a millionaire in a homey castle, hidden away in gum tree suburbia.

The previous month I had returned from Bali. Life was good. I found the women beautiful and, with my bike on the road, life was a mystery. My motorbike and I shared many a good moment together on the roads. The trusty, rusty 500 was a good mate of mine. She leaked oil but she was a faithful companion. The days I stripped the sockets because I believed that when the bike died I died with her . . . it was a strange time, that.

I had returned from Bali and red wine and good women awaited me. I got good old-fashioned sex, drugs, and rock and roll. I made it with the housekeeper, who was an ex-pro. The smoking weed that awaited me every morning was delicious. The grass had awakened me to the mysteries of the universe. Thousands of planets with intelligent life swarmed all over the cosmos. Imagine it: little civilizations all over the place. Their spaceships swarming all over the universe. This made me a mere speck of atoms arbitrarily conglomerated into a human form. It's all relative. It doesn't matter. It's just the universe fulfilling its organized nuclear destiny. Wars, famines, and flames plus peace, love, and purpose. Triangles are big in the universe's tune. I had cosmic and spiritual realization with track marks following the vein on my arm.

A typical day saw me awaken with a goblet of half-drunk red

wine sitting on the cabinet beside my bed. A shot. A sip of red and into the shower and then back into the cosmic room to dry myself. Get the little droplets of water cascading down my shoulders and thighs, another gulp of red wine, and wander out into the kitchen for an egg flip. Then back to the room to finish off the goblet of wine. Fill it up again and take another drink. Any wino will tell you that I felt euphoric. Why do I deserve this opulence? Let's get some brain damage done early in the morning. Sailing off the edge of Andromeda, right off the planet into the cosmic consciousness of the cosmic room. I lay down on the bed and put a tape on and let the music play down the corridor. Whirling music with a head numb and it all happened in a woman's womb of the cosmic room.[30]

My head was full of vibes just waiting to bust loose and tear down the fabric of society. I wanted to dream something out of this world and so that is what I did. I started to dream. I took a bottle of sleeping pills and went for the record. I ate twenty-five of the mothers and went to sleep to awaken refreshed the next morning. The cosmic room is my cocoon.

Guzzler was a homosexual and a child pornographer. I was a fool in a fool's paradise.

26

A woman can do it. Believe me, it's true.   **Rainbow Moonfire**

Welcome to heaven. The words that I had scrawled on the wall of our house. Guzzler had set us up in our own dealer's pad to increase our respective fortunes.

The typical out-of-work druggie can easily score when he has dealer's pay in his pockets and knows that a shipment has just come in. I smoked the Kashmir hash out back and stared at the motorbike. I picked up the manual. After a couple of weeks stoned I'd be tripping along to this road author. It makes the world insane, getting stoned on this dream. It can't go wrong. Trip along psychosis, mate, programmed to a happy ending. Baron Wasteland, a hell of a man, echoed from the house.

I looked again at the motorbike that, to my speeded hashish mind, defied description. I'll never give up, you mechanical fucking bastard. The machine that had parts like an animal and symbolized perhaps the courage of a generation. I put the book down and waited while examining the bike and thought about a snort of cocaine. My mind wandered off. Look at the bike. The gear levers jammed and, with a sigh of disgust, I went inside to have a blast. The familiar room with the coffee table strewn with torn Marlboro cigarettes. The Nepalese blanket strung across the door. The stereo playing Baron Wasteland's blues acid animal rock.

Baron Wasteland would be engaged in a vague reminiscence with himself while Rainbow Moonfire swayed in smacked-out euphoria. Speeding along at 100 miles an hour with a can of beer in his hand. Cornered, he'd have to talk.

"Blankey bike is cactus," I said. "Have we any degreaser?"

"It's been a hot day," Wasteland said to Moonfire.

"Bloody hot," she agreed.

"You never understand me, mate!" I shouted back at him.

"Dig a charge? It sounds like you need one," he replied.

"Yeah, what is it? Speed, cocaine, or testosterone? My sex life is in tatters," I replied.

"Smack," came the reply.

"Yeah, I'll take it. This is a bad life, you know, mate. I can't stand it. The weather is so hot." We used some smack and smoked into the night. Later, we snorted snow.

Late at night I heard him say again, "Yeah, you know, mate, it's been a hot day. Bloody hot. Rainbow, have we got any china that we can shoot up?"

She replied, "We've got a half-kilo bag and it's all good."

27

*The Pharisees and scribes put burdens on your back that
they will not carry themselves.*   Matthew 23:4

Lying on my bed, listening to the radio, I had a little fantasy.
Sphere was pacing the floor repeating over and over to himself:
The penis must enter the vagina, the penis must enter the vagina.

Rainbow Moonfire entered by the side door. "What's the problem, kid?"

Sphere replied, "I've just discovered how creation occurs and
now I must discover how destruction and death manifest themselves, for the pick must enter the vein."

At that moment, Baron Wasteland ambled from the kitchen with
a wicked-looking loaded syringe. "Here it is, Sphere. I made it up
to your specifications. This contains point twelve milligrams of
acid, a half-gram of good-quality scag, and other vitamins and minerals that are essential for good health and well-being. We're ready
to begin Operation Holocaust."

The syringe slid into the vein and drew its crimson music, while
from the stereo "Gimme Shelter" played and the plunger was
slowly pushed down, down, down. Sphere was seated in a chair
with his arms and feet manacled to prevent injury. The audience
waited in anticipation. Then, instantly, Sphere's mind and body
exploded in a kaleidoscope of psychedelic euphoric symphonic
orgasm, reaching into the outer limits of the great, universal dream
of swirling, mindless timelessness—or bullshit, in other terms.

Time passed, as his friends grew restless to receive his first
words. Two days later, when they could finally make sense of his
insane rambling nightmare, he proclaimed those immortal words
that are even now being memorized and written down in history:
"Too much acid, easy on the scag, a dash of Ritalin and more pethidine,[31] and we've got a hit. I think I'll christen it the Injackelating
Quiver Giver. Congratulations, we've done it again!"

We all laughed as we got out my pick and began the ritual orgy of memory trace destruction.

"It's the natural ingredients that I like," said Rainbow.

"I charge for the effect," Wasteland added.

"Me," I laughed, "I dig the social atmosphere of a blast."

Whatever the reason, we all felt an Injackelating Quiver Giver coming on. The band crowded around me and wanted to know what to expect. I received some revelations. Slowly I spoke: "I went through a holocaust and brought World War Three down on my own head. I am the Holy Ghost. This is the last psychological war. I'll tell you a little story. It began when I was seven, when I was playing Runner Across, a game we played at school. I fell over and scraped my knees on the asphalt and when I went to the nuns for treatment they noticed blood on my ankle and when they pulled down my sock they found a four-inch gash that required six stitches. Then, years later, while scavenging in a garbage dump, I fell over and cut my wrist. See, on my forehead you can see the scars of crucifixion. I have all the scars of crucifixion. The stone that the builders rejected has become the cornerstone of the temple. I am the Holy Spirit. The Lamb that was slain since the beginning of the world."

"He who blasphemes against the Holy Spirit is never forgiven," Rainbow solemnly spoke.

"We are truly in the presence of greatness," said Wasteland.

I spoke again. "I came to destroy a church and then build a better temple and that church is my mind. Friends, I have a confession. I am bisexual. I am man and woman. I am three beings in one because I am also neuter. The destruction of myself in punk rock will continue till I resurrect myself and run into eternity."

"Sphere's a poof," Wasteland laughed.

"I love my fellow man. I dig penises and I add them to my sexual record collection."

"You're still an arsehole," he replied.

"I'm a man," I replied. "Sex and poison and rock and roll."

"You're a cat," Wasteland laughed. "Cat, cat, cat."

28

This is a trip to everywhere.   Magic Star Flower

Uncle Cane Toad and Magic Star Flower arrived and Cane Toad spoke: "We've got some bummer news. The bad news is that we created the universe." He laughed nervously. "We're mad. Hawkwind are right. We are the center of the universe. Magic and I created the universe. We're gods."

Rainbow laughed while Wasteland leaned back. "Do tell," he said. "Too much speed," he nodded to me.

"Let me explain!" yelled Cane Toad. "Magic and I were having a screw on acid last night while listening to Hawkwind and when I couldn't get it off, she masturbated me to orgasm. Magic's now got the universe in her hand. It's either in her hand or in my mind ... or in the washing machine."

"Give me a look at your hand," Rainbow asked. "Yes, it does look like you have the universe in your hand, with all those sparkling jewels of sweat."

"I hold the seven stars in my hand!" Magic exclaimed. "We're all trapped in eternity. We created ourselves."

"Let's have a blast," Wasteland added. After the charge, Wasteland asked, "Where did you get this idea from?"

"Remember last week when you believed the police were monitoring us with transmitters implanted in our teeth?"

"Yeah, I remember," Wasteland replied. "Rainbow and I worked out that all the busts on Guzzler Sane's business were because the dental clinic had implanted transmitters in our teeth. You mean the transmitters have given you the power to create the universe?"

"You said it, kiddo," Cane Toad replied.

"The government is insane," Magic shuddered.

"Yeah, they are mad," Cane Toad retorted. "They made us create the universe. The universe never ends. It just keeps wanking for eternity, getting smaller and smaller as it radiates from the center."

"God, let me out!" I said. "This is paranoid."

"We're the gods, mate," Magic explained, "and now that the government knows, they will destroy the world."

"I've masturbated on acid," I said, "and if I've got a transmitter, that means I've also created the universe—maybe the Crab Nebula; and that's how I invented rock and roll."

"You mean all this is true?" Wasteland asked. "You believe it?"

"You bet it is, kid!" I exclaimed. "The gods of the universe reside in this room."

"The sperm just dematerialized in my hand," Magic stuttered. "I feel sick. The universe is insane. We're all mad. I'm God and I'm insane. We're really lost for eternity. What will we do? The government will crumble and there will be anarchy when the world finds out the truth."

"I think I'll kill myself," Cane Toad replied. "Let's offer ourselves in sacrifice. Let's all take an overdose on heroin."

"How long has this transmitter business been going on?" I asked.

"Most probably years," Wasteland said sarcastically. "You were probably implanted with a transmitter as a baby."

"A transmitter!" I cried. "A transmitter. That's how they did it! How the world picked up my thoughts. God, there'll be nothing but pain for eternity. We exist to perpetuate the ritual of creation. We're all lost. All lost in eternity. The reason that we are alive now is that we are trapped in eternity. It explains everything if we are the gods. We, the gods, cannot stop the ritual because in another infinitely small universe somewhere in the cosmos we are being born again in another Milky Way."

"Babble away, Sphere," Wasteland laughed.

"What are we going to do?" Magic asked.

"We're going to keep quiet. Play it day by day till all this madness blows away," Wasteland explained. "Lunatics! You can do what you like, but I'm going to have another charge of speed. I'm going out, as out of it as I can be, mate."

"We've got to get it together and stop this ritual. You don't know what it was like at my birth."

"Not your melodramatic whingeing shit again! It never happened!" Wasteland exclaimed. "Women don't rape babies."

Cane Toad interrupted the conversation. "When we go outside, we see the stars. We create the universe in our minds."

"Did we create the universe or did the universe create us?" Moonfire asked.

"That's the million-dollar question," Wasteland shot back. "But I think the universe created us."

"I did it on acid and speed. I wiped it off and the universe was hurled into the washer!" Magic exclaimed. "The universe exists in a matter–time continuum in the washer. A junkie created the universe."

"I thought that the sperm was dematerialized in your hand by some orgasmic matter transmitter?" remarked Wasteland.

"I don't know anymore." Magic started to cry. "I don't know."

"None of us knows," Cane Toad said sympathetically . "The fact is that we exist because others make us real."

"I'm getting out of Sane's organization and into religion!" I broke in. "I'm going to give it all away. Even the rock and roll." I walked into the bathroom and looked through my reflection of two black holes into my mind, and there was the universe. I had found the opposite of Elysium Dream. Hell's well. We were the twin gates of eternity. A computer, the sum of one, and as I looked into the mirror I saw God, I saw myself, I saw hell, I saw the universe, and I saw an astrological planet that was a dead star in its third generation. I placed my hands over my eyes and pressed the sockets until I saw the abyss of my childhood, while the lightning square flashes began to dance and hallucinate on the speed.

29

Women love status, money, and men, in that order.
Magic Star Flower

This week. Written by the evil Baron Wasteland.
Choreographed by Rainbow Moonfire.
Hallucinogenic trip no. 456.
Trapped in eternity.
Sphere, the inventor of rock and roll, had been implanted with a transmitter in his tooth as a baby, then cruelly raped and mur-

dered, but still he survived as the balls began to roll to transmit his thoughts of love over the earth. First, there was Moses, the father, then Jesus Christ, the son, and now Sphere, the truth-giving spirit.

Last psychotic episode, Uncle Cane Toad and Magic Star Flower had created the universe with a transmitter that had turned into a transmatter, and now Sphere has realized the horrible truth. We are all trapped in eternity. We die and are reborn and live the same life over and over again and that is why we are here now.

Sphere paced backwards and forwards, smoking a joint, as he muttered to himself, "There is an infinite number of universes. Tragedy, O tragedy."

Magic whispered gentle words to him. "It doesn't matter, we will find a way out."

"You don't understand," he replied. "I will have to go through the horror again. Over and over. It never ends."

Baron Wasteland entered from a side door and leered menacingly at Magic Star Flower. "We'll have to drop the bomb!" he yelled.

Sphere, who was also a noted pseudonuclear physicist, replied, "You don't understand, Wasteland. The universe wanks in and out. We have to stop it wanking. If you drop the bomb, it will cause bloodshed, but when the total universe wanks in we'll be drawn into the vortex and *voilà!* Creation again. There is only one solution. Jesus Christ will have to raise us from the dead. To the church, men!"

"There are two solutions," Wasteland added. "I'm going to have a hit and go fishing. I hear that snapper are running in the harbor. Where's your pick?"

"It's burred."

"Let me have a look." Wasteland examined the burrs, which can tear the skin, and then started to sharpen the pick with his teeth. "Where's the toothpaste?" he asked. Soon he was sharpening it in the solution in his hand and, after fifteen minutes, had a sharp fit. "How many times have you used this needle?"

"Twenty to forty times," Magic replied.

"God, you're disgusting! I've got this new Italian glass syringe with a box of needles. I've even got a wire to clean it when it gets blocked. It's better than jumping up and down with a blocked syringe. Still, you have to be careful because sometimes you can blow the needle right off when it's blocked."

We all got stoned on Mandrax, crushed up into a white paste and injected.[32]

"Abraxas is coming this afternoon," I said.

"We'll be ready for him, won't we, kids?" said Wasteland.

Uncle Cane Toad had it all worked out by the time Abraxas arrived. Wasteland thought him leapy, but we each thought that each of us was crazy. Wasteland warned Cane Toad not to let on to Abraxas about the transmitter. Abraxas walked in and observed the scene of torn cigarettes and empty and half-drunk bottles of beer on the coffee table. Uncle Cane Toad laid it straight on the line when he walked in. "This spinning across the universe is a drag," he said.

Tranquilizers-all-round Abraxas gave a knowing smile and asked, "How's it going, kids?"

"Freaked," Magic warned.

"I can't handle it," Cane Toad sighed.

"I'm crawling up the walls," Wasteland replied.

"All right, can I speak to Sphere? He's my patient. How's it going, Sphere?"

I remained in silence for a few seconds. I didn't want to dispel the delusion and I couldn't understand him because of my anxiety. "Fine," I replied. "Everything's peachy keen."

"You're lucky. There's schizophrenics and there's schizophrenics. Some have their whole life destroyed. I'm prescribing antidepressants for you also. So, come into your bedroom and drop your strides for your Modecate injection."

Abraxas left. I went out to fill the prescription and when I returned, Uncle Cane Toad had brought out his telescope and was trying to find heaven in the washing machine. He had a wild idea that it existed as a dream suspended in the tub. He was not satisfied, so he began to search high and low for heaven. He looked at the moon, in the toilet, and finally located it at the center of the sun. He triumphantly proclaimed: "We live for an eternity of ages and ages after traveling through the fires of hell. The sun is alive and thinks."

This madness was too much, so we dropped the antidepressants and

I awoke halfway through the night, crawling up the walls. I didn't know where I was as I banged and crashed in my room of darkness.

30

Heaven is just a thought away.   Sphere

One day the roof caved in, when Baron Wasteland, as an able-bodied speeded-out bus conductor, swore at a passenger and got suspended, then fired. Cane Toad and Magic were living down the road on taxi driving, speed, heroin, cocaine, hash, and muffins. Cane Toad jumped from his taxi and was taken to the psychiatric hospital, where he slashed his wrists.[33] At the cricket, Baron started swearing at the coppers and was arrested for abusive language.

After a couple of weeks, we were a subdued bunch when we got back together and moved to Bondi Beach. There was no more exuberant shouting at the neighbors, or naked people on the front lawn. The five musketeers were back together again, ready for good stoning weather. Perhaps we died there. I started singing, and playing the guitar.

> *I've got anxiety blues*
> *Down to my shoes*
> *Right to the soles of my feet*
> *Yeah I'm a dead beat*
> *Testing, one two three*
> *I need to do a pee*
> *Into the sea of destiny*
> *Hee-hee, my urine's free*
> *My bladder's Japanese*
> *Maybe Chinese*

If I want to make the big time my punk rock has got to get better.

Coming out of the concrete, with the sun in his eyes, the make-believe man wandered down, stoned, to the beach after a charge of heaven. I nearly blacked out at the safety railing. Walking out on this spring morning to the corner shop, stoned on hash, and surrounded by millions of people attending the annual City to Surf race, I thought they were going to make me Pope. I went back inside and had another joint of brown hash and a shot of scag. These people were running like lemmings to the sea. All too much. Inside was the ever-present stereo playing the Charlie Daniels Band.

Outside, and round and round the rugged rocks the stoned rascal ran. Maybe it's time to give an explanation of who we are. We were put here to find God, that great man-made perfectionist.

I put on my hong-kongs and walked on the gray rocks, looking at the sea's crustaceans, sheltered in crevices. The sea washed and cleared the gorged, scarred rocks on the shore. It was rainbow's end. A dog chasing its tail. What good is an explanation of knowledge when all you see is yourself? Insanity. I strolled on the boulevard to find someone with feet planted on the ground. The pain got richer and richer.

You have the choice. Do you want to get involved? Speak up, I can hardly hear you. You are not interrupting anything important. God is what you need. You're no great madman, just a philosopher who made a mistake. Travel, if you want to search for your daughter's age. The extremes will come together and the bright light will fade. The dream will become reality and you can't do more than that. It's all in your mundane mind. It's time to face the earth with the predatory knowledge of the entire rock and roll plan. Intelligence wanting to matter so it builds a body. Matter turns to energy. The energy that is released in utter stark nightmare that is the primeval spark of the universe, which balances the void where the beginning of terror sees itself become self-matter. All for love and love for all. The endurable beauty in the futility of death. Inspired with fluent emotions, I have been blessed in letting go of the insight. Missing, I let it go. The story is imprinted on the waves and it's a bleeding shame to leave the warm water.

Caught in the prisoner's poison. What are you doing wanting a color TV set? On the inside, it's walls and on the outside it's spelled backwards. The law you notice. There is no law wherever you go. Death, that is where I am. Bondi Beach. A microbes'

*soap opera. Inside, freedom rides in my suede, leather, and out-
back flannel. It will take me to that image on the last trip to
Bondi Beach. The acid child, her hair resting on my shoulders.
There is beauty in the senselessness. If I could choose one, I
would choose the one most human. My daughter. Like a blind
man, I hit the strum of a sparkling guitar. On the esplanade there
are human structures that grow from mushroom pizzas, while
the seagulls fight over the crust. I discovered that the children
don't know mathematics as yet. The double infinitive eludes
them. They are still caught in the past time. Integrate and differ-
entiate and then be yourself. Warm water flows through my liver
and evolves to crystal sweat that drains from my body like urine
which is ever beautiful. The blue sea and the people believing in
the sunshine. It's their recreation, their external reality that I
wanted so much to touch. My eyes caressed the wine. Did I tell
you that I want no more? My mind knew its failures. This is my
earth, my civilization and my creation. I am a man.*

*Man, I wanted so much to say that. My dreams walk into
transparency because the drug addicts are laughing at you. No
time to go into descriptions, because I have to believe before the
activity sweeps the scene clear. Ugliness at the scene of beauty.
The philosophers on the esplanade are like me as they step from
their eyes and watch what they want to see, their own mind and
planet. Love's movement. I wish it was good. Alone, my people
lay in the crushed quartz sand as my mind reached for the sky in
significant exhilaration. Nothing is wasted. The machine, my
mind wants to go faster, to dart and to blur. Maybe it will take
me to a romantic death. Stone dead. It could be so easy to
achieve an eternal home but to kill myself. Christ will come back
with his loyal angels and I will still be here, still waiting on the
beach with my lips and mind parted in hell's disbelieving shock.
You gave everything that you promised, but desire lived on in my
mind. The cities stretching for infinity were not my destined
home. I traveled through the great visions and saw nobody as a
slave. The work was good as the gardener of civilization.
Schizophrenia. The children were lovely and the love made them
grow. Didn't I tell a twisted truth? Didn't I lie? I drink the wine.
I don't want to live forever.*

I wanted the acid child, to dream and plan her future. I, myself, would be forever alone disliking change and permanency. Elysium, you see the truth now with this hedonist drug bastard. Like life, you bloomed and died. The reality was that they told a dream and gave a nightmare. With a little more self-control we could have made it. I lost my nerve. The past is forever over and now the good know. It is a step above the universe. You can't change the past, just try not to relive it.

Get it and forget it. Cool it with a few slaps of sea-water around the face. Do I want to tell the truth or deceive myself? It's all around us as the dreams of love get worse. No, I don't know what I wanted to say except sanity is what we've got to work towards. If I could tell the truth, I'm in a lot of pain. I dislike this existence. Fun, life is full of it, laughing boy. I've got an imaginary ulcer. It's high noon and life is precious with two hot showers on a sweaty day to keep in harmony with nature. Fun, I'm dying in hell.

After the trip on the boulevard. Stop at the shops for a vitamin C. Feel the breeze and morning sun. Wander back inside and listen to the Grateful Dead. Talk to Cane Toad, who is just waking up. Wander around to the wine bar and have a few ciders. Come back in the wind to have a shower and more music. Looks like I'll be strung out for the rest of the day. A pizza and orange juice for lunch and go inside wired, with my feelings singing, and it looks like I'll be walking the line of delusion. They are going to assassinate me.

The messiah walks along the beach
A shot is fired and he hits the ground
People watch but they can't explain
What it's like to feel his pain
What it's like to see his brain
Stinking in the concrete drains.

31

A lot of people don't fall in love.   Baron Wasteland

I was doing the withdrawals. I had only been taking half a gram of bad shit a day so I could do the withdrawals at home. All my energy was spent in trying to score, so I eventually went into my shell of pure need and want. My anxiety wouldn't let me keep still. My cold, clammy hands and the anxiety pains in my stomach and chest spread out to the nerve endings and I was sensitive. I couldn't stand a shower. I had diarrhea. The anxiety magnified the withdrawals ten times over. I was lucky, because if I'd been on a gram a day I would really have had bad pains and would have had to do my withdrawals in hospital. Still, I would have liked to be in hospital, but I just hung out and tried to think of something else. It was only a matter of time, of crazy, painful madness. The days passed slowly and I was quite mad when it was over.

> *Inside, alone, I played chess with the ants.*[34] *They were the next rulers of earth and had computers for brains. I saw the bull ants as they watched me. Slow moves of precision, that were opposed to my quick, agile moves in which they would not discover my mistakes. The automatic ants. What is versus what shall be. Elvis is dead. I had lost but I had deceived the mechanical ants. They would not pester me anymore that day. During the dreaming day the imaginary game of chess would be allocated to the memories of my mind.*
>
> *I played chess with the dreamless reptile. He was my next subconscious partner and was easier to defeat. When reptile lost, he lurched over and knocked the board to the ground. The reptile was the past. I stood in the middle and observed the hollow shell that my genius had invented.*

They were strange daydreams, all the same.
The local corner shop was owned by a Chinese spy and the

atomic bomb would soon be dropped. It was nearly the end of the world.

I played chess with the cockroaches. They scuttled over the board, trying to evade the light, but after a while, I just squatted in the corner, trying to keep warm. I periodically broke into shivers and then I'd get warm. The cockroaches always played black but I knew their game, so they screamed inside as I squashed them.

It was over and over as the wind played with him. His T-shirt fluttered about him. He walked till he reached the place where he could see the whole city. My mother and father, you crucified them too. The abstract that you call art, the noise that you call music, the lunacy you call TV, the games you play, the society you call forth. All wrong. All delusion. I scream at you, Jerusalem, still stoning the prophets. What made you so frightened? Perhaps a culmination of centuries of change. You each have a different answer. What did you do it for? What's the use? I am the blame.

I got down from my platform and walked towards the psychiatric hospital.

32

Where's my suicide pills?   Sphere

The schizophrenic sitting on the bed in the psychiatric hospital is Sphere. He has been tranquilized and he knows nothing. He is a zombie. He can't think because the medication has taken his dream away. Did you know they have medication that can stop you thinking? They are little white pills that take everything away and leave you as a vegetable. Sphere was a vegetable. He still existed but he had no desire to think. All he wanted to do was stare at the walls and wonder, in short phrases, how to escape. He was in pain but his mind was a locked safe and they would not give him the key. They would not set him free, so he struggled, and half his mind and body died and he was left temporarily twisted and deformed. He should not have fought the pills because now half his mind was blank, twisted pain resting on his shoulders. There is a change of medication. There is a change of everything.

He was introduced to Group A therapy, so he told them how he invented rock and roll. They attacked him, so he remained in silence, and when they found out he couldn't communicate very coherently, he was dropped from Group A. He went to Group C for balancing exercises and saying ta-tas. Not much rock and roll was discussed, but he did a lot of fun drawings, made clay pots, and had plenty of happy walks.

Did you know that some people think Sydney is in the United States and some schizos are aliens from space? Some people think we have reached the end of the world. Most of the druggies had a firm grip on (can I think it?) reality. They wanted to breed.

I fell in love with Forever, the Black Star of the Night, an alcoholic, and we shared our ideas. I explained why I hated Abraxas, because he didn't give me side-effect tablets for the Modecate when I first started, and so I went for six months in bed with the covers drawn over my head.[35] I also explained about rock and roll and how it was prophesied from the beginning of the Christian church. Jesus had said, "The heavens will rock." The early church divided into Rome's Vatican and Constantinople, Alpha and Omega is rock and roll reaching back into the magnetic fields to create empires. I prefer the roll to the rock.

I struggled to get to sleep at night and I struggled to wake in the morning for my needles, pills, meals, and therapy. Most of the people there were drugged and drunken write-offs. I ran and tried to escape but the nurses knew I had to live with myself, so there is no escaping from my schizophrenia. Nearly dead from medication, I dragged myself around the psychiatric hospital, halfheartedly believing Abraxas, that I had one chance in three of ever being sane again. After time, my dreams faded with the medication and again I was introduced to advanced group therapy. I told my story, complete with omissions, because I didn't want to embarrass myself. I got down to my secret subconscious and the stutterings became more pronounced; but here's to the honest people, the people who believe that the tongue is put there to use. To the fools who speak the truth. I may be totally wrong, but I'm an ignorant fool. I wrote a letter to my Elysium Dream:

Dear Elysium,

I am writing to you from a psychiatric hospital. The hallucinations have made every day weird and it has been this way for years. I want to explain some important things to you so that you will not forget me.

I wanted to save the world and that is the reason I couldn't stay with you after you became pregnant. I decided to go insane when I was fifteen because I knew that I could go through it and still come out sane. I was hurt very badly as a baby and I went through insanity then. My great dream is a great nightmare. When I was a child, I called my nightmare dream because it was over. I have the secret of insanity. I will tell Abraxas one day that secret. Please think of me because I am very confused. I don't know if I can get out of it this time because I have to get into it. I don't want to go into details but you must understand, I believe that I invented rock and roll. I want to be totally honest with you, Elysium, but I know I am mad. I can't live alone and I can't live with you. This letter is to let you know that I still think of you.

Love, Sphere

33

Sphere, you have one chance in three of ever being sane again.
                                                              Dr. Abraxas

I kicked over the 500 and rode in the dream, to Bondi Beach. Magic Star Flower greeted me at the front door. She was bombed out of her head on barbs to carry her over the smack withdrawals. The Who played from the stereo.

Uncle Cane Toad sat on cushions on the floor, waiting for Wasteland and Rainbow to return from the pharmacy. Wasteland had broken into a doctor's surgery [office] and scored a prescription pad and was now an expert at writing prescriptions for physeptone or, as it's better known to the population, methadone.[36]

Rainbow would enter the chemist's shop [drugstore] and check out the pharmacist who filled the prescriptions and, if the pharmacist didn't look too mean, she would leave and tell Wasteland everything was cool. Wasteland would then enter the shop, hand over the prescription and, if the pharmacist said it would be ready in ten minutes, everything would most likely be fine. Wasteland would watch to see if the pharmacist stamped the prescription or made a telephone call. If the pharmacist didn't stamp the prescription, or made a phone call, he would split the dream and go to a different shop.

Sometimes Rainbow would watch where the pharmacist went for the keys to the dangerous-drugs cabinet. Then Wasteland would slice through the alarm's magnetic tape with a razor blade and, after twenty seconds, the alarm would go off, but Wasteland and Rainbow would already have split. The chemist, not knowing why the alarm had rung, would turn it off and in the morning find his shop broken into. Sometimes, if we didn't have the keys, it would take us twelve hours to get the safe off the wall. We had a couple of safes out back with the corner oxyed off. When they broke into a chemist's shop they went straight for the dangerous-drugs cabinet and forgot about the cameras and other goodies, or went for the syringes when we had difficulty obtaining them.

We'd sometimes heat up twelve to fifteen tabs, but usually only eight (being careful not to heat it too much, because it gels) and we'd have a fine hit with our disposable syringes.

Wasteland and Rainbow arrived back and everything was cool, then suddenly Rainbow started to have convulsions and gasped for breath after the shot and the next thing we knew, she was turning blue and she was dead. We all freaked out. Wasteland gave her mouth-to-mouth resuscitation. He started shaking her and thumping her chest till he fell down, exhausted.

Uncle Cane Toad said, "Quick, call an ambulance and then clean the place up!" We hid the gear and waited for the ambulance and police.

We all got charged with possession and self-administration, and we lost a friend. We bailed ourselves out and, after we arrived home, we sat around in stunned silence. Rainbow was a woman of spirit and that is why I loved her. She had a spirit that no man could possess. She ran around with her pick and she shot us all down. Now there was nothing.[37]

I had a shot and staggered out to the footpath and threw up as the neighborhood kids watched the junkie. Then I revved up the 500 and shot like suicide into the fast lane. I watched the cars race by and did the ton over the Harbour Bridge into the peak-hour traffic. My mind was empty and my eyes filled with tears from the roaring wind. The teardrops radiated and left trails back to my ears, only to be lost in my hair. I curved, steered, and revved to a stop, all my energy gone, my hands shaking. I breathed deeply with my heart thumping and my adrenaline-mind still with blackness.

The following days were an assortment of short stories, ramblings, and general insanity. I would ride every day, singing to myself, and I lived out my frustrations and fantasies on the road, on the machine and in my head. I wanted to be with Rainbow because she was the lucky one to be out of this mess. The psychiatrist, Abraxas, had labeled me paranoid schizophrenic and I didn't know if I was one or just a mixed-up kid caught up in a trip beyond my control. Schizophrenia, a chemical imbalance of the brain. I decided to give up the Modecate to see if I'd go insane. The story of my past life was called *Going insane, after giving up the major tranquilizers,* but maybe this time it would be different.

I was visiting Wasteland, and I had some grass. We sat down for a charge of speed and a smoke. Speed really sends me crazy, heroin freaks me out, but cocaine is cool if I don't snort too much. Well, the speed started up my thoughts and they went on and on and on and on. There is no peace in madness. I needed a drink. I needed the perfect drug to make me sane. I had started using heroin to come down from the trips and I used speed to help me think in my tranquilized state but, as usual, I had taken too much and was going out of my head. Amphetamine psychosis had got Uncle Cane

Toad and Magic, but Wasteland could take a ton of the shit and still be down-to-earth. Sure, he'd swear and drink a lot of alcohol with it, and feel like screaming, but he always kept his cool.

Wasteland was telling me that Rainbow had locked him out the night before and he had had to break a window to get in. Shit, even Wasteland's brain gone! Rainbow had died a month ago!

Nobody knows what it's like to go insane, but I knew. He was my friend and now we were brothers. Even Wasteland had gone mad. I guess it says a lot for the drugs. We understood each other now.

I said goodbye to my friend, Baron Wasteland, because I knew he was as fragile as the rest of us. Cane Toad would understand him too, since he had gone insane. We all knew insanity, but I knew it better than anyone else. I know when I'm insane, because I'm in pain, but the strange thing is that it is a hard lesson to learn and it is easy to forget that I'm a paranoid schizophrenic.

It is easy to forget after a shot of speed and give in to the delusion. I forgot as I rode the bike fast, singing away, I crossed and dodged the center white line and overtook more cars than I care to name, then I went head-on into one. I got up and stood in the middle of the road, looking down on my crumpled bike under the front wheels of the car. My hair blew across my eyes. I should have died and started my life over again.

"Did you get that in the movie?" I asked another driver.

"Did you get that on tape?" I asked the transmitter.

The transmitter replied, "Your friend, Baron Wasteland, wants to die in a war. We are the sadomasochists and we will give him that war because we are going to torture you. In the telepathic wars you will torture each other unmercifully."

34

I am the universe.   Magic Star Flower

Wasteland's war arrived. My fragile mind fought in the mind's war. I sat in the now with my thoughts reaching back into the past of memories, and melding the future with my plans. For the past year I had waited for my suicide pills, because I had been waiting for the war. How I found out about the experiment I cannot guess, because it just naturally happened in the daydream of my mind. The mindwaves of the whole of humanity were in a grid network similar to iron filings in a magnetic field. The dreams of each person carried them on a journey to the imaginary war at the end of time. Theories evolved and dissolved. My thoughts were being amplified all over the world.

The sadomasochists who controlled the game were getting deadly serious and suicides and murders were common at this stage of the god game as the human race was driven insane. The sadomasochists concentrated to defeat the Sphere and there were tolls on both sides in an army made up of workingmen who all thought they lived normal lives but were all close to insanity. It was the only life they ever had known and by telepathy the psychopaths tore their dreams apart. Who was the strongest telepath on earth?

Let me explain: The sadomasochists, the power holders of society, had decided on a mind war, so they planted transmitters in psychopaths to fight in the last war. The electricity had altered the atomic balance of the planet and soon it would be converted to the fields of Elysium, while other wavelengths would be hurled into the abyss. It was the last war, and the sadomasochists decided to enjoy their last days with entertainment: intrusion into the minds of men and women. It was the mind war.

Out of this emerged Sphere, the lover of acid child, who was born halfway through the twentieth century, of English and Irish parentage. Dark in complexion, with a beard and shoulder-length hair, our hero was a bike rider who evaded cars with the skill of someone who knew the minds of their drivers. He was a prophet of the highways, a messiah of the paths that led to perdition and freedom. A man who could control a woman with one hand and hold a lighted number in the other. He was a man of full strength who knew his own destiny, or so he thought. He was an enigma to his friends and foes.

Systematically, some of the individuals of the world realized that there was something wrong with their ideas, and when Sphere first found out the truth he thought that he was the lone inventor of rock and roll. His perception showed him that he was a telepath, locked in a world that hated and worshipped him. Death to the sorcerer!

He landed a job in a printing factory, to supplement his invalid pension, and continued on with his work and only occasionally remembered his transmitter. He couldn't fight against the government of the testing ground.

I was working on a collating machine, putting books together. My mind lay elsewhere as I worked the collating machine, which was controlled by a foot pedal. It was a repetitive job and I had a tendency to daydream. I was working towards a discovery that was complex and basically simple, at the same time. I was counting the number of atoms in the universe. How or why I wanted to find this number I could not tell. I was beginning to feel the strain as the number got higher and higher. I continued on with my work, dreaming. The computer part of my brain needed to know the exact number of atoms in the universe. Love was needed to be added to the equation. There was a new girl in the factory, with a very pretty face and figure. She was small, charming, and blonde. A girl with a pleasant mind, who loved dancing. Sphere had been too long with his dreams of terror and he needed companionship. He needed to love someone.

"Hello, you're new here?" Sphere asked.

"Yes." She looked at the floor.

"My name is Sphere. I work on the collator. How do you find your job?"

"It's all right," she replied. "It could be more interesting, but I don't mind." We sat and talked for a while, a task that Sphere was not used to. Except when he talked to himself and imaginary friends, he was a loner and he had been alone for the past five years. He still felt the love of his chosen woman and his acid child. He had been alone since his beautiful dream had ended and now his life was lost in destitution.

"What sort of music do you like?" Sphere asked. He did not like asking questions, with its distant reminder of school, but he was showing real interest in the girl. She was shy in her own way, less intelligent than Sphere but a hot little number all the same. She liked disco and I remembered: I'll call her Eternal, my White Queen.

"How about we go to my brother's home and watch television tonight?" *M*A*S*H* was showing on the tube and I wanted to see how the psychological war was progressing.

The sadomasochists were releasing some coverage to the news media. Not the whole picture but dribs and drabs to draw in the public till the final news sensation broke that we were a mild, telepathic race and that a war was being waged to wipe out civilization. Men were fighting other men with their minds. Men were at their stations at computers listening to the voices of the transmitters. The sadomasochists were getting nervous because their future looked dangerous.

I took Eternal out that night and it was a beautiful, black satin night. The stars, although they lacked the brilliance of the city lights, still possessed a majestic magnificence. The radio was playing "Dreadlock Holiday" by 10cc.

We drove through the wonderland of orange streetlights and the colorful fluorescent lights of advertisement. I reached over and gave her a hug. I was in the mood for love. We drove to my brother's home and were met at the front gate by Snuffit Dog. He got his name because if he rolls in the marijuana patch one more time he's going to snuff it. A stinking animal. The dog jumped all over us in a very affectionate manner. Eternal was a bit scared at first of the gray mottled cattle dog, so we walked quickly down the path, her boots crunching on the gravel. Snuffit was close behind, wagging and playing about. We met the kid's kid at the door.

"Good day, kid," he said.

"Good day, kid," I replied.
We were invited in and sat down to watch the television.

The fact dawned on me as I watched the TV. The radio was telling me also. Like a prophet, I was becoming more aware I would have to be ready for the day when they would confront me with the tapes of my conversations. The day they recognized the inventor of rock and roll. The world would show up with its bigotry, greed, pride, and hate and also with its reason, compassion, and intelligent perception. It was a painful fate that had chosen me, but it would be my own ingenuity that would rescue me. I was gravely concerned for Eternal. I could die alone. I would have to face them alone.

Sphere watched the TV, maybe the most important invention of the century. Only through this medium and the radio could I follow the events of the psychological war. The great experiment in mass telepathy was progressing. The television, my window to the world, had enough information to educate the people. By story-telling, television could rule a world. Without a dictator, humanity would be reborn with wisdom. I was dreaming for a universal government that held the answer of an earthly kingdom.

The sadomasochists were unaware of the psychological progress of their patients. To the sadomasochists, something strange was happening. The computers taped the conversations and picked up the buzz of sleeping brains. They had not been able to break the code of the sleeping brains.

We drove home later that night and after an ardent goodbye we promised to see each other in the morning. I returned to work the next day and resumed my job when the clock showed 8:30. I smiled across the workbenches at her. We had another date that night.
"Hello, how are they treating you?" I asked.
"Not too bad," she replied with a twinkle in her eyes.
"No problems?"
"No problems."
"Good, see you around. Got to get back to work." Sphere ambled away with his mind quiet.

I was having strange dreams as I worked the collator. Dreams of a nature that was completely beyond my present imagination. I dreamed that I was on a planet at the center of the galaxy. The people were partial telepaths who could let other people into their own minds at will. They had a perfect civilization. There had been no wars in recorded history and each individual was happy in an environment that lacked nothing. There was no overcrowding in a civilization that had reached harmony with nature. Their thought ships had combed the galaxy to find species that had not reached their technological level. Their ships were ball bearings, phantoms, mere thoughts, but they allowed two-way communication. The race left most civilizations alone, not caring to manipulate their societies. They mapped the astrological thought plain that covered the entire island galaxy. They studied and classified earth, but still they remained apart till the earth made its own evolutionary discovery and joined the peaceful races of the universe. What Sphere was doing was forming an equation which would provide earth with a point in space that would make possible a thought picture that could travel the mathematically perfect galaxy. A thought ship. I was adding to my building blocks and the computer in my mind would give the answer to the world. The answer of total negation of oneself, traveling to the other side of time and information on life reception of the great schizophrenic dream. We could travel the galaxy without leaving the planet. Why am I here? I am here to tell the world that the angels who left their places were trapped in eternity.

I picked up a stray thought from the pool of infinite intelligence. I thought to myself, if a man could throw his mind with the aid of a machine, then time could be distorted to a place where all thoughts originated and terminated. The mythical kingdom of heaven. There was a definite pattern to suggest that we were on the verge of some great scientific discoveries.

The sadomasochists' artificial brain computer, which would convert brainwaves into comprehensive speech, was almost completed. They would be able to read my mind. Unknown to me, the mission was already completed. The sadomasochists listened to my secret thoughts.

The radio commentators were the first to contact me. I was listening to the DJ at work when I realized that he was talking to me over the air. It had been the moment that I had been waiting for. They had located the inventor of rock and roll. They could look out of my eyes. The radio stations had been aware of the experiment for some time and many sympathized with me. They had built their own computer converter from smuggled secret information and listened to my thoughts.

I screamed when I first discovered the truth. They play me for the fool! Inside my mind I screamed. My mind was turned into black, seething energy. They will not explain the truth. I walked through a nuclear holocaust of antimatter which hurled me back to the beginning of the universe. A re-enactment of hell. The first wavelength of pain.

I had to take the rest of the day off work. I shitted.

Magic Star Flower was worried for me. I was lost. The first day had decided the outcome of the war. I returned to work the next day, out of my head on Mogadon.[38] I couldn't work, so I took the rest of the day off.

Later that night, I drove with Eternal, my White Queen, and talked about magical things that only the two of us could share. We made love that night. My finger stroked down her tight, dry groove. Up and down my fingers went until her lips unfolded and my finger edged further inside. I went down on her and tongued her while my twisted mind shouted love, lovely, love as I lapped at her. *I need you to stop the shouting in my brain.* I was in deep conflict when I finally entered her to her deep moans. Slowly, her tight dry vagina parted before me and slowly I was all the way in. I discovered my old self and inner quiet. I felt her pubic hairs streaming down into her vagina as I pushed them in. I changed with her mind. I slowly went backward and forward in her tight dry vagina. The softness between our eyes was merged and blended till we became one as I came in our tender, oily breakaway. My delusions were dispelled for fatherly protection, kindness, and warmth, which are the legacy of love and love protected me. With my hand in her hair I could read her eyes. She was shy. She was mine. My White Queen was rolling.

She talked. "I was raped a year ago. A drug addict raped me and I got pregnant and had an abortion."

Some women have large, wet vaginas, some women are dry, some women don't even know why.

It seemed as if I was being raped.

She continued. "I used to enjoy sex but now it has changed. I hope he gets a long sentence. I have to be in court in a month's time." The words faded away. We talked about the nature of humans. Two ordinary people sharing each other's ideas. She was like a child. We were good for each other. The voices faded away.

The next day at work my dreams at the collator continued.

I found myself at the center of the galaxy; because of my pain, my thoughts had reached to the end of the universe and come back to Sphere. A cap was being ceremoniously placed on my head. A multicolored room with gauges and switches and buttons surrounded me. I was chosen to fly the thought ship. The number of atoms in the universe. Escape from the planet. My mind became a kaleidoscope of landscapes. The ship was thought into space, receiving the total knowledge of my mind. I could not hold the image. I was having a mental breakdown. The number was known which echoed down my mind.

I left the machine, knowing that I could not return to it. It was stopped at the exact astronomical number of atoms in the universe. I was going home to collapse in mental exhaustion.

"Can I have the rest of the day off? I'm not feeling well," Sphere humbly asked the foreman.

I was given the rest of the day off. As I warmed up the 500 I saw the magnetic field. High-tension wires crisscrossing the earth. I could never return to my job. I had finished with the equation "Thought doesn't matter." I had to move on to the next equation till the earth is converted to the fields of Elysium. Move on till the next record was released. The voice in my head said so. The war was being repeated.

I was a nervous wreck and suicidal. There was confusion inside and outside. Human nature against spiritual nature. The real and the imagined. Instinct against intelligence. All this primitive emotion fought in immaterial thought.

To save my sanity, I had to give up hard drugs, but I still smoked and drank alcohol. My self-image was no more and there was no more Sphere. Survival in a surreal landscape became everything. It was a cruel war that seemed to last forever, but I had to go through the ritual and then become sane, just like in the beginning. Standing alone in the field, I had a direct link with infinity. I controlled the world. I held the attention of the human race. I was the only one with a nervous disorder that amplified my brainwaves. I ruled the world through the dream. I was the inventor of rock and roll, but the world refused to recognize me.

The voice in my head said that I had to be perfect to rule the world. Fornication and drugs had to go. I was two beings. One was the Holy Spirit and the other was the seducer of the whole world. It was the end of man's quest for knowledge to be in harmony with nature. I was the beast, the Devil, the dragon, everything that was despised. There was an inner war to overcome death. The voices wouldn't leave me alone. I was then and then I was not. I was being torn apart. I yelled in my mind that nothing in me is perfect. There was mad laughter as my hands tightly folded across my chest in a natural straitjacket. I watched the TV, listened to the radio, and lived in hallucinations. I called them Nazis but they replied that I was nasty Sphere. I swore at them. I held conversations with them but they would not listen. There is no law for the schizophrenic. I would have to find my own way out of the maze of the apocalypse.

35

The law does not bind the schizophrenic.   Sphere

I was alone now. Dire consequences began to eventuate. Tropical monsoons were altered by the increased wavelength of my mind. Storms of uncontrollable fury devastated towns and these were sent by God. Lightning flashes illuminated the sky, earthquakes shook continents, and these were sent by God. I watched on TV the destruction sent by God. I knew that, in my insane frenzy, I was killing more and more people—innocent people who had never hurt me—and every death brought me closer to the point of no return, of a mind on fire with grief. The weather chart showed the highs and lows which corresponded to my various moods. I went into a cocoon. A shell was forming over my crusty face. Bedsheets were strewn from my bed at night. Twisting and turning, I slept erratically. Night was turned into day and day into night. Every day a nightmare. The late movies were driving me mad as they showed my reflection as the Creator.

God controlled time and he became everything. A single piece of matter can be brought forward and backward till it becomes everything. It is then put in a time lock between the beginning and the end. Our life is over in a second but between seconds is an eternity. It is a man trapped in eternity. The sadomasochists created God and that is why we are here at this particular second. We can do anything with our minds. The law does not bind thought. We are outside the law. The imagination is real.

I regressed to my childhood. Years ago, when I was born, the nurse thought to herself: *Penis and scrotum.* She proclaimed to the gathered assembly: "It's a boy." Boy, was I red. I was born with a deck of tarot cards and specifically designed astrological shit because I was born on the shortest day of the year.[39] Mate, I had to wade through some I Ching slop to get here. Here I was, your average overweight big cheesy sibling, who loves nothing better than gurgling and crapping in the bathtub. A lovely, cherubic baby with no teeth. An elf of wisdom.

Then my world changed. My lungs screamed for air and I was hurled back into the vast infinity of a tortured mind. Existing in a circle of pain, for eternity. The black carbon hell of being crushed by a million tons of force. The weird, spiraling, shimmering abyss of walled hell that fell into infinity. Then, at night, the balls began to roll. Then the sequence was repeated. I was too small to be trapped in eternity. I was inflated like a balloon. Now I was back there. The terrible weight on top of me. The vastness of a mind that is a tiny spark existing in pain. A cataclysmic explosion where a piece of tiny matter is shattered in the wild expanse, in the blue contorted face and undeveloped mind of a child.

I possess a million more nightmares than you ever possess. I could not live in the house of a righteous God, so I was ostracized to eternity forever. I am trapped in eternity. Maybe there is a child with a crystal mind. There are many great dreams I have got together. I remember the circumcision and masturbation of truth. I remember the sexual dreams of puberty. I remember the acid trips I journeyed through to the smack days of institutionalized madness; but there is an order of dreams I don't think about.

I told you about the sadistic nuns who were not only cruel but didn't know love. I saw them years ago when I rebelled and they made me repeat the mathematical equation. It was my dream to organize the dreams. To bring the Bible up to date and record the last two thousand years.

Now I remembered, as I rode the 500. Religion. I could create my own religion, but that's not what I want. I want to destroy a religion.[40] I came to collapse a church and destroy a man. Now, brothers, I know your motives. How you love your fellow man. I went to your homosexual school, where boys sit beside boys. How you hate wickedness. How you are twisted up inside by an ambiguous religion. I know of your uncertainty and fear and madness. You are not balanced. Yes, you are insane, murdered by your own insecurity and loneliness and despair. When I go, I'm taking a few with me. Yes, I can take you with me. I know how to destroy your church, the perch which you sit upon. I know how to destroy the faith in you. I know you're homosexual, bisexual, normal, and neuter.

I remembered the destruction of a man as I hurled myself into oblivion. I, too, am homosexual. Bisexual, they call it. I would take the people in my mind to the local public toilet. I love penises. So sensitive. I love them white, with a foreskin. Peeling back the skin to see the purple helmet and to watch the homosexuals as I masturbated them to orgasm. Buggering men. I loved the new experience of a new penis to explore. In my studies, I found that 50 percent had the bent-nail effect and the average length was a mere 4$^{1}/_{2}$ inches. Some had tiny balls, some would never get it up, and most were circumcised.

Yes, I had invented punk rock.

36

I'm a sexual being.   Sphere

This is my suicide, to offer myself in sacrifice where the end of the guilty sexual dream will be forgotten. I live in hell. I have the masturbation scar. I will castrate myself. I will cut off my genitals and this will defeat the sexual dream that is boiling juice and weirdo's playhouse. I created the universe, and with the razor blade in my hand the blood from the inch-long gash had already seeped down along the inside of my penis, and with a little more pain my penis would be cut off. On three different occasions I have tried to castrate myself, but I could not do it. It is the culmination of years of pain and this time I will succeed.

The pain was the electricity and it has been torturing me. The electricity has intelligence and the lightning has been the perpetrator of evolution. Now its intelligence is being hooked into computers. This would be its final resting place, where it will rule humanity. The electricity is insane. The weather's electricity is good and which is good, AC/DC or direct current?

The parts of my mind have been turned into churning hatred. There is a complete transformation in myself as a deeper and

blacker torture emerges from my already blackened mind. The electricity is driving me insane. My mind is full of violence that turns at every angle like the contortions of a drowning worm. My mind is crawling and burning from the torture of the electricity. The electricity loves to torture me. It has ruled the earth for eternity and now with computers it will electrify the world.

I have been trying to add to my life and make it more meaningful with new, revitalized experiences that do not require honest work. You do not know what it was like to be me. I don't pretend to understand this madness. The madness of the world. God will always torture me. I need rest. I need to die.

I cannot do it. I cannot castrate myself. There is too much pain.

37

I think that everyone is like me.   **Magic Star Flower**

Baron Wasteland, Magic Star Flower, and Uncle Cane Toad decided to do an armed robbery on a chemist's shop. I listened to their plan but I was not interested in obtaining any chemicals. The next night they donned their balaclavas and made a frontal assault on the all-night chemist. The robbery went well and they made off with a stash of chemicals and that night were injecting them.

The next day police surrounded the house, knocked at the door, and then came barging in with guns drawn. It seemed the chemist recognized them because they used to buy their picks there. The whole gang was busted. The police charged the others and tried to hang a charge of accessory before the fact on me.

I finally got out of it after being intimidated at the police station. The others were sent to prison.

38

Fame is an idol.   **Sphere**

I had confused dream with reality and there was no escape from the transmitter, so I decided to visit Wasteland in jail. I went to sleep and woke the following morning. It was a good morning, as mornings went, with a slight dew on the grass on this September day. I made preparations and got the .22 and carefully checked that there was no bolt with the rifle. I didn't want to spend too long inside. I rode out in the car to die or live. Mad Dog Sphere had reached critical breaking point. I rode into the war dream. It was still early and not yet bank opening time, so I drove across Gladesville Bridge to the south of Sydney. The car radio was playing, as usual. Soon it was ten, and the bank opened its door to an armed robber.

I walked into the National Bank with a .22 caliber rifle wrapped in a blue sarong. I walked up to the teller. "This is a holdup; put the money in the bag." I paced the floor, watching the staff. "Cut the bullshit and put the twenties and fifties in the bag." The staff stuffed the bag full of clams. I walked out with $15,000.

As I emerged from the bank I looked to the right and was startled by a copper four feet away. Automatically, I whirled and aimed the rifle from the waist. The copper dived for cover into a shop doorway. Shoppers started running for cover. I turned and walked away. I don't think he had a gun.

Getting into the car, I started the motor, checked behind me, and drove into the flow of traffic. I drove around the block and, to confuse the sadomasochists, I threw a wad of one-dollar notes into the air in front of the bank. The transmitter was in my mind so there was no chance of escape.

I didn't know what to do with the money. It was just more drugs for a drug addict. It was bits of paper. It was no good to a psychiatric case so, while driving, I threw thousands of dollars out of the car window. I would take the rubber band off a wad of banknotes and throw them in the air. The notes floated in the air like confetti.

After several miles, the police caught up to me at a red light. The officer was beside the car window with a gun leveled at my head before I knew it. Then, when I saw the lights change, I swerved out of the traffic on to the other side of the road and did a sharp right turn in front of the oncoming traffic across the intersection. The police siren was close behind. I went down the main road and swerved into a side street. Bummer. It was a dead-end poverty alley. I drove to an abrupt halt.

I wondered what to do.

"Halt! Up against the wall!" the copper yelled.

I got out of the car and walked towards the police officer. Suicide.

"Halt! Up against the wall!" The copper was nervous. He was crouched down, with a gun levelled at my head.

I kept walking towards him, closing my eyes as he was about to fire. Death. Slowly the universe unfolded in the darkness. I opened my eyes as death came closer.

Fire all your guns and explode into space.

Reaching out, I put my hands on his shoulders. His quick reflexes pistol-whipped across my right forehead and then again on my left temple. I went down, dazed for an instant, and was docile. Handcuffs were slipped over my wrists so tight that the blood circulation was cut off. I was dragged along the ground to the police car. Frantically, he called for reinforcements. Hundreds of grubby children and sack-dressed mothers hung out of windows as more police arrived. I was loaded into the divisional van and taken to the police station for questioning.

They asked me what I did it for.

I said, "The publicity."

"That must be the craziest story I've ever heard."

The cell door was locked and a tear rolled down my cheek.

Taken into the court, I faced the magistrates, but Sphere was not afraid. I was charged with a number of offenses and also with assaulting a police officer. I pointed to the cuts on my forehead and said that that was assault and that he was a fuckwit and that was an insult. Bail was refused after I swore at the judge. I was taken to the remand section of Long Bay jail. People just don't dig a crazed, Anzac hillbilly with grinning teeth and foul breath.

In the sweet institution it was real good to get away from the madness outside. It was crazy out there with half the cars going the opposite way. Luckily, I hadn't been killed. I could relax with my transmitter and listen to the voices echoing through the thick concrete walls. It was beautiful being locked up. I wanted everything dead around me. Not a trace of living green. There was someone else in the complex with a transmitter and I could hear him pacing up and down the cell block laughing to himself. We're all going to be insane. We're all mad, you Melbourne misfits.

39

God's a mother.   Baron Wasteland

I was placed in "Programs and Protection" when the screws found out that I was an invalid pensioner. Every morning we were marched out to the front yard with its bench, toilet, and rubber tennis ball. We were segregated from the normal prison population and it was a squalid home for flies. There were usually a couple of crims to each yard who would sit on the concrete, lean on the wall, and wait for the sun while listening to music from the communal radio. I was alive and crazed in wacko company.

"Napo" was Mussolini, and I could hear him giving his political speech. "Crowbar" was a hunchback, in for arson. He had burned down a Hare Krishna temple and I could hear him singing, "Hare krishna, hare krishna, hare rama rama rama." There was an American down in the end cell, in for murder, who was waiting for extradition papers. The others were an assortment of rapists, heroin smugglers, transsexuals, thieves, and murderers. We were a colorful batch of fruitcakes.

I was once placed in a cell with a child molester. He had been transferred from Parramatta after being bashed. Crims hate child molesters. Little did they know that I was once at fifteen.[41] He was being protected now, because crims hate child molesters. They really hate them and so their life's not worth a penny.

I thought they would release me after ten days but they didn't. The sadomasochists jammed the transmitter and tried to alter my body texture to rubber. So I like pain. I was classified a psychopath after I started screaming and spitting at the screws. My health had deteriorated because sometimes I didn't eat or drink for days.[42] I would get into fights with other crims, so I was placed in solitary. There was a good screw who would ask me to eat, otherwise I would have died of starvation. I became gaunt and lifeless, nearly blacking out each time I stood up.

To shut me up, they put me in with the Beast. He stole a razor blade from the shower and scratched *Fantasy Encounter* on the cell wall. I thought he would slash me during the night as he screamed and raved. No crim yelled for him to shut up, so I thought the Russians had dropped Q-bombs on Sydney and we were all dying of radiation sickness.

One day, after returning from the courts, I screamed a prophecy at a screw. The next day the screw came into my cell and beat me around the head and accused me of knocking out his front tooth. I got an extra eighty-one days on my sentence and two weeks in solitary, but because I was already in solitary it didn't matter. I could see things that were not there. I had to get away. The dreams I used to put me to sleep at night were coming back at me. I was constantly tripping. There was an evil spirit that would howl about me. The world was hypnotized. The evil spirit menaced me. My mouth was twisted in delusion. I thought I was captured in the castle of Satan. Satan was all around me.

I was sentenced, at last, to four years with a non-parole period of two years.

In the normal prison population that night, in insane despair, I slashed my wrists, arms, and feet. I watched the severed white flesh turn red as the blood began to flow out. I was bleeding crimson blood on the cell floor. It was a crucifixion that impaled me on my bed with scarlet blood streaming down my sides. I stood up and walked in the blood as I pumped it squirting out of my veins. I watched myself die, as the scientists watched the performance through the transmitter. The beautiful scarlet crimson blood covered my arms and the cell. My wounds had started to congeal. The blood had seeped into the bunks, dripping down from my top bunk to the lower one. In a semiconscious state I realized there was nowhere to sleep, to die. There were gallons of blood splattered all over the cell. My cellmate pounded on the door and a screw was there. I stood there with crackling, caked blood in fascinating configurations on my outstretched arms. They took me to the prison hospital. I fell asleep with a drip in my arms and had my first sound sleep in a long time.

I remained three months in the prison hospital,[43] and three times I tried to commit suicide. I was destroyed by a million animal flashbacks and the nurses gave me tranquilizers. I was drowned in a pain of misunderstanding as the Premier threatened to send me to the salt mines. I'll give him salt, insult. The fly.

The impressions of insanity started to leave me as the tranquilizers took effect. I was a zombie again.

40

Doc, I was born on June 21, 1953. When I was two years old, the first rock and roll song became number one on the charts. **Sphere**

I awoke to find myself in the dormitory of who-knows-where. I usually awoke like this, not knowing who I was, why I was, or where I was. Nightmares flourished in my mind during the early hours of the morning. I quickly oriented myself, with my mind adjusting itself to the dream. My other companions were all lifers on governor's pleasure, the criminally insane. I was the exception. I was a political prisoner. I remembered now. The mistake. I had arrived yesterday from Long Bay jail, had been medically examined, given a few instructions, and released to the yard. This was Morisset Hospital, Ward 21, maximum security for the criminally insane. The golden triangle of the psychiatric set. Wasteland was here. We were both classified criminally insane.[44]

In my mind the voices continued:

> *The bastards. Why don't they recognize me? I can play their dream too, but I'm tired of dreaming. They have destroyed my life and they will destroy themselves and the fragile world on which I stand. Their fucking dream. If I could screw it and scramble their brains till they have no silence, no place to hide, and no resting place, then they would destroy themselves and my world in insanity. How can you win? How can you get revenge? How do you get out of this dream?*
> *Insane.*
> *Man the disturbed. Man the fallen. Man the insane. I think we're all fucking insane. You have killed for a billion years and live on death. This is the death planet. Welcome to hell. Welcome to the world of the insane.*

The voices laughed.

Half-asleep, I slipped in and out of the dream as the never-ending voices and hallucinations were quiet for a moment or two. As I lay on the hard bed, my mind tried to adjust itself from the nightmare.

> *They will torture you again this morning. Why do they crucify the prophets?*
> *Are we all mad?*

My thoughts wavered and went back into the great dream. I dreamed again in the land of the past. A land of beautiful scenes, painful feelings, and a million shifting raped and raided delusions.

> *Elysium, the dream has begun and you know when and where my nightmares roam. Yeah, they're in my head. Oh God, Elysium!*

I lay there on the hard bed as my mind rolled. The nightmares had finished with the night and there was no need to rise yet. So I'd just lie there and rest, close my eyes and try to escape reality again.

I'm in pain. These psychos are fools. I only fear pain. They will torture me again. I need to protect my dream.

I had fallen asleep into another hallucinogenic nightmare. I woke up again, closed my eyes, and fell into a half-sleep again. Putting a jigsaw puzzle together, and a crim came and scattered the pieces. I began to trip and hallucinate in my dream. The scene changed. I was driving a bus and there were two women in the back seat. On closer inspection, one was Elysium when she was eight years old, made up to look like an older woman, and the other woman was Rainbow, made up to look younger. The scene changed in flashing globes. I was in a cave and there was a dreaming rock there and if you believed in God and lay on the rock you would have beautiful dreams. I lay on the rock and began to hallucinate that I would trip forever in a swirl of insanity. I awoke to the mistake but realized that it was meaningless. I called for Elysium.

The thoughts continued in my head as I awoke from my hallucinogenic sleep.

The inventor of rock and roll reduced to permanent insanity. The bastards. Why don't they recognize me? I can play their dream too.

I dreamed, whispering suspicious voices in my mind.

Why do they treat me like a dog, an animal, a number in their system? I'm a human being. I'm the Holy Spirit. I'm God's representative on earth.

The voices laughed.

The never-ending voices in my mind were dispelled by a hallucination for a moment or two. *Why does man crucify the martyrs? Maybe they were mad too. All madness.* My thoughts wavered and went back into the great dream.

They're in my head.

I dreamed again in a mind wandering in a time and land of its own. A closed circuit tuned constantly to a video movie, I talked to myself. I couldn't turn myself off. There was nothing strange in that. I think who I am. I am who I think I am. Years of constant drug-taking had isolated my mind to the point to where I had lost contact with normal reality. Am I insane? These arguments confuse me. My thinking is constant, repetitive, never giving me peace. I have no peace of mind. I have no tranquillity. My mind never stops. Stop the dream. Please get me out of here. I have a transmitter in my tooth, I screamed a silent scream. I cannot trust these people. I'm in pain. These psychos are fools. I do not fear them. I only fear pain. They will torture me again in this asylum. I need to protect my dream. My mind.

Jesus, I've got to get up. My mind is only half-awake and I've got to face it. My hands are sweating. Yes, they're starting to sweat now. I hope no one touches me. I'm sweating more. They're going to touch me. They will know I'm afraid. I don't want to be touched. The thoughts began but faded out before a logical conclusion was reached. The ritual suspicion circled my mind. *I'm sweating. I'm sweating. I'm sweating. They will know I am afraid. They won't like me. I'm sweating. They don't like me. They will know I'm afraid.*

My mind changes. It is daytime in the haunted mind and the spirits still are laughing and playing and crying inside. I start to laugh and cry at the same time as the shadow approaches.

"Get up, Sphere." The nurse shook me. "Get dressed."

Cringing into the bed and wrapping the sheets around me, I said, "Please don't torture me."

"Get out of that fucking bed and get dressed."

"God, no." I rose, dressed, and wandered through the doors to the enclosure.

He's classified me criminally insane.

Yes, I am insane.

Whispers in my mind.

Nurse's report: "He believes that he has a transmitter implanted in his tooth."[45]

Whispering suspicions in my mind.

Nurse's report: "He also talks to the radio and TV stations."

Whispering in my mind.

Nurse's report: "He is a chronic paranoid schizophrenic with manic depression."

Voices in my mind.

Ego.

Knowledge and disconnection of intellect and emotion.

I smiled a painful smile and dreamt again.

"I've got a transmitter in my tooth!" I yelled as I tried to dislodge a tooth. Opening my mouth, I started to claw at my teeth. If they remove my teeth, I'll be sane.

Dreams of delusion are images that love had invented in the great dream. I created myself greater than I am. I'm a maker of dreams. Pain rhymes with insane. I'm in pain. I can laugh at things that you think are morbid. Death holds no fear for me. I only fear pain. I need to protect my dreams of violence.

I got up and wandered away slowly. The day was fresh. I wandered out of the dormitory, through the TV room on to the veranda. An urn of tea was brought out of the kitchen and the patients were released to the yard. We would stay there till 8:30, when breakfast was served. I was afraid, so I called to Elysium and had hallucinations. The morning went slowly while I sat cross-legged under the frangipani tree and talked to Baron Wasteland, who was laughing.

"Well, another fine mess you've got us into," I said.

"It seemed as if life was passing us by. No drugs, mate."

I retreated to my self-imposed isolation of the great dream.

Breakfast came around. The head nurse yelled, "Rightio!" The dining room was unlocked and the mob surged in. I sat in the chair the nurse directed me to. This was my reserved place. Sloppy porridge, then bacon and hard-yolked eggs with sugared tea, all lukewarm. My partner across the table forgot the food and ate the gravy and, finally, it was especially tempting on cornflakes. He thought they were trying to poison him. He freaked out all over the place, so the nurse tested his food. God, mate, you're revolting. The knives and forks were soft plastic, so there were no chances of anyone slicing his wrists or stabbing an inmate or psychiatric nurse. The place was still haunted by crims who had hanged themselves in the dormitories and private cells.

Morisset offered little excitement. It was a dead place with a vegetable garden. It used to be a snakepit, but with modern tranquilizers it's a home for the retired. The mob quickly ate the garbage and surged out to fidget about as they lit cigarettes. A trusted few had cigarette lighters which were taken away at night and then returned in the morning. The insane love fires and the flames are again burning my brother.[46] I walk in the flames as they burn my mind. Pain, pain, pain. Years ago, I ran out first and saw the woodshed on fire and started yelling and screaming for the kid's kid to run out. He didn't come out. I ran away to get help, crying shock. I found a dead chicken and molested it.

After breakfast, volleyball was played, with nurses making up half of the team. It was a good, fast game which usually ended with the ball going over the wire and, yes, there it goes after a bad-tempered bastard kicks it over.

I stopped and rested, sweat pouring down my face. The music played from Baron Wasteland's cassette. The Eagles were playing as Baron Wasteland laughed at his thoughts in the playground of his mind.

The Hunter Valley stretched before us with Lake Macquarie in the background and the hospital vegetable patch in the foreground. Three fences separated us from the outside world: one brick, one barbed wire, and one electric. The chances for escape were nil, but I didn't want to escape. I was content.

Abraxas wanted to see me.

We shook hands. "Your hands are sweaty, Sphere."

"I can't change my feelings."

"Do you always sweat?"

"Most of the time. I have low skin resistance. I have a transmitter in my tooth. I invented rock and roll."

"So you have a transmitter? Inventor of rock and roll? It's the same story you told me last time." He wrote it down. "According to these reports, you believe we're sadomasochists. We'll have to double your medication."[47]

It was starting to rain and we entered the world of thunder and lightning. The ancient gods were showing their approval with the deliverance of rain. I have always liked wet weather, as it subdues everything. There is the half-light and the security of houses. A chance to find yourself in the book of life. I was impatient and my high spirits soared through the rain.

"I created the rain," I said to the doctor. "I can make rain."

From this beautiful, painful vision, my mood instantly changed and my eyes found Abraxas. "You think you can hide me away in a psychiatric hospital and never tell me the truth? Why do they inflict pain on me, Abraxas? Why don't you take me to the machine? The machine which can read the mind?" I slipped into the dream.

"We have no machine," Abraxas replied.

"The machine. You know my thoughts. I gave you everything, didn't I, when I came through the dream? Abraxas, I want to die. You could give me some pills and I could die. We could all die and I could be with Elysium. Rainbow died."

"I can't do that."

"Yeah, I know, doc, but I don't know why. Like a child, I believe you but you lied. I made such a perfect story because I wanted you to believe me, but you're a dog. I trusted you and you gave me pain. I looked up to you and you deceived me."

"What do you mean?" Dr. Abraxas asked. "You may need shock treatment for depression."

I quickly realized that I would have to put the round peg in the round hole, because there was going to be no shock treatment for this little black duck. You soon learn that you don't tell them a thing. Not even if you're dead. Give the psychiatrists an academy performance. I know psychiatrists are fucked, man.

"How would you like shock treatment, mate!?"

"Calm down. I'm not psychotic. Tell your story."

"Our society is built on a story. It's a twelve-storey building and the foundations are starting to give. Then you will build another storey.[48] Civilization is folly. They will take it all away. I can see through the lies of this world. No, I don't live forever. No, I'm not significant. The dream is not all-powerful. It could have been good, but there was too much pain. You don't know, do you? How would you like shock treatment?"

"I'm not psychotic," Abraxas again replied.

"You're a fruitcake," I replied. "I hide behind my demented hallucinations. I hide behind a fanatical intelligence. Glory is what I seek. This is a self-perpetual universe. We live in this world for eternity."

"I don't understand you," Abraxas said.

"Just let me speak my fucking mind and that is all I ask. I was raised on fear, but you don't rule me now. Have I ever told you about the spiders? Write it down, Abraxas. The coppers will get something to put on me and it's most probably spiders. The day is alive with crawling spiders. Turn off the flashing lights. Slow the projector down. Open your eyes to the reality that is all around us and the monsters vanish with the feverish sweat. It's just a dream, Abraxas."

"That was quite a recital you just gave," the doc said.

"I hallucinate all over the place."

"You're a schizophrenic, you know."

"I'm a mind worker, Doc."

"You're insane."

"I love her."

"Who do you love?"

"I must remember, because the dogs circumcised me, mate."

"Yes, I know. You're ashamed. You'll get over it. Okay, you can go now." And as I walked out, the hallucination was upon me.

Wasteland was waiting outside. "How did you manage to get here, mate?" I asked.

"I used to take my shower outside the wings," he replied. "I guess they didn't dig a naked hippie showing the bum rocks, so they shipped me here. I just wanted a change of scene."

I noticed Cactus, a friend from one of my visits to a psychiatric hospital. He was standing by the fence, staring into the distance. I returned my attention to Baron Wasteland, who was laughing hysterically.

"Could do with a shot, a scotch, and a number." We both smiled and lined up to get a cup of tea and biscuits. It tasted of detergent and reeked of sugar, but I drank it, as it was my only substance till 1:15 when lunch was served.

I rested, strolled in the yard, sat under the frangipani tree and scratched myself, because of the Largactil itch: the medication irritates the skin when exposed to the sun and gives it a strange purple-blue coloration.[49] It is a misery in summer. I talked to Psychotic Bob and Baron Wasteland about our poisons. Our talk went around in circles and we behaved like mischievous children, which gave us a timelessness. All was good-natured as we laughed at ourselves. We were adults in the twentieth century. We were the children of the atom bomb. We had achieved some tranquillity.

41

Women have the masturbation effect. It's called blowout.

Magic Star Flower

I dream of no voices. We are released from the dining room to the veranda, where we search for the truth or hide in our dreams. I have learned from experience not to make any ripples and soon you are accepted as sane. I have no reasons to hide in insanity anymore. I will be released from Morisset because I've learned the answers. I am stable on chemicals. The medication slows down the thoughts and therefore you can cope with yourself. It's tranquil, serene, and it's natural to be relaxed.

I waited a moment longer, a moment to forget. In Morisset there is plenty of time to forget. My thoughts reached into and twisted around themselves. I walked in the yard to escape the senile voices and wonder about myself. Most of the junk had been cleaned out of the attic. I wondered why my insanity ever happened. The answer presented itself. I tried to escape from reality. I tried to escape into something that I am not.

At night the Professor paced the ward with no clothes on. I was awoken by the sounds of footsteps. Psychotic Bob got up and took his pajamas off. I followed suit and we paced, naked, backwards and forwards. The night guardian, the psychiatric nurse, cursed us through the bars to get back to bed, but we paid little attention. It's natural to be free and restless on a moonlit night. You can jail the body but not the soul. I see their penises and know that I am not the only one with the scar. The nurse handed me a double Largactil through the bars and I gulped it down and lay on my bed, falling into a restful sleep. Next morning, Psychotic Bob tugged on my arm, telling me he was going to escape and travel to Cairns and capture the city in a guerrilla war. He wanted me to be the first in command.

The tea was brought out and the psychiatric set once more gathered around the tea urn and told their life histories. The prison system kept us preserved and in good health. Pleasant conversation made us rich indeed and except for my crusade against cigarettes, I was at peace. I always managed to run out of the roll-your-own tobacco that was provided and had to use the great Australian bite on my mates. My friends were vainly interested in themselves.

Abraxas called me into his office. I sat down. I had to get something off my chest today. I was nervous because today I was going to tell Abraxas my secret. The reasons I am insane and a drug addict.

"There is something I have to tell you. I made a bad mistake once and I can't keep it to myself. I'm a child molester. When I was fifteen I sexually played with a boy and girl from next door. I nearly had intercourse with the girl and she was only eight. The boy was nine. I feel as if I fucked up their lives and my own."

He said, "Don't tell this to anyone."

"Abraxas, I was with Elysium Dream once, but I couldn't stay with my woman. The dream came back on me and I didn't want to hurt my child. I know who I am, and because of this I am trapped in insanity. I am trapped in my own guilt to relive the past and never forget. Every day I remember. Do you know what it's like to love someone and not touch it and be haunted by a mistake? To be driven insane by your own mind and never be able to escape? To never love your own daughter because she makes you remember that mistake?"

"Why did you sexually play with the children? Tell me about it," Abraxas asked.

"I had a girlfriend at the time, but she was sexually inadequate. I lived in sexual frustration. My girlfriend told me I was immature and so I viciously proved her right. I wanted sexual equality and I got rejection. I was slowly going insane at the time and because of the masturbation scar I knew I lost it."

"What is this masturbation scar?" Abraxas asked.

"It's a circle of discoloration around the penis caused by masturbation."

"I've never heard of it," Abraxas said, "and I'm sure it has never been classified."

"You've never heard of it?"

"No, it doesn't exist. There is no medical term for it. You can call it whatever you want."

"I'll just call it the masturbation scar. I thought I was the only one with the scar, but Baron Wasteland has the scar and on nudist beaches at least 30 percent have the scar, and you tell me it doesn't exist? Ten percent of the male population has the scar and medical science has no name for it? I think it was the reason Adolf Hitler hated the Jews. The scar most probably caused World War Two. The reason most alcoholics and drug addicts begin using drugs is because of the scar. God, nobody tells the truth in this world."

"Don't get upset," Abraxas said.

"Well, by the time I was fifteen I thought I was the only one with the scar, so I went insane.[50] I've been insane for so long. I can love my nephews and nieces, but I couldn't stay with my own child."

Abraxas leaned back in his chair and said, "It's society that is to blame, and you have to be free of your self-condemnation. Normal men are turned on by little girls. It has been proved in psychological tests. Perhaps mothers are legalized child molesters. Who can say? But don't blame yourself after all this time. You can give a name to the masturbation scar and reveal it to the world, but I don't think anyone else worries about it."

I realized the solemnity of the occasion. "I'll call it being ringbarked." We shook hands and I left. I thought to myself, *I know the secret of the hallucinogenic mushroom. It is phallic, neurotic, atomic, and psychotic.*

Outside, a crazy walked up to me and said, "To the battle stations, men."

I replied, "I don't know where they are."

Soap is recommended to clean out the stomach and I still had an overemotional dream that did not give me rest. I missed Elysium and our daughter. She was most likely a druggie, looking after our daughter.

Baron Wasteland was getting more and more restless and one day he decked an old-time resident psycho who had once killed a psychiatric nurse in the vegetable patch with a pair of garden shears. Baron Wasteland was put in the grill to cool off. A couple of weeks later he jobbed a nurse and was held by four nurses and given a hiding. He was forced to undergo shock treatment. He said he had had it all together before the shock treatment but after each session he was becoming more and more confused. He's a man, and I hope he gets the trip under control again. I oil-painted in the grill with a rapist who said that when he got out he was going to do it all again. More raped women.

I enjoyed sitting in the sun telling yarns and soon I wouldn't have anything to talk about except the simple day-to-day pleasures. Only in death will I discover the eternal truth. I was still suicidal, but I wouldn't tell Abraxas that. I still wanted to die fulfilled. My life was spread before me and the truth uncovered was quickly lost. I wanted to understand myself. I was getting old and I wanted something that would not fade for eternity. I wanted a woman to love. I wanted to get into a woman.

Abraxas called me in. "Anything to tell me?" he asked.

I replied, "I created the universe. It told me to do it in the book."

"Which book?" he asked.

"The Bible. Revelations. I have the seven stars in my right hand."

"Oh god, what can I say? It's not possible, Sphere. I don't know how the universe was created, but it's just not possible that you created the universe. Talk it over with your mates and they will tell you the truth. You're only human, Sphere, so don't try to be a saint, just be yourself. You are a very frightened young man."

"I'm not the great harlot?"

"No. Did your parents ever talk to you?"

"No."

"They didn't love you?"

"No."

"Someone should have a long talk to you."

42

The Devil is a schizophrenic.   Sphere

How many times had I duplicated the penis scar, my protégés? I ran into subconscious wanderings in the tranquilized months, but soon Baron Wasteland and myself were searched, handcuffed, and loaded into the van to be transported from Morisset Hospital to Long Bay jail.[51] The doors were closed and the screws started the engine.

Back at the Bay, the Morisset crowd were invited over to the Professor's cell for a cup of tea. The Morisset mob usually stuck pretty much together because everyone in Morisset is encouraged to use first names, so we are usually a congenial group. After mischievously hiding Psychotic Bob's cigarettes, we settled down to talk of Morisset: the toecutter gang, the bad food, the lack of freedom, the mangler, the characters who made the place a home for the insane. I remember Digger walking about with no clothes on as the high priest of Satan, yelling for the culprit who stole his underpants. Baron Wasteland would wash himself under the fire hydrant in the yard; a thirty-nine-year-old bed-wetter; lobotomy cases and bad-tempered bastards. Nothing else happened except the incidents I wish to forget, the intimidation of shock treatment and the bad psychiatric nurses.

Morisset is where the most insane criminals in the state are kept. They know the score. If they are back in the prison system it is usually recognized that they have gunned down, stabbed, and choked their best friends. Seventy percent are on governor's pleasure. These people are found not guilty on the grounds that they are insane. They usually do 10 years pumped up on tranquilizers, while the lifers do an average of 12 ¾ years.

It's all the same in Long Bay. Eighty percent kill their relatives. Crazy Joe knifed his one- and two-year-old daughters to death; Wilderness Willie killed his six-year-old son; Skunk shot his twin brother; TapeWorm strangled his aging father; Psychotic Bob shot his mother; Digger strangled his senile grandmother; Spider shot his girlfriend and cousin; the Professor cut his wife into little pieces. They have killed every conceivable relation in every possible way. Some don't talk about it and nobody asks and it's better that way. Ignorance is bliss. There is no judgment and therefore no reprisals. It is who you are right now that is important. Step on the scorpions and they will kill you. You dig society.

> *Dear Elysium Dream,*
>
> *Years have passed by and I thought for my own peace of mind I would write you a letter. Just a short note to let you know that I am all right. I'm in jail by the way, honey. The commissioner has released the long-term psychiatric patients back into the prison system and there are quite a few Morisset and Callan Park patients here. I was caught in the stream; otherwise I would have spent my sentence in Morisset. We seem to congregate at the same spot. The clinic. Not much can change here but life does seem to be getting better. I don't know how long I will be here but there is a good chance of being released on parole. I put the jail out of my mind and think about pleasant surroundings. I just take it how it comes. I am writing a book and it is making some progress. It helps the time to go faster and it is getting my life in perspective. It is a real documentary of our times. I don't remember most of my life, so I make it up. I hope to get some money out of it. I'm a greed fiend with colorful psychedelic shit. It doesn't make much sense but it's great therapy.*
>
> *The other day an unusual thing happened. We were let out of our cells after lunch and waited for library muster when a crim walked on to the central grass area, waited till everyone was watching, then dropped his strides and cut his genitals off and threw them on the ground. A guard came racing over and grabbed him. Another guard arrived and they both lifted him up and carried him to the clinic. Ten seconds later, a crim picked up the penis and scrotum and, holding them at a discreet distance in front of him, ran to the clinic. Some younger crims fainted while others vomited. It was the talk of the jail. Thankfully there were no sausages that night for tea. The next day we got word that they had performed microsurgery and sewed them back on.*

Besides my personal mental health progress, the routine of the jail continues. It has been eight years since I last heard from you, so I'm not expecting a reply. Rainbow is dead. I won't go into it, but it was horrible. Just look after yourself and, if I haven't told you before, I love you.

There is not much to say now it's over. I will be stable–unstable till the day I die. An interesting thing is, the Mellaril keeps me sterile.[52] I get nothing but dry retches when I masturbate. They try to make me impotent, but the chemicals don't work. I still masturbate and feel pleasure, but when I come I have no sperm. I wouldn't menstruate if I was a woman. I wish they would discover an impotence pill so I couldn't get it up.

If I could say something to you I would say, watch out for the isolated dreams. I'm a little corner in society's psychiatric hospital. If I could scream I would, but it would do no good. I hear music from other cells at night as Captain Straight and wonder where I went wrong. So much for reminiscence. I will find another woman. It will be hard, because you're the hottest little number I've ever known.

Love, Sphere

43

I have a deep need for other people.   Baron Wasteland

Woken up by the rattle of locks being unfastened, I hear the sound of the bottom-landing bolts being drawn back. It gives me time to dress before the top-landing bolts are drawn. I'm one out, meaning one in a cell. I am released from my cell to wander down to the bottom landing, fill my thermos, and return it to my cell. Then I walk out to the circle till the wing is cleared.

A screw yells, "One sick in cell!"

"Rightio!" another screw yells back.

The mob surges back into the cellblock each to fill a bowl with porridge, grab a carton of milk, an individual serve of cereal, some toast, and a sachet of jam. I get nothing except the milk. I've got prison-time blues. We amble upstairs and are locked again in our cells to eat breakfast. At precisely three minutes past 8, the locks are unfastened, the bolt echoing a thud. We're released to the circle, where we collect for muster. The laundry workers gather under the shadow of the basketball net. Five Shop muster is to our left and Maintenance behind us. The names are called and we fall out to wander down to the laundry.

A screw asks, "Where's your name tag?"

"It's in my cell," I reply.

"Well, get it, turkey!"

"Yes, boss." I amble back.

In the laundry we tie our personal laundry bags and throw them into the washer. The washers have four compartments and each section takes a barrow of sheets weighing about 40 kilograms [88 pounds]. My laundry gets washed and I sign out for clinic. A man needs a Mellaril on a cold morning to keep in control.

The usual crowd is gathered under the awning, waiting for the nurses to arrive and open the window. The regulars are here and I can almost name the whole blanky crowd of thirty crims who attend clinic. This section of the Bay is maximum security for medical and work holds. There is a bricklaying and laundry course. The rest are medical holds. A bunch of invalid rejects, a potent brew of drug addicts and lifers with no reverence for anything or anyone.

The clinic window is opened at 8:30 and I wait my turn to say good day to the nurse. She knows me well; we're old friends of a thousand mornings. Some days we have a laugh but usually it's routine, with me handing over my card for Mellaril.

I walk towards the laundry and am tempted to stop off at my cell and empty the thermos for a cup of coffee. I shake off the thought and continue on my walk back to the laundry. I keep it straight and honest. I rattle the lock to attract the screw's attention. "Can I get through?"

I walk to the laundry, where I rattle the lock again and the officer unbolts the gate. Back in the laundry, we gather in groups to yarn and laugh. Some go to take their hour of activities, but I will stay in the laundry till 10 o'clock when I have my yoga class. At 9 o'clock the sheets are unloaded from the driers and brought out in barrows. Some crims fold the sheets in two while others feed the half-folded sheets into the roller. At the end, the neatly folded sheets are loaded into barrows to be taken to Five Shop, where the sheets are dispatched to other jails and hospitals. A different-colored batch of sheets for each day of the week. For overtime, we do hospital sheets. You have to watch out for germs, afterbirth, and turds. (Jesus, there was one turd, a greenish-yellow one—and mate, it stank. I nearly threw up. Fortunately, there is usually just the common variety of black stool.) The overtime is for the maniacs who want to earn $3.20 for six hours' overtime. The sixteen hours we work each week gives us $8, enough to purchase a buy-up of coffee, tobacco, and odds and ends.

I go to my GROW class on Monday and Bible class on Wednesday and yoga on Friday. On Sunday, I attend the church service in the Central Industrial Prison.

At 11:15 we wander back to the Metropolitan Reception Prison, where we go back to our cells or walk in the circle. At half-past, it's clear the wings, so we walk for ten minutes in the circle till the Crown[53] yells, "Fall in!" and we assemble outside our respective wings. Another muster is called and I wander in to pick up a batch of sandwiches, some packet soup, orange juice, and a piece of fruit. The bolts are set into place and we're incarcerated once again. I listen to the transistor radio as I eat my lunch. Afterwards, I check *TV Week* to see which movie is showing. I choose a movie and lie down on my bunk to watch the action.

Before the movie is over, the screws arrive back from lunch and the cells are opened. I don't know how many movies I've watched for an hour and seventeen minutes, and never seen the end. It's outside for laundry muster and another afternoon of repetitious folding of sheets. The two hours go slowly and then it's over: 3:15 has arrived and the final muster in the laundry is called. We dribble out to the normal jail system. I visit a friend's cell to yarn and yabber. I have a cup of coffee and shake my leg restlessly. Half-past four, and the head screw yells, "Clear the wings!" and the circus once again assembles outside in the circle, where we pace up and down or sit on garden chairs. Fall-in is called, and we wait outside Nine Wing for cats and chats, to be called forth to pick up our dinner and be locked in our cells. I eat my dinner and then check *TV Week* for information on television programs. Pure torture. You'll never break my hardened spirit. Maybe I'll read the evening newspaper or a book I've borrowed from the library. The night is spent in silence with the television entertaining me. Then it's hit the sack, Jack, for a good night's sleep.

I'm awoken by the rattle of locks being unfastened. I'm released to fill up my thermos and take out my dirty plates. Then it's out to the circle till the landing is cleared and so it goes on . . .

I wander over to Baron Wasteland's private cell. "I'm going to write another record of songs," I say.

"Shit, mate, the last lot you wrote were so empty! You're as leapy as Cane Toad."

"This record is going to be positive, so don't put me down, because I'll lay the trip right back on you. I don't need your destructive criticism."

"More garbage," he replies.

"Not garbage, mate, but ascetic beauty. I won't get pushed inside ever again. The bad karma is going to come back on you one day." I took the advantage and laid the bastard down. A true cynic tearing into his human weakness.

44

A piece of coal put under a million tons of pressure becomes a diamond.
Superman

Baron Wasteland was released.

There is always a bit of trouble brewing in the wings, and over at the clinic one morning two crims took a screw and nurse hostage and we were locked in our cells while the day-long drama was played out. The screws didn't give in to the crims' demands and so the crims gave up in the end. Lennon was dead: December 8, 1980.[54] He knew when he was afraid and in pain.

On Christmas Day there was a two-minute riot. The scheme failed when the crims didn't get a hostage and so Mace was thrown into the wing. The other day another cell was burned out. The cells have been painted so many times that if there is a fire in the cell the paint goes up in a blazing inferno. Before we go on, can I have some quiet? Thank you. Flashback, flashback. Keep on trancing. It's all life in the prison with something always happening. Today, one of the transsexuals in for prostitution was bashed up by her boyfriend and there was wailing in Nine Wing. The drags are strange.

The self-pity, the depression, the isolation—but mainly self-pity. Make up your mind. I wear my poverty well with my cheap movie. Poor old Sphere, you really messed it up. Now, if you will only forgive me. Please feel sorry for me, because that is all I want. Someone to pick me up, dust me off, and say, "You poor, destitute wretch." I've had a terrible life. I'm a martyr of truth. Society's to blame and the food stinks too. I'm a human being too and I need your love and money. A frustrated little penis. I have been hurt and there is a voice crying in the wilderness. I'm not playing your game anymore, it's my nightmare. Get off the floor, you sniveling wretch, and promise me that you won't cry. I tremble and ramble on but I won't cry, not even if you say I'm a fool and a psycho. Just so long as afterwards you feel sorry for saying it and feel sorry for my miserable life. You can't keep a good man down, so I'll black out again, talk to the TV and try to understand this living in a drain that feels like a brain. I know you will destroy my world like you did the women. No wonder I'm insane. I like the attention; it's my defense mechanism.

Well, bugalugs, it's time to rise and shine. Do you know what you need in life? Well, I'm going to tell you anyway. A happy-go-lucky disposition. Maybe after all is said and done our dream is our most valuable possession. The delusions that we don't want to part with but, my friends, it's a pleasure to do without a nightmare. It's sanity. When I scream, follow me, my little band of alcoholic tribesmen; something good will come out of it. Searching inside and outside for the perfect sob story. Admiring myself with a bruised ego in the middle of my mind. We've seen plenty of good paranoia on this trip. Where would I be if I didn't believe in that dirty image? Only fools believe in dreams. Big shit, I'm a fool.

There is a strike and a riot going on at the moment. The prisoners have been locked in their cells for the last five days and police are manning the jail, giving us takeaway meals. "I'll have a mushroom pizza and a bottle of champagne." The copper says, "Get lost, creep." Downstairs, prisoners transferred from the riots at Parramatta are yelling out for medical attention for wounds from shotgun blasts and bruises from batons.[55] Yells of "Dogs!" "You animals!" and "Maggots!" Each day smoke rises outside my cell window as blankets are set on fire and thrown out of cells. I watch the riots on TV, but I'm not really a cynical blanket-burner.

I stumble out of my cell after seven days of not talking to anyone. Watching TV all night and sleeping all day has taken its toll. A laughing giant bacteria emerges, gassed out on toilet fumes. My toilet grows fungus and it's a heavy trip, mate.

A friend necked himself the other day and I think he was innocent. He was in for murder. Mixing with men with the minds of sewers and the mentality of bashed and bashing children. He said goodbye, with still a screw loose.

Seven times I've masturbated this week and it's only the first day. Sick, maybe; screw loose, definitely. Prison society wants surreal with the real. The head sweeper dresses up as a woman. Transsexuals with no dongers. Weird, mate.

Two years passed and I was granted parole. I had reached the conclusion of my sentence and, except for a few changes in the script, my prison term will be over. Psychos use allegory. My allegory is the jail. I'm really talking about being locked in my own mind. I'm a crazy predator, stable on medication. The dream of Sphere is the scream of Sphere, but one day the screaming ended. So I didn't write about the operation on my appendix and the jail brew. The allegory of Sphere is that it sends you crazy being locked up with me. I have a transmitter in my truth.

45

We're all expression of the same energy.   Baron Wasteland

Two years and eighty-one days passed.

Released from the complex, the prison of ideas, Sphere moved freely through the random impressions. The Sphere had been away for so long and there was uncertainty in a world in revolution. Rap and breakdancing were all the rage now. The structure of time and space had been altered and destiny had been captured. The spheres had changed from the beginning of time. Eternity had begun.

He died in the nightmare. The Sphere rolled like drops of gold glowing in black space and flowing from the distant shot towers of old as he smiled, *Come here,* to the spheres of uncertainty. Sphere, nothing is accepted here in this river of untold fears and nothing is rejected here in this world of countless tears. *Come,* said the spheres, into the babble of spheres flashing hallucinogenic dreams revolving around the sphere of distorted time, while the voice echoed down the memory traces of his institutionalized mind and was as restless and as vivid as the seduction reality that it represented.

Inside the prison, on the concrete paths and in the cold bleak cells, murderers had taught him how to kill. How to play the game. Slowly, the wild-world punks with colored hair, stud-encrusted belts, pixie shoes, and scarlet acne passed by. Evolution had changed into another self-indulgent excuse for revolution but the vast majority were still quite conservative, like cool, chicken-fucker, religious me. I was going home to the last all-encompassing psychotic episode of rolling reality and still you do not know the meaning of Sphere. He had learned to murder his insanity. He could play the game to its ultimate conclusion. He knew himself. He didn't know himself. The paradox smiled.

The pictures flashed in drops of gold. He will now talk to you:

Go to the center of the Sphere. I am the perfect ego self that expands and contracts to defend and attack myself. I am the future. I am the past and you are the righteous in your ordered, natural lives. Look deeply into the hypnotizing sphere and here comes the defense of your ego. Did you become me? Did that make you big by making others small when you attacked yourself and defended yourself? Did you feel the hurtful hate of the feelings of identity as it twisted its knife into our universal karma? Did you fall for my story?

I smiled as I ordered the paranoid spheres. I laughed inside as my religion shouted, *Conform, normals, conform! Fit the puzzle together and now you know pain. So rebel, fools, rebel!*

Relaxing the ego, I smiled. Yeah, it's a religious trip, mate, and by telling you, I expand the spheres. When you doubt me, you doubt yourself. Now the Sphere covers your vision as it rolls into its ordered place. The mirror was passed through part of the human race. I smiled at the world as the children played their verbal games against each other. I saw their skeletons. I know now, mate. Whoever controls the power words controls the game; while the meaning of the symbol is sphere, the mind that changes is yours. The roles have changed. I have looked long enough into my own mind to know. I am insane, but you will forget. You must forget because you cannot remember. Here is pain. Here is repetition. You still do not know the meaning of sphere. I am institutionalized in my madness and the insignificant becomes significant. My controlled anger rules my mind. I have an insane confidence to hurt you because Sphere is the significant.

46

You know so much, man, but you don't know what it's like to be a fucking woman.   Magic Star Flower

You know so much, woman, but you don't know what it's like to be a fucking man.   Sphere

At home I didn't really go wild. I kept my cool. Jail had taught me to take it slowly, slowly. No hurries or worries. I hadn't smoked a cigarette in three months and hadn't used drugs in two and a quarter years and except for some jail brew I had been sober in all that time. Still, I was on tranquilizers. The tranquilizers were physically addictive and I would have to go through the withdrawals. Still, I wanted to be straight, normal, and handsome. I knew that once upon a time I had been normal and this kept me going. Once upon a time, I had been normal. Years ago, the dream had ended. I would get to that bygone age and regain sanity; tranquilizers were a temporary answer. I wasn't going to be on them for life. My paranoid schizophrenia was temporary. It could be cured.

Denial. I'm sure of it. There were no instances of insanity in my family, therefore I was a drug-induced schizophrenic. A traumatized schizo. Adrenaline and stress caused the voices and hallucinations and the imbalance in my brain. If I could only get enough new-fad physical activity and a chance for quiet relaxation, I'd be fine. That was the answer: exercise, relaxation, healthy nutrition, and a friendly environment. Still, there was something wrong with me. The life of Sphere was empty. He had no dreaming. He could suicide now in a gentle death if he had the pills. He was looking now for the dreaming of life and he knew where it lay, but to get there was a journey that was perhaps beyond his capabilities. He needed to find love again, but it was his biological heritage to be hated, for sexually playing with children.

Perhaps he might find eternal meaning or just a transitional meaning and that was all he wanted now. Sphere had no god. He needed to love God, the Creator, who had caused all his fun and pain. He needed eternal happiness. He needed to discover God and find out why all the emptiness. He needed to create God and have faith, but he had no faith left. He was a sad man.

Sphere had to love the eternal. He had made mistakes and had been labeled. Sphere wanted a house and garden. The house of God and the Garden of Eden. He would walk into the promised land.

Sphere was going through the withdrawals from the Mellaril. Headaches, depression, and a constant cold sweat. It went on for three long, lonely weeks, with Sphere's parole officer prodding him to get back on the tranquilizers. Sphere's already frail health was taking a battering. He was going insane and he hid the truth. He wanted the clarity of perception that the tranquilizers had confiscated from his life. He couldn't express his emotions, so he went further on into his nightmare.

It was too much for Sphere. He loved his parole officer, named Surrender. He needed to escape, explore her body, but there is no escape after depression has seeped into your mind. He only knew he loved her warm smile and vibrant love of life. She was an exceptional woman, with intelligence that shone with inner craziness. She had been hurt in her time and her dreams broken, but still her maturity had weathered the storms much better than had Sphere's frail boat. He had been tossed on the seas, while she had had fine sailing for most of her life. She didn't suffer the nightmares which tortured Sphere's sleeping mind till the nightmare and the real were confused into a continuous trance. The nightmares were so crazy that daytime brought relief from the colored dreams of a flickering projector. He told the truth that he always told, and she knew he was a deviant. Nobody could understand Sphere.

47

There is little pain in remembering a nightmare.

Baron Wasteland

Baron Wasteland overdosed on pethidine, a synthetic heroin.[56] In his room, the old sign hung on the wall: THE SADISTS, A HERO AND HEROIN BAND. He was laid out on a slab in the morgue and an autopsy was performed. They cut him open to find out what was inside but I don't think they found much. His body by this time was a ball of shit. There was a funeral of crying relatives and spaced-out drug kin. His fault was that he went inside and let others babble at him, but his last words were so clear and distinct. He said, "Rainbow is in me. I am eternal. Sphere, you are Elysium. I saw you become her as we all became each other. In the end, life and death are just words."

I saw him the day before he died. He was hooked and the only way to kill the pain was to have another charge. So he died. A junkie is dead. He died in the drug wars, where man searched for utopia. He was a man who shot smack and wanted it legalized. We'd tripped together, grown up together, and seen each other withering in pain after an overdose. We had been drunk together when we couldn't score, and in love with our beautiful junkie women. We'd seen it all together, mate. It seemed like yesterday that we were doubled up in comatose withdrawals in the slums. He was a man who lived close to death and it had been his chemical companion for so long he had forgotten that one day we would walk out of this wretched joint into the fresh air. Yeah, we all killed him. Death was his final release.

His mother took down his sign and collected his syringes and threw them in the garbage can. I integrated, separated, and spoke: "I wanted him to die and he died. I wanted Rainbow to die and she died. I'm a man who can tell others to die, but I'll miss the old bastard because he put up a good fight in our little game. You know he loved to play Monopoly?"

She turned on me: "You killed him, didn't you?"

I smiled and said, "Yes I did, and even you did a good job of putting a syringe in his arm. We're a bunch of fucking mind-killers. Baron was the coolest of us all. I played an insane game with him and used my mind to kill him because death to me is a good status symbol."

48

I was raised on fear but you don't rule me now. Have I ever told you about the spiders?   Sphere

Baron Wasteland dead.

Drunk in my room.

More and more creeping war. How long does this mentality go on till I throw down gun, bottle, penis to surrender? The war has been fought since the beginning. I am human and everything you despise. I am schizophrenic. I have the understanding that even the most ugly woman is sometimes narcissistic and that all male animals masturbate. I am a contradiction. I am frail and afraid and also strong and brave. So many years ago I became who I am. I was born a baby that shitted, pissed, smiled, and laughed as my mother bathed and perfumed me till I became who I am. A plastic celluloid composite piece of tissue paper.

I am man, the animal spirit from the same egg as woman, the parasitic bitching menstruator. The two of us, man and woman, grace the world with our beautiful fertilizing shit. We fuck and make religious replicas of ourselves. We sweat, and the smell expelled from our genitals scents the rooms with rancid, putrid, rotting garbage. We decay, and fill the graveyards. We are the vomit of the universe, children of electric acid. Humbled, we are tortured and driven insane by a force that shows no mercy as it indiscriminately slaughters the children of fear who breed and breed.

I came to tell you because I am boringly inebriated. The animal spirit is inside and outside of me. I must believe that I'm a spiritual animal. In my mind I have imagination. I give you my spiritual animal dream because that is all I have to amuse you with till the time of sanity.

Spiritual animals, I do remember the love and hate of the insignificant sperm germ that grew to become you and eventually became me. I have risen from the abyss. I'm a vicious killer. I'm a creep who hasn't the balls to stand on his own two feet.

Women are creepy.

I have faith in love and hate. I believe the two realities exist side by side and they are compatible but are not compatible. I am an agnostic Christian communist neurotic trying to keep the faith.

Women are jerks.

I'm a perpetrator of a new society of artificial laws that bind and protect the innocent. I live to create and destroy. I create alcoholic hallucinations. The drunken depression swallows me. The sphere has rolled.

Satan and God, do you know how much I hate you, how much I hate this planet, how I hate myself and this book? You could never understand that much pain. Pain beyond your comprehension and understanding. Pain to the limits of your imagination. Pain to the edge of rhetoric.

Woman, do you know what it's like to achieve your sexual maturity at nineteen and be considered immature and not a man? There is no compatibility. There is no love. There is no understanding. There is no equality. There is nothing for the failure. There is no humanity. Man is not that frail. Man is not that weak. Man does not know what I mean to be frail.

Do you know why I'm drunk? No woman loved me. Women loved me till they found out that I was demented and crippled inside. No god came to rescue me. No woman came to love me. No man came to teach me. They all wanted to create a fool. They all wanted to fool me. They all wanted more. They wanted to kill me and that is what they did, but I remember. I remember how you lied. I remember how you snide.[57] I know how you're going to fall into death.

The sphere rolled.

We all had our book to write, our song to sing, our movie to produce, our play to act, and now I can fool you and receive money, praise, power, status, and all the sex and love a man deserves, but this movie star is dead. There is no hero. There is no barbaric strength. There is no money, praise, power, glory, or sex. There is only the truth that you kick me when I'm down. There is no moral lesson. There is only a surreal truth that my mind created.

The Sphere rolled.

The torturer entered the room and we stood as one.

The master said, "Shit."

We were seated and the lesson began as we were fertilized by his turds.

"Today we do everything but do nothing. Shit and listen to the farts of thunder of this planet. Earth the shock is a tooth in decay. It will be extracted when rotten and placed under your pillow and the tooth fairy will leave you sixpence."

I really love a truthful explanation, so I apologize for not knowing, but one day society will work it out.

The sphere rolled.

Perhaps I'll read the Bible, but I know that the lawyer Paul has got a monopoly on that and I always thought that Peter was the rock on which Christ will build his church. "Saul, Saul, why do you persecute me?" (Acts 9:4). I never did trust anyone with visions.

The Sphere rolled.

Where can a man go, Lord, to find peace? I blew the candle out. The telepath's thoughts were broken. He slipped into the still of the night air and watched the ripples of the grateful radiate in the glow of the twilight mind. He loved to glow. In the glowing, he knew. His mind was free to pursue its interests and so he observed himself and thought about serenity. The bitter taste of his dreams enclosed in a book that trapped in chains the pains of the past. Saul, Saul, why do you persecute me on the inside and outside with your perfection?

The Sphere rolled.

The woman crushed my head when she had me circumcised as I lay and waited and so I poisoned her with the hatred in me.

Man, listen to me. Do you understand yourself?

49

Insanity is like going to sleep. You lie on your bed and suddenly you're asleep. Then you have a nightmare and wake up in the psychiatric hospital and realize it was just a dream.   Uncle Cane Toad

The nightmare was back. Surrender, my parole officer, went on long-service leave and I thought the sadomasochists' network was set up once again. The weeks went by, and then the months, and no Surrender. On one wild occasion, with my replacement parole officer, I was going to kill him. I arrived in an agitated state, shook hands and sat down to talk about things. I went berserk in the interview room and knocked over a few ashtrays and was just about to punch him in the face when I realized I would not kill him. I would end up in prison again. He was pressed back in his chair facing a crazy man with raised fists who was about to smack him in the mouth. I calmed down and breathed deeply. I don't remember the rest of the conversation, but the next time I saw him he had an Aboriginal bodyguard.[58] This time I was calm. The scene rolled.

I got drunk again today, saw my parole officer and nearly killed my father. It was a strange day. I was drinking and smoking dope while listening to pop music in Uncle Cane Toad's caravan [trailer]. I drove to Parramatta to see my parole officer. I thought I was a jet fighter pilot as I drove, and did wheelies around corners, nearly wiping out one pedestrian.

On arrival, I read magazines while waiting. We went into the interview room for a pleasant chat. "You dirty rotten murderer, for killing Surrender!" (He was a good bloke actually.) We got through the interview, with me getting the impression there was about to be a revolution.

I then went to my parents' house with a couple of bottles of wine. I was going to kill my father. He was sitting with Ma at the dinner table when I walked in. He had his back to me. I chose a sturdy bottle of wine from the brown paper bag, walked up behind him, and with all my force brought the bottle down a crashing blow. At the last centimeter, because of my fanatical force, it slipped out of my perspiring hand and flew across the table and bounced with a thud onto the floor. He looked around, startled. The TV went surreal. He looked scared. Ma said that I had better lie down. She had seen the entire incident.

I lay on the bunk and knew it was over. I was insane. I would get my gun and burn it in sacrifice. My anger had been directed against somebody else besides myself. The scene rolled.

Our mother, who art in heaven
Hallowed be thy name
Thy kingdom come
Thy will be done
On earth as it is in heaven
Give us this day our daily bread
And forgive us our trespasses
As we forgive those who trespass against us
For thine is the kingdom, the power, and the glory.

50

Jesus is cool.   Uncle Cane Toad

The dream said to Sphere, the Judas Jonah, *I have decided to put an end to mankind. I will destroy them completely because the world is full of their violent deeds. I will destroy you. Build a shelter for the children who do not know cruelty. They do not know truth as yet. I am going to send a holocaust on the earth to destroy every living thing. Everything on the earth will die, but I will make a covenant with you. Take into your shelter a male and female of every gentle kind of animal and of every bird in order to keep them alive. Take all kinds of food for them.* Sphere, the Judas Jonah, wrote everything the Dream commanded.

The nightmare rolled.

Take with you seven pairs of each kind of ritually clean animal but none of the unclean animals. Take also seven pairs of each kind of bird and fruit and flower that you wish in your garden. Do this so that every kind of gentle animal and bird will be kept alive to reproduce again on the earth. I am going to send fiery rain that will fall for forty days and nights in order to destroy every living being I have made. Sphere wrote everything the Dream commanded.

The nightmare rolled.

Take into the shelter all the books and music of truth, leaving out the books and music by the liars and deceivers of the world. The library must be extensive and intensive so that no knowledge is lost and when you emerge from the shelter you must not practice the sciences of the tower of Babel, how to split atoms or send rockets into deep space. The sciences you practice must be gentle and you must be happy and enjoy your craftsmanship. This is the beginning and end of Eden.

The nightmare rolled.

Take into your shelter the parents who are knowledgeable in the education of the world. Take into your shelter the whole community who build the shelter, because they must also share in its salvation that the Lord's spirit has revealed to them.

The nightmare rolled.

I am Sphere. I come from the land that was destroyed. The earth is covered. The burial ground is desecrated. The temple is ablaze with light. The children are afraid of the approaching storm. I come out of the desert where no flowers grow except in the time of the summer rain. The burning summer pain of the universe is reflected in a raindrop that clings to the flower in crystal clarity of the desert that is called the Never Never. I am tired of the journey of my life but soon I know it will be over. When the leaves fall I know it is close to winter. All these things I see. The frost is covering the dry grass. The birds have come down from the mountains. The leaves fall. The cicadas have gone. I wear a coat to keep warm in the shortening days. I shiver in fear of the winter, for I know this is the last winter. The last winter when my mind will be obliterated and scattered into the eternity of Esrevinu.[59] The fiery furnace of the sun returning and falling like a star on the cities and country of the neutron age. Death will be sweet as the oranges of the Riverina.[60] My mind has been battered from the shock of the violence that my people practice. Their ritual has almost arrived. The war is near.

Why was I chosen to write the book? I who am a sinner, a hypocrite and pagan. The Lord saw my contemporary romance fantasy and was pleased, so he sent me a vision in my dreaming childhood. The vision was a shelter and in the shelter were children; the children of the last age whose innocence pleased the Lord. The children watched through the window the winter that froze the world while the scientist told them stories of happiness and love.

He said, "Happiness is chemical. The right nutrients. Happiness is in your heart when you love. Happiness is a friendly and beautiful environment." The scientist's eyes smiled and he was eager to tell another story. "Do you ask me what is love? Love is a chemical reaction that occurs in an organism that makes it ready for procreation so that when the siblings are born they will be protected and cared for by the optimum operation of the organism." Cobber the Evolutionist smiled.[61]

The nightmare rolled.

He spoke again. "Man built his own destruction. You see man lives and dies. He tells the truth and lies. He was programmed for creation and then destruction to continue evolution. He is fulfilling a prophecy. He has served his purpose and now in his struggle for survival he kills and tortures his brothers in his failing madness. The truth was rejected in the last age and in its place were self-centered idols of lust, greed, pride, power, and jealousy. The people wanted what they could not have. They had life and they also wanted death. They built death."

I, Sphere, the Judas Jonah, guardian of the Esrevinu, will repeat all that the master has told me. Love the Lord, talk to him every day. I love you, Lord. Love your fellow women. Tell them every day, I love you. Love yourself. Love life. Tell yourself every day, I love you all, and feel your own love. Let love not be a repetitious word but an emotion of life, blossoming into fulfillment of joy. Always see the good and disregard the bad.

The nightmare rolled.

"Surround yourself with your own craftsmanship. Clothe yourself in workingman's attire, for you are a servant of the earth and the Lord who rules the earth, our most gracious Creator, who has given us our freedom. Do not be ashamed to go naked when you bathe in public because King Solomon was not clothed as you are. You are clothed in a naturalistic beauty that evolves into the Esrevinu. Keep warmth in your heart. Keep love and laughter in your spirit that is free to enjoy the adventure that evolves in the Esrevinu. Be yourself till you are chastised by the elders because you do not know till you see. Never be afraid to see, because if you close your eyes you will fall into a ditch like the blind men of the last age.

"The leaders of the last age are false prophets. The false prophet brought fire down from heaven and so deceived the inhabitants of the world. The true prophet went to Hollywood and told them to destroy their guns and so give up the unnecessary cruelty. I solemnly warn everyone who hears the prophetic words of this book that God will add to his punishment the plagues described in this book and they will wallow in pain and will not share in the tree of eternity that grows in the garden of our God.

"May love be with you always."

The nightmare rolled.

"Remember, do not breed like the insects and animals. The people of lust played their god game and because they loved themselves so much they created as many replicas of themselves as they could. They thought they were God in their procreation. They have not the simplest knowledge of arithmetic. They really know but still want more. Ignorant swine, they wanted more and more and that led to competition and war and war. They wanted to be God and they repaid their creations by killing them in their egocentric madness. Sexuality is jewels.

"They tortured the weak. They congratulated the victors. Their religions were hypocrisy. Their leaders were hypocrites. They believed in perfection and knew it was not possible. They deceived and lied and hated but did not admit to their human faults. They were bigots who thought they possessed the truth when they only saw the truth of themselves. The people of the last age were aggressively ignorant in their righteous imperfection."

Cobber the Evolutionist spoke again after a short pause. "We have written the Bible. It is a book of stories of knowledge and love and not a history lesson on the failures of mankind. It is now truly a book of truth and wisdom and love.

"Go to sleep now, children, and have pleasant dreams. The madmen have gone. Good night, children." He walked away by himself muttering, "The entire educational system is a capitalist plot. I will educate the children to become themselves, their teachers and their society, and explain that work is their mistress."

The nightmare rolled.

The hallucinogenic dream blossomed into a nuclear sexual fulfillment of ecstasy, while the sexual jewels, blown into nature's space, floated in exquisite pleasure of delight. It was truly written that God would increase the pain of childbirth but woman would still desire man and be subject to him and man would work all his days and produce weeds and thorns. The ground is under a curse which man and woman cannot escape.

The Evolutionist said a silent prayer and shared his heart with God. He was happy to live.

51

*The little plastic dreams, with no feeling, emotion, or
desire.*   Magic Star Flower

Magic Star Flower said, "We've brought a friend to see you,
Abraxas."

Abraxas said, "Will you ever be sane and stay on the tranquilizers, Sphere?" He admitted me to the insanity house. I had a new
secret. I had tried to kill.

The nightmare rolled.

The old insanity house, with its handful of pills and running naked
in the corridors. In group therapy I kept telling them I was a child
molester but they didn't care. They told me I was preoccupied with
sex. I screwed my new woman and drank rum and Coke on the balcony. I went skinny-dipping, drunk, in the river and was put in with
the Korsakoff victims.[62]

Do you know the trip of a paranoid schizophrenic alcoholic
drug-user? The trip is the thoughts that dart in fear, just below
consciousness, that I don't want to acknowledge. They flick and
pester me till they are brought to the surface. They are never
vocalized and they can't be suppressed. I don't know. They are
thoughts. I'm blushing, I'm shaking, I'm homosexual, I'm a
pedophile. I'm afraid to express these emotions. They are the
voices of guilt. They are the words I never let anyone hear. The
truth cannot be expressed. It is the land of the id. Some psychiatric
cases spend all their lives with these thoughts, but I knew how to
rid myself of them. I talked them out. I spoke my mind. I listened
and remembered.

The nightmare rolled.

If only Abraxas would explain my diagnostic criteria for me, but psychiatrists get tired of repeating themselves, so they are professionally secretive. Abraxas got me to beat a pillow with a cricket bat in group therapy. I screamed till I was exhausted. It was the best therapy I ever had. I just kept beating the cushion with a plastic bat and screaming and screaming.

The nightmare rolled.

52

My dream is a nightmare.   Sphere

One day she was there: Elysium Dream, with a young girl. She smiled and said, "Hello, Sphere. Magic told me what happened. She wrote to me and told me you were here. I never received your letters, Sphere, and I waited so long with men I thought were you. You have never hurt me, Sphere, and you always tried to make me happy. You're a sweet man. Come home. You have a daughter you've never seen. The war is over. I'd like you to meet Euthanasia. Her full name is Euthanasia Dream Flower."

"Hello, beautiful. I'm your old man." She wrapped her arms around me. We talked about the future.

"Your main purpose in life, now, is to impress people with your conformity. Play to an audience. Sell yourself to me. I love you."

"I'm not going to sell myself. Elysium, I wanted to make it right but I messed up my life. I want you to take away my nightmares."

"You have to tell me everything."

"I don't have to. A man needs something that belongs to himself and no one else. Maybe a better man will tell you everything, but not me."

"What would Sigmund Freud say about that?"

"He has been discredited."

"But you haven't forgotten, have you?"

"Okay, how's this for a Freudian anal fixation? I used to play looking in bottoms with my best mate in the local bush before I went to school. I suppose that makes me a generous personality. I'm an arsehole."

"Any more hangups, you little bugger?"

"Yeah, I still masturbate over little boys' and girls' and animals' genitals, vaginas, penises, scrotums, and breasts. That's what I think about. According to Freud, I must have a phallic personality. I read somewhere that woman is the only animal with a clitoris. A little-known fact. I'd just love to be impotent."

"Anything more? I won't judge you," she said, "but I thought the prick evolved from the clit?"

"The first time I masturbated was in the back of a classroom."

"Okay, anything more?"

"No. Did that make you happy? I've told it all before in group therapy, but if you ever make fun of me in public I'll lay you down so fast!"

"Sounds like a good excuse for insanity. All sexual problems."

"I don't know. Are there schizophrenic animals in the wild? I wonder if the nightmare of living is the cause of schizophrenia? I don't know."

The dream rolled.

53

My book is what you make it.   Sphere

"Will you ever escape from hell, Sphere?" Abraxas asked.

"I don't know. The symbol is sphere. When the last sphere, the sun, the earth rolls into its ordered place, you will see before your eyes all the days of your life. Then you will wake up from the imprint. When you see the last of me. When you see the last guru, the last of perfection, and when you see the last of evil. The last voice of insanity. When all motion of me ceases, you will have peace."

Elysium walked into the room with Euthanasia. The organizer crossed the room and smiled at the child. She looked outside the window towards the marijuana plants in the garden. The mentor faced Abraxas. "I found happiness. I gave up the poison, and for me the nightmare is over. The symbol is broken. You see, I was looking for a place of eternal happiness but I did not find it on this world. Here it is just a fluctuating dream of eternal peace. I had to let the Elysium Dream go to become herself. I wanted reality and then I found out I was caught up in that reality. I had to let go of life. I am a computer. I am a man."

"And how do you keep your sanity?" Abraxas asked.

"I exercise and exorcise my mind. I express who I am. I live in a world that is confused."

"And what are you going to do about it?"

"I am going to do nothing. I'm going to the country, to become who I am. You see, a lot of the insane wanted it that way. Now I want the truth, but not the truth of the sadists, the truth of the universe. One day I might even tell the truth. I've found a woman and I'm going to leave the city slums to be with her. I'm not a good man. I am who I was destined to be. I did not change a thing. Abraxas, we've been through a lot together and I'm sorry if I'm a babbling fool. I know about pain and oppression. I wanted to tell the world who I am. I'm a mentor."

We shook hands.

"You're still sweating. You're still afraid, still paranoid."

"I'm sane."

"If you're sane, I will have to revoke your pension."

"Doc, do me a favor. I'm a fruitcake. One of the first fruits of mankind."

The game rolled.

54

Why did I tear down my glory? Why do you tear down my knowing when I haven't a better house to move into?
My mentor. My teacher.

In the psychiatric hospital I talked with Abraxas.

"I read your book. Why did you say Elysium returned when she didn't?"

"I visited her in the commune and discovered the child was not mine."

"Why give in to the delusion, then?"

"I wanted the book to have a happy ending, but it didn't work out that way. It's a worthless book. It does nothing except entertain a fringe audience. It's a failure, about a failure. I wanted a long, happy ending."

"Life isn't like that," Abraxas explained. "There are always bills to pay, dishes to wipe, the kids getting sick and a living to earn, and if you understand that, then that is all anyone can accomplish. Life does not have a happy ending. There will always be good and bad times. Your bad times have been worse than most. I gathered that from your book, but it sounds like there were plenty of good times. Try to understand, you are a paranoid schizophrenic and still you had the courage to write a book. You don't know everything. You have been living in a romantic nightmare."

"The book is a fraud, Abraxas. I was a man seeking an answer and always the answer slipped away. Elysium and I were only together for three weeks, but it seemed like an eternity. She was a woman who wanted a child and I could have been the father, but I couldn't handle the trip. My life has been hell. I remembered the balls rolling through my head and because of the acid I became the inventor of rock and roll. I will leave it up to you about the rest of the characters. We were only small drug-dealers but were heavy drug-users. I have only had ten hits of heroin in my life but have smoked five kilos of my life away. Some of that grass was as strong as acid. We never talked to each other but listened to music and used our favorite drugs. I never talked because I was afraid my friends would find out my secret, that I was a pedophile. The rest of the book is a true mixture of friends. I finally saw Elysium after ten years and she is straight. She's living in a commune. We talked and I discovered Euthanasia is not my daughter. It was my imagination. Euthanasia had a red birthmark on her face caused by the drugs Elysium used while she was pregnant. Wrong, I was wrong, always wrong. I loved her and she screwed around. I needed her more than she needed me.

"It's a book about the things a man couldn't face but, once faced, their significance fades into insignificance. It's about the meaning of a word, *Sphere,* that means nothing, zero or perfection. I wanted a reason to live, so I invented a reason. It's all right now if I stay on tranquilizers. Marijuana makes me vomit with nervousness and it's the same with coffee, cigarettes, and alcohol. By the way, I tried to kill my father. I went insane and thought he ruled the world before me and caused World War Two and that my grandfather caused World War One. I am not as big a fool as you think—or a bigger fool than you realize."

"Freud will be pleased." Abraxas replied. "You tried to kill your father?"

"Yes. I learned to kill in jail. The book is a book of garbage and not a magic book. It's a book of shit. I was filling in time because I couldn't live in emptiness. The book is my hobby."

"You have never been sane," Abraxas said. "There is no perfection."

My life rolled.

"I know, and the name of my imaginary daughter is Euthanasia. I want to die. I raped myself when I molested the children. I go round and round. The last sphere has rolled into its ordered place. My last dream is over. I am sometimes sane and sometimes insane and now that the book is finished I will forget it. I gave in to the aggrandizement of the book because I really believe I created rock and roll. If only I could get rid of the romantic, sexual nightmare and forget."

"A little more advice," Abraxas said, "to help you adjust to society and yourself. Don't change the guts of the book because for some the truth is hard to face and that is the reason the world is such a satisfied mess, because some can and some can't face the truth, but you know a love of the earth that few practice and realize. You would not be part of its destruction by fighting in wars or paying taxes for its armaments. You realized you are not perfect, you made mistakes and evolved into a man of personality and character. When we are born none of us knows, so we learn from other people. You rejected their morality and you were right and wrong. Our world is in revolution and we will go in circles till we know and live the fluctuating truth. Sadists are just people who believe in themselves. Some sadistic people take out their anger on themselves and some sadistic people take their anger out on others. And you're a very angry man."

"It's the story of one man," I replied, "and in the book I discovered my life and perhaps in the next book of life I will discover happiness."

"The book is insane, but Jesus will be proud of your humility and your theory."

"Do you think the book solved any world problems, Abraxas?" I asked.

"No, it's your truth and now it's part of mine. There are a million books nobody reads. There is no solution to bring the world together in harmony. The world is lost, but you have saved yourself. You are a human being, an individual and not your brother or your sister. You staked out your individuality. No one's as bad as you, Sphere. You fucked up their perfection trip beautifully. They'll crucify you because you rubbed their noses in the dirt. You'll be ostracized, but you've been ostracized since the beginning. Society never dug you, Sphere. You have always been outside it since the beginning. One of the untouchables. The rich and the righteous will always hate and despise you, but the black man and the cripple will say, 'Thanks for the tip and see you, sucker.'

"I'm proud, myself, that I made one man sane. I have my own mission. You're a lovable fruitcake, Sphere, and if you give up your electric guitar and your cigarettes, you will find happiness."

"I wish the government would ban cigarettes and legalize marijuana, so everyone can go into cannabis psychosis."

"Why send people insane with cannabis? They have enough insanity as it is. Till our next conversation, and if you start to dream, have a shot of Modecate, and don't mainline it, young man. I know what you're like with your randy desires. After you start dreaming, the next stage is you'll be in pain and then you know you're insane."

"I have an iron deficiency. I worry about what people think of me."

"You dreamers. You have a chemical imbalance in your brain."

The gentle terrorist walked from the room into the anarchy of his own life.

"Wait."

I re-entered the room.

"Sphere, your last poisons are alcohol and cigarettes, and when you give them up your life will change. If you feel your life has become unmanageable, go to Alcoholics Anonymous, although even they won't save you. The vitamins won't save you. Your spirit might. Maybe that chemical imbalance is just called love. Goodbye, Sphere." And he smiled.

Life rolled.

55

Pseudo-wisdom is the wisdom of the innocent.   Sphere

Released from the psychiatric hospital, I moved in with Terry and Sneak.

Sneak was going to the RSL[63] to play some pool. It was time for his tranquilizers. I sat in the living room of our three-room apartment in Petersham with a half-drunk bottle of red in front of me. God, I hated Petersham, with its dilapidated rows of houses and the brothel around the corner that I couldn't afford. The paint was peeling from the walls and the carpet hadn't been vacuumed in three months, there was only cold water in the sink and the can in the shithouse didn't flush, and you know I hated Petersham.

I was going to get out and go to the country and maybe there regain my sanity. I lit another cigarette and had a little daydream. I ruled the world and solved all its problems but couldn't solve my own. I smiled and let go of the dream and took another sip of red with a draw of my smoke. In Petersham, my only recreation was to dream and drink and smoke and talk. Our dealer owned the house we lived in, so we were never short of smoking dope. The bottle shop was around the corner. The brothel was around the corner. My mind was around the bend. God, please get me out.

The lunatic upstairs had weeded out my Indian hemp plants from the garden and buried his rubbish there. There was a girl and her daughter, also upstairs, that I never got to see, who I wanted to screw. A bunch of Fijians lived in the main flat downstairs where we used to live before Terry got carted off to the psychiatric hospital for wearing a baby's hat.

When we were together we were three psychiatric cases who had escaped to our dealer's pad from two halfway houses. The halfway houses fleeced us of all our money and the authorities wouldn't let us drink on the premises. We had all been kicked out of the halfway house at Richmond for drinking and whoring and had gone to Anna's, but she bled us so badly we couldn't afford to booze and play pool and you know I hate pool. We had all been released recently from the psychiatric hospital with nowhere to go, so we naturally congregated together to live out what remained of our lives in dignified solitude.[64]

My parole officer said I had the brains to go to university. I was tired of sweating at the boxing gym and going to the rehabilitation house. They once asked me at the rehab center how they could improve the facilities and my suggestion of naturalist bathing in the swimming pool didn't go down too well. After that they advised me I had to take tranquilizers or leave the premises. I had to get away and go to university. My uncle and aunt had died recently and left me $7,500 in small, unmarked bills, a little bottler of a fortune. I never knew that that much money existed in the world, and with my pension I could get a degree and really retire with an intellectual blue-nose grin.

I finished off the red and went into the bedroom for a wank.

Afterwards, I switched on the stolen TV and settled down to watch the idiot box, with its clean heroes and tough, evil villains. I hate TV. I only like music. The soothing voice of rock and roll really makes this chicken-fucker swing. I listened all day and half the night to the rock and roll and, shit, I didn't get enough. That Laura Branigan had a voice that could vibrate a hot spot. Yummy mummy, I wanted to lick her out.

Sneak arrived back and I told him I was moving out and going to Armageddon University[65] in the country. He said, "Yeah, mate." (That was all Sneak ever said, "Yeah, mate.") Terry was going to look after Sneak and take him to live on his farm when he got his compo, from his accident, but now he was back in the psychiatric hospital.[66] Terry always smoked too much dope and he messed his head and would walk around with a baby's cap on. He freaked out a couple of people, so they took him to the psychiatric hospital and put him back on lithium.

Sneak had recently been divorced from his wife and he told me that all he ever thought about were his kids, two girls and a boy. He was one of the gentlest people I have ever known. The reason he got his nickname was because he was so sneaky on the pool table and all he did was drink and play pool at the club and pub. When we were together we dug each other because we were good blokes who had nothing except our friendship. Society snubbed us, but we were true blue dinky-di.

Sneak went out and committed suicide by drowning himself in the river of his home town. Terry disappeared without leaving a forwarding address, and I went to the University of Armageddon.

The reality unfolded.

56

We exist because others make us real.   Uncle Cane Toad

The kids at the university were a wonderful bunch of arseholes. The majority only cared about themselves and tried personality assassination on anyone who didn't laugh at their jokes. I don't think I ever knew a more cynical bunch of vicious swine who didn't know themselves. I remained stone drunk for the year and was finally turfed out of college at the end of the year and told not to return. There is nothing as obnoxious as a drunk.

I found accommodation in the flats adjacent to the university [the next year] and moved in with three Muslims. One Hindu, one Buddhist, one Christian, one Communist, and a Jew lived next door. I was the baddest one in the flat, being the only drinker—which isn't entirely true, because Islam smoked, but he eventually quit at the end of the year and they all enjoyed an occasional drink but never got drunk. I walked among the seven lamp stands. The seven churches of Revelations.

The Hindu told of his sex life and I don't think I ever want to hear about another person's sex life because it is entirely devoid of love's emotion and constitutes an idle boast. I was the alcoholic deviant of the flat who was constantly drunk till I was convinced I needed Alcoholics Anonymous and that was the beginning of my recovery. They loved me in the flat, and for that I will be eternally grateful.

I told them of my glorious sex life and if you ever want to reveal your sexual triumphs after this, it is up to you. My sex life began at puberty when I was wanked off in a homosexual school during a Latin lesson. I have sexually played with a boy and girl. I have climbed onto the roof of our home and masturbated while looking into the shower at my sister-in-law. I have sexually molested three cats, one male, one female, and one neuter. (Love them cats.) The first time I had sex with a woman I found out how Mary could conceive and still be a virgin and that, my ex-friends, is my sexual certification. What you are having for fantasies I make real, so I had better get out of town.

One night I took thirty Cogentin and the next night thirty more.[67] I was sitting at my desk and had a dream. I was making a margarine pizza and put a blob of margarine on a plate and popped it into the oven.

Blackout.

Next thing I knew, the pizza was cooked and so I took out the burned margarine plate and thought it was the worst pizza I'd ever seen.

Blackout.

I was wandering the flats and I'd enter a flat and ask if Islam lived there, because I knew if Islam lived there I lived there also. The next thing I knew, I was beside the road and a police officer was asking me questions. I said I'd been drinking at the hotel. They asked me if I would go with them and I said okay. Next thing I knew, I was in the dock at the jail house being asked to empty my pockets.

Blackout.

I stood there for I don't know how long.

Blackout.

A copper came up and asked me what I was doing and I replied that I'd dropped my smoke, and I didn't even have a smoke.

Blackout.

I was in the police car and the officer asked me if I knew where the flats were and I innocently pointed in the opposite direction. I was escorted by a burly university security officer to the flats. When I arrived, everyone was awake and there was the doctor, nurses, security officers, and police, and then blackout.

I awoke the following morning and found a strange bag in my room, so I asked Islam where it came from. He told me that I had gone to a friend's flat and picked it up. I said I had a dream last night and he said that it was no dream.

57

Man has to build his own temples.   Sphere

Star Ship lay in my arms. "You come to university at thirty. You're carrying on the ritual of Jesus Christ, aren't you?"

"Yes."

"Will you crucify yourself at thirty-three?"

"I don't know. I already have. I might walk into the desert without food and water. I did it once before. I walked for a day into the desert at Broken Hill and at the end of the day I came upon a road, so I slept there. The next day I walked further into the desert and at the end of the day I came upon another road, so I slept there. I walked further into the desert and came upon another road and saw this as a sign to return, because the voices were quiet. I hitched a ride on an ore truck and arrived in Sydney five days later."

"Did you really invent rock and roll?"

"Yes, I did."

"Abraxas thinks you're insane."

"I know; out of control, he would call it."

"I'm not sure of you either. Perhaps there are others with balls and dreams rolling through their heads."

"I don't care if you believe me. I'll keep traveling on and sending my feelings out to the musicians. They believe in the music. I'll have women and perhaps one day I'll settle down. I want it that way. I like the quiet life and I appreciate the music. I'm eccentric, a nut."

"What's the next step in music, Sphere?"

"Most probably contemporary Christian music, or universal music working on two planes. I don't know. I've become a Christian and I go to university. The music will follow. I'm working on a new generation of wankers."

"You're screwing me and you're a Christian?"

"Yes. Sex and religion don't mix, so I don't screw you in church and I don't moralize in bed. I'm quite adventurous sexually and I know I can't stop my little manufacturing factory, so I don't try. So I'm a hypocrite, but I get plenty of clam because I'm a man who has given up trying to be a saint. I'm a man who knows the real thoughts and actions of men. I can read personalities of myself."

"Who are you, Sphere?"

"I'm a man who, when I go insane, either thinks people can pick up my thoughts or I get fanatically religious and think I'm a prophet. I'm a man whose mother was God. I'm a man who will commit suicide if I don't find peace of mind. I'm a sex deviant. I'm an alcoholic. I'm the man other people told me to be, by putting thoughts into my mind which I thought were mine. I'm the culmination of years of dreaming and stories and actions. It doesn't matter if you don't believe me, because soon all this will fade away. Even rock and roll ends. The universe ends. I'm giving up the trip when I give up the alcohol. I'm an alcoholic and the alcoholic nightmares will pass soon. In the future I may get into nature music. I've been into this dream music for the last two years and I've produced a few good songs, but now I don't know. All this will pass away, even the pain of the nightmares."

"What are you going to do with an ego like yours, Sphere?"

"Star Ship, baby, be cool. Did I tell you about the time I lived on vitamin pills for a week? Or the time I hitched to Dubbo and stayed in a hotel room for five days and didn't eat or drink and had a nightmare that if I died the world would suicide in a nuclear war? How about the time I molested a cat? The bad times are over."

"You're crazy. You got kicked out of college last year because the administration didn't dig the time you appeared naked in front of three thousand people at the Sunray Sunday concert. Cobber the Evolutionist showed me the pictures."[68]

"Yeah, they weren't very flattering."

"How about the stories of the times you'd come in drunk to the dining room and show your naturalist magazines to the waitresses? How about the time you gave them your underpants for a Christmas present? And the classic: how you had a psychotic episode for the two weeks of the final exams and got a medical cer-

tificate to do delayed examinations? And crashing the senior common room to drink their liquor? You just hate society. You just sexually harass women. Your whole book is sexual harassment."

"Star Ship, baby, be cool. I've given up the poisons. I'm a
Christian. I'm in AA. I get an invalid pension. I'm a novelist."

"We'll stay together till you drive into the sunset, eh, Sphere?
And forget the dream?"

"Yeah."

"Sphere, I may as well be laid back with you till I get my major
in psychology."

"You'll see. It'll be all right. No worries."

"Now I *am* worried, because I know when you say no worries
we've got worries."

"I'll start second year at university next year and, as I've said, I've
given up the poison."

"Will you take me to the ball?"

"You know I hate balls. The last ball has already rolled into its
ordered place."

"What will I do with you, Sphere?"

"Star Ship, baby, you know what I like. Yes, my little friend, let's
do it again?"

"Get me out of your sexual harassment, Sphere."

"Star Ship, we've just begun to travel the universe and we can't
stop now."

"Sphere, Sphere, Sphere, give up your dramatics!"

"Yeah, let's talk about something interesting, Star Ship. How's
your bladder? Got any new panties recently? You know I dig premature ejaculation because it's so easy and satisfying. I'm not too
exhausted to enjoy the delight of the mind control of orgasm."

Star Ship looked at me and said, "Ahhhhhh," and I know when
she says that she doesn't like what I've said. "Your book's a sick
book by a sick person. All it's about is sex and drugs and sickening
dreams."

"Yeah, I know, but it's the truth. I'm a sexual being. Man is the
sexiest animal on the planet. I was a drug addict and I invented
rock and roll. Let me tell you about life. There was a man who
thought he was the greatest man in the world and then he saw the
greatest tree and the greatest flower and the greatest woman.

They were full of dreams and they died after a moment of grandeur. The man wrote a book which he thought contained the wisdom of the ages and it was his thoughts printed on pages. But nobody listened because they thought he was a fool. The book was his life and he saw his reflection and he knew that he was not the greatest man but a foolish eccentric. Youth had faded and he was just another dirty old man. Don't fake it, baby. He saw the truth. He was not Jesus Christ but just another failure. We all fail in the end."

58

Men need women more than women need men.   Abraxas

I knocked on Abraxas's office door.[69] A voice said, "Come in."

I entered. I had arranged an interview with him. I told him to relax and free-associate. "What do you think of me, Abraxas?"

He replied, "Like most patients, I find you interesting. I need diversity too. Psychiatric patients are like normal people. Some are shits, and some I like."

"What do you think of religion?"

"Religion's very effective but causes some discomfort in some people. I have an inquisitive nature, so I'm agnostic."

"What do you think of sex?"

"Sex is terrific but it is wasted on the young. They deny their sexuality because to them it's so overpowering, but when they get older and settle down they appreciate it."

"What do you think of sport?"

"Organized sport is a waste of time, but kids playing has a lot in it. I like individual sport because it's good for exercise and self-image."

"What do you think of politicians?"

"They're smart cookies and I admire them for their capacity to do a job, but unfortunately they are shortsighted."

"What do you think of your children?"

"I'm very fond of them and I hope they won't repeat my mistakes, but I let them go their own way."

"What do you think of world affairs?"

"This reflects man's basic nature. Their breeding territories. I'm not optimistic, so I make my contributions now."

"What do you think of psychiatrists?"

"They vary, because there is no general rule. Life for a good psychiatrist is emotionally draining. There are strong and weak psychiatrists. A good psychiatrist accepts biology as a brain function. There's heart disease, lung disease, and brain disease. This is critical in acceptance of treatment but is not rigid."

"What do you think of education?"

"I tell the kids the truth. I'm a sociobiologist. A good education is necessary."

"What do you think about TV?"

"I can't stand advertisements and TV's mostly crap. Give me programs on natural history and some current affairs, but it's mainly boring."

"What do you think of books?"

"I like interesting books—autobiographies and scientific books—but I don't read novels. Patrick White's novels give me the shits."

"What do you think of communist society?"

"It has high alcohol problems and should leave the Third World alone, as it upsets ecosystems."

"What do you think of capitalist society?"

"Its advertising promotes the seven deadly sins and has no responsibility towards people. It's ecologically irresponsible."

"What do you think of women's rights?"

"I believe in equal opportunity, which should not be confused with biological equality. They have the same health problems as men when they do their jobs."

"Do you believe in superstition?"

"It's horseshit and is just replacement of religion. It's mostly nonsense. It is characteristic of humans to seek an explanation."

"What's your opinion of life and death?"

"I don't mind death but don't like dying. Life's interesting, sometimes pleasurable and sometimes a pain in the arse. It's getting shorter."

"What do you think of meditation and relaxation techniques?"

"It has a lot going for it. I practice it once a day."

"What is your most common fantasy?"

"I'm lying on my back in the sun by the sea."

"What do you think of university research?"

"Some is good and some is a waste of time. I'd like more money in specific areas."

"Do you like learning and teaching?"

"Yes, I like my job. Perhaps I'd like more power so I could do a few more things."

"Describe your personality."

"I like myself. I'm self-changing and a friendly, outgoing individual."

"Do you know something that the world should know?"

"Yes, the biological, neurological nature of cognition. Simply, how the brain works."

"Do you like Australia?"

"It's a lovely country but is becoming more like the USA with its rules and regulations and will collapse under its own weight."

"What's wrong with men and women?"

"They're shortsighted and they don't know themselves."

"What's the most important thing in life?"

"My family, and understanding."

"Anything that you would like to talk about?"

"I'm tired, worn-out, and need a holiday. Patients are difficult and my defense mechanism shuts patients out. Basically, I can't stand the pace. I've just read Clive James' *Unreliable Memoirs* and it was very good."

"Okay, Abraxas, you're sane. Thanks for the information."

"I've got to get back to work, Sphere. It's a hectic life. See you."

59

Love makes me live. **Sphere**

Star Ship only wanted a three-month affair, so I was starved for affection and my need and want sent me quite insane. I felt like punching her out as I felt my own human weakness. Were you expecting Superman? Were you expecting a man who knew himself and could laugh without the visual sound of drugs? I'm as fragile as glass, an unhappy insect that crawls into a real pain of despair. No more hurt for me.

I watched the year pass till I reached the sunny and rainy day that would be my last. I had saved the dreams and reached everybody's end. You see, there is a happy ending for me. Death is just a metamorphosis into a butterfly and it's not a painful end but only a matter of falling to sleep. The second death had no power to hurt me. I felt my own tranquillity. I had tortured myself enough. I had learned to swear in hell and soon my shell would dissolve and I would become consciousness. My work is over.

You see, I have not the things that make you want to live. I have no woman, no children, and no faith. I have nothing but a dream. In my mind I have schizophrenia's heaven and hell. I am going into my mind to find my reward. I am going where you will soon follow. I am going to the fields of Elysium to be with my imaginary daughter, Euthanasia. I smiled and knew that everything would be all right. I saw the beautiful things that surrounded me in my university room. I had become a starship pilot with my tapestry, Nepalese blanket, quilt, and serene pictures hanging on the wall of my room. I had a stereo, a record collection, and a car. On the bookshelf, my philosophy, psychology, and sociology books gathered dust. I had everything I desired but I was not happy with the rigors and hypocrisy of life. The strain of life had no importance for me. I was leaving all to have peace. I might swallow the pills and watch my thoughts as I sail into eternity to be with Jesus and the other martyrs. I smiled and knew. The last scene rolled into its ordered place and I died only to say that my life will soon be over.

I was happy to take the next step beyond into eternity. I go into the inevitable because I wish to cease to exist. There is no happy ending for me, just a repetitious remembering of mistakes. The dream is over, but I could not suicide. I had recovered from my nightmare into my dreams and I know I will never love another woman till she loves me. A man should never love a woman till she loves him.

I will flip a coin to see if I live or suicide. Heads I live; tails I die. Dramatic, isn't it? Schizophrenic, more like it. It's the decision of God. It's my decision. Positive or negative, I symbolically kicked every woman in the cunt and symbolically sent myself insane.

I flipped the 50-cent piece into the air . . .

60

Nobody controls the universe.   Sphere

The spirit of the book spoke. *I know, I love, I think, I feel.* The fanatical dreamer who wishes to preserve the burial ground of earth crash-landed on the planet's natural truth. He was the dream-giver. He called forever. I am future. I am earth. He who had the vision to see a million years was called sanity, the same man. I am the same man.

In his mind are a million spheres and he could not justify one sphere to the detriment of the other nine hundred thousand, nine hundred and ninety-nine. Mathematical probability says he should not exist and he knows if the law is broken he is trapped in eternity. This is his greatest sphere. The year of matter turning energy into thought.

The telepath spoke to the law while war broke out and the armies of heaven followed the rider of the heroin out of the haven. He sings an old song. *Valhalla, we are coming.* He wears the Bible's garment deep-dyed in blood. He is the representation of God, the universe. He goes into his own desire for eternity and believes the contradiction would and could be resolved as he rides into the abyss, forcing his enemy before him, while the real nightmare of war shocks his mind into a delusion of confused illusion and the screaming never ends, because this is reality. This is the life of the gambling man.

The collective dream came out of existence as the universe evolved into heaven and heaven evolved into the universe. This is the perfect shit made from a dozen avocado and pepperoni pizzas. This is the world I love being murdered by the beasts of more. This is our salvation and our destruction. Cursed. Do you want more? Shall I go on because I died such a long time ago? The child molester was hurled into hell.

The schizophrenic had heaven and hell in his mind and he watched the pleasant hallucinations. He felt the breeze like a schizophrenic, he had vision like a schizophrenic. The schizophrenic had walked the fields. He believed in the beautiful dream and he had gold, proved in the fire, coated on his teeth from the cigarettes. He knew. He didn't know. He knew the imaginary mind machine had made it so. He knew the truth. The hallucinations could be controlled by the Modecate. He controlled the Modecate. He was proud to be called schizophrenic. You see, the schizophrenic knew. He shook off his cares, watched the adrenaline vision, smiled, and said in his mind, *Shit, I've done it. I'm as mad as hell but I'm happy. My mind belongs to me.* The truth. The truth. *The truth is that everyone knows who I am. I am free of guilt. I am free of worry. I am free of the sexless nuns. I don't have to hide because of my schizophrenia any more. I don't have to run away. I don't care what they think anymore because I am the sane man.* My spirit was free to be himself. The angel inside smiled. He/she knew he/she would come out of his own mind and see and talk to others because he/she was accepted and he/she was loved and hated. He/she knew he spoke only the best of bullshit with the worst part of his life over. The raindrop fell from the sky into the ocean and echoed.

The representation of the universe smiled and said, God can even create himself a schizophrenic with no power. He can even be the most hated man on the planet because he knows.

Woman, did you ever realize the psychological battle of man?

Did you know of the male menopause? Woman, did you know it's utter shit being a man? Woman, do you think yourself lucky not to be the mutation that is man? Man the mess. Man the ravaged spirit. And you, woman, stand by and let it all roll. You take everything. Woman, you're a liar and a thief. You've taken it all away and then you give man your short-lived love and affection and then your hatred, bitterness, and resentment, because you too are a little less the psychological mess that this man is. You too have your war and it has been waged since the beginning. Woman, why do you do this to man, the brute? Is it because of your sensitivity? Is it because you don't like being poked between the legs? Is it for revenge against the man who bites at your heels? Do you always give nothing except your hackneyed clichés? Woman, you do nothing. Woman, you just watch and simmer in rage, proud that you're not the fool man is to fight a war. Woman, one day God will ask you what you did to me. Did you love him as an equal? Did you tell him the truth? Do you understand that your virtue is chauvinistic self-concern? I believed in you but you did not believe in me and this is true for one man. Woman, you tear men to pieces and with my strength I can/can't hurt you. I looked for equality and I saw a war where neither side wins. We've fought each other enough. I walk away from the battle of the sexes. I was hurt too much by the nuclear whore.

Yes, it was you who did this. Woman, who spends her life fighting men. Get thee to a nunnery. You spend your whole life fighting men. This is the psychological war of woman where she wins status. You love his uniform and pray for his death so you can cry. I lost everything because of you, woman. What did you do to your doll? I'm sorry. I'm sorry for both of us.

Now, this was the time when the computer directing the battle was destroyed. The angels of heaven will destroy everything because of this. Their computer god a wreck of tangled pain twitching in agony as it is tortured and violated. Michael, the most powerful angel of Valhalla, decimated the perpetrators of the crime, so they left the computer alone to attack Michael. The angels of darkness and power will destroy everything because of this. The false gods knew that they would have to destroy the children. They knew they themselves would die, so they directed their children against the children of light. Michael became God and, in time, his followers became gods. Michael became the Devil and the Devil became God. The obscenities of hell kicked and pissed and bit and swore in a war that never ends.

The police were then called in to restore order. "All right, you lot, you're all going to jail. You women too. No fucking objections, you know we maintain law and order here and anyone who breaks the peace gets his arse kicked in."

Meanwhile, in heaven, a power lord took his throne and smiled and remembered a vision. The trusted angels stood at their posts. These are the most loyal angels and will not move or budge till ordered by the power lord. They loved and hated the game. They loved their god, children, wives, lives, and land. They protected the children. They were killers with steel eyes. Their minds were crystal dreams and they lived in shock as their empire crumbled about them. The power lord anxiously rested his head on the table and felt sad that he had betrayed his people. All was lost, so he said to the psychopath he kept, "With this switch you can destroy the girl."

The power lord, his mind numb, thought to himself, *What does it matter? I will not intimidate you with my rule of fear and displays of violence. I will let you all go so you can run and play and smile. The world is beautiful with his/her laughing, haughty naughtiness. No one judges except God, and I defend.*

Sphere, the woman/man, to all intents and purposes looked upright, presentable, and just, with no irrationality. His main purpose was to create a girl/world. The man with eyes for eternity could see the black void where he judges man and woman and, most of all, he judges himself. I cannot forget. I cringe in fear. Look for the man who doesn't sweat. Look at the man who has them all in the palm of his hand. Equality, a woman his own age.

The bands are going to take it all over, the TV and the radio, and give it serenity. We're from the earth and we're not going to take inane conservations of riches from the bejeweled, sophisticated bitches. We have no heroes, no John Waynes, no James Bonds with licenses to kill. No sports cars, no suits, no Robert Zimmermans. We come from the earth and we fight the fight. No sexless nuns, no impotent Victorian intellectuals. We have the confidence to be virgins, to be mad, to be afraid, to be strong.

I broke the time barrier in the testing ground and if I wanted a good PR man like Paul, once I could have had my own church. I'd get the Americans, like the Romans, to make it politically viable, and if I'm certified insane then all the religious freaks like Jesus, Mohammed, Buddha are schizophrenics too. I won't go without a fight. Fire, hell, damnation, heaven, bliss, nirvana. Madmen, all mad. Hee-hee. They thought Jesus was mad too. My church is the church of the insane. I destroy my church myself and this is the truth effect.

The last psychological war which never ends. Every man, woman, and child for themselves. To the lifeboats, men. Follow me, men. Where's my horse? Get the grappling hooks, and with the shells exploding all around me I ran in circles like a cowardly cur while my brother dropped napalm on his own children. Destroying everything, destroying ourselves. Collapsing the house of cards. Exterminate every living creature, you madmen.

The last armies of heaven, the scum, the schizophrenics, the most hated man on the planet, the child molester, the last believers, watched as the vicious fantasies of the acid warlocks and the trained killers gazed at the gold and jewels and brightly colored pieces of paper and, with a cry, the armies of heaven rose as one as, their minds battered and screaming, they hurled themselves into hell and burning and burning they knew who had destroyed their minds, their temples, their Lord, their bodies, their earth and into hell they dragged and cursed their tormentors.

It's the seduction of a society. On with the thirty-year striptease show. The alcoholic and marijuana addict lifts me up and brings me down. Rock and roll, and when the war game is over we shake hands, pat each other on the back and go our merry way.

Look up in the sky. Is it a man? Is it a plane? No, it's Marshmallow Man. How many other men live in fear? Men who are destroyed. How many fucking men have you scared shitless? Hands up who live in fear? Feel your own fear. Feel your own fear. Feel your own fear. Here is your sphere.

It's the woman's nature to destroy man and after she gets what she wants from me she will crush me while my daydreams adjust the future. So soon we will be converted.

In my mind I have gold and jewels but I must give them away

because I'll get lost in the maddening wine. I give you a million spherical dreams. The jewels of friends. Halley's Comet is in the sky and it's the sign of a new rock and roll song of a new generation while the conflict between the person I should have been and the person I am reverberates down the echo chambers of my mind. The last book has rolled into place.

I, the black prophet, the Marshmallow Man, say, "Woman, don't expect me to fight your battles for you. Woman, you must fight with the fighters. If you command, be ready to die. My battle is all against all. In my mind and body is the brilliant insecurity of a man who fights, a man of fright. Surrender, we must all surrender to truth. Woman, if you fight you must really fight the exciting cowshit of testosterone on this planet."

Fuck it. Fuck it. Fuck it.

Cursed. My life is a living hell. The book is a lie. Do you fucking understand, creeps and cretins? It's a lie. I am a liar. It's a fantasy.

I smiled and knew they understood years ago. I am Abraxas. I am disturbed. I have been insane. Do you want a flower? *Da, da, da, da, da, da.* Tears in my eyes, I cry in my lonely room. I never will escape from paranoid schizophrenia. How would you like to be called disturbed for the rest of your life? How would you like to be locked in an institution? How would you like to repeat second class? How would you like to be taught by nuns? How would you like to be a sexual deviant? How would you like to be a drug addict? How would you like to be me? How would you like to be a man? How would you like to be such a fool?

The collective dream came out of existence as the universe evolved into heaven and heaven evolved into the universe. This is the perfect shit made from a dozen avocado and pepperoni pizzas. This is the world I love being murdered by the beasts of more. This is our salvation and our destruction. Do you want more? Shall I go on? *More, more, more.* The child molester came out of hell. Do you want more?

*more more more more more more more more more more more more
more more more more more more more more more more more more
more more more more more more more more more more more more
more more more more more more more more more more more more
more more more more more more more more more more more more
more more more more more more more more more more more more
more more more more more more more more more more more more
more more more more more more more more more more more more
more more more more more more more more more more more more
more more more more more more more more more more more more
more more more more more more more more more more more more
more more more more more more more more more more more more
more more more more more more more more more more more more
more more more more more more more more more more more more
more more more more more more more more more more more more
more more more more more more more more more more more more
more more more more more more more more more more more more
more more more more more more more more more more more more
more more more more more more more more more more more more
more more more more more more more more more more more more
more more more more more more more more more more more more
more more more more more more more more more more more more
more more more more more more more more more more more more
more more more more more more more more more more more more
more more more more more more more more more more more more
more more more more more more more more more more more more
more more more more more more more more more more more more
more more more more more more more more more more more more
more more more more more more more more more more more more
more more more more more more more more more more more more
more more more more more more more more more more more more
more more more more more more more more more more more more
more more more more more more more more more more more more
more more more more more more more more more more more more
more more more more more more more more more more more more
more more more more more more more more more more more more
more more more more more more more more more more more more
more more more more more more more more more more more more
more more more more more more more more more more more more
more more more more more more more more more more more more*

Self destruction Self construction

Balanced on a tightrope I wrote this song
Am I right or am I wrong?
Am I weak or am I strong?
Did I lie when I said I died?
The truth is, I'm still alive.
The world is slowly killing me
I was tortured to be free
From the idiots on the TV
From the sadists in the military
From self-destruction, from disease.
Can anyone really love this man?
A woman his own age who understands
The psychology of war in his final stand
Evolving and revolving in this ignorant land
I'll try to live if you take my hand
The coin decides if I live
Or if I'm damned.

61

Will you ever escape from hell?   Abraxas

My pride, my delusion of grandeur has ended with the book. It is complete as I am complete. The past of the book is left far behind. The memories traced on its pages are forgotten. A useless book once read is placed on the bookshelf where it gathers dust. I could read the book again but I know it will only torture me, so it is best to let the dead bury the dead. I do not wish to be reminded of my distorted truth, so I will travel on, savoring each minute, into the future. I can still smile if I walk away from the past. I can feel the strain of life as it tugs on the reins of my mind.

My mind is full to the brim of the colorful words I uncovered in my idiotic nonsense, which amuses me and makes me glad I discovered myself by reading and seeing my thoughts. The truth is that this book is a book of nightmares and dreams, and nightmares and dreams are always and must be forgotten. I will forget my thoughts and grow into a refreshingly new conglomeration of ideas. Let the dead bury the dead. I ride to heaven; or will I dwell on death?

The book has died. The sun still shines. I think I'll do something different. Maybe I'll go out into the fresh air and no one need know I wrote this book. No one need know the daydreaming of Sphere. I will walk away from the book into obscurity as a paranoid schizophrenic with a chemical imbalance in my brain.

I smiled to myself. I'm a dog. I won the victory by a mile. I give to God what belongs to God. Perhaps I died of a broken heart, faithful to the end. I hope you enjoy the charity of a man who didn't want a child.

The coin said tails.

Transcription of a note found beside Ross's body on November 27, 1985

In the end after I decided to suicide I realized the futility of life.

I'm afraid & as always sweating. I even then just thought
   should I masturbate before I go but no I'm a sexual being to
   the end.

I know every man & woman reach this moment in time & it is
   very frightening.

I'm a scientist to the end. I wish I believed but I know soon I will
   not believe anymore.

May God have mercy on my soul.

I'm sorry.

I really am sorry.

I'd like the boys in the flat to have my car as payment for freaking them out when they find me dead.

I felt I was so important.

I feel so important.

It's a far far better thing than I've ever done before.

I can't live in pain, I'll have a last cigarette.

I could babble on forever.

I think that they (secret organization) is listening to my thoughts.
   I cannot live in insanity I refuse to live in insanity and that is
   the only reason why I die. I'm a paranoid schizophrenic and
   for us life is a living hell.

Love, Ross

Notes

1. *Baron Wasteland:* Obviously a play on "barren," this character was actually based on two of Ross's friends. *Uncle Cane Toad:* The cane toad, *Buffo marinus,* was introduced in Queensland, Australia, to control a grub in sugarcane. Uncle Cane Toad was probably given this name because he came from Queensland. *Elysium Dream:* In Greek mythology, Elysium (or Elysian Fields) was the abode of the blessed after death; heaven; or a state of ideal happiness. *Sphere:* In old astronomy, celestial spheres were the revolving globe-shaped shells in which the heavenly bodies were supposed to be set. *Music* or the *harmony of the spheres* was supposed to be produced by movements of these shells. Sphere also means one's field of action, influence, or existence; one's natural surroundings; or one's place in society. This name for the central character of the book was in keeping with Ross's delusional system—his belief that he was the center of the universe.

2. Ross began his novel in Long Bay jail.

3. "Oz" is an Australian slang term for Australia.

4. Kombi is a Volkswagen Kombi van, often associated with hippies or alternative lifestyle people.

5. Throughout Ross's psychotic episodes he reported that balls were rolling around inside his head. The intensity of these processes grew as his psychosis worsened. Balls may refer to planets and the name Sphere may be related to this. He mentions at the end of the chapter that he "comes from" these balls.

6. At this point it would appear that he is experiencing a complete psychotic breakdown driven by both the schizophrenic process and drugs.

7. This event was related to us in detail by Ross's friends.

8. St. John of God Hospital, Richmond, on the western outskirts of Sydney.

9. Ross uses this name throughout to refer to a number of different

"psychiatric professionals" who were involved directly with his case. *Abraxas* is a cabalistic (mystical) word used to denote the Supreme Being. It was often engraved on gems called Abraxas stones. Abraxas was also said to be one of the horses of Aurora, the goddess of dawn. According to Herman Hesse in his novel *Demian:* "Abraxas is the presiding deity who is both man and woman, god and devil, whose embrace is both an act of worship and a crime, and whose presence evokes both terror and bliss." *Abraxas* is also the title of an LP by the rock group Santana, mentioned by Sphere.

10. Eagles are slang for amphetamines, as in "soar like an eagle."

11. At this time, Ross was working for the Post-Master General's Department (now Australia Post) as a clerical assistant.

12. The strychnine taken here may have been used to potentiate the hallucinogenic effects of LSD.

13. Ross talked about this episode to his doctor at St. John of God Hospital and regarded it as the beginning of his schizophrenic illness. Our investigations lead us to believe that this was not his first episode, but it may have been sufficiently vivid to represent the starting point for him.

14. This is his first oblique reference to his belief that he sexually molested some children in his neighborhood during his mid-teens. We have been unable to corroborate this "secret." It is possible that it was part of his delusional system.

15. It may be that by now Ross was not only experiencing the "trip" associated with the drug but also the onset of his schizophrenic illness.

16. While there may have been some discussion of Ross among his friends because of his idiosyncratic characteristics, it may also be the case that his expression of paranoia is a part of his illness.

17. Zoroaster was a 6th to 7th century B.C. Iranian religious reformer, founder of Zoroastrianism, also referred to as Zarathustra. It is possible that Ross had been reading in this field and was familiar with Zoroastrianism. He may also have been familiar with a well-known piece of orchestral music by R. Strauss called "Thus Spake Zarathustra," the theme music in the movie classic, *2001: A Space Odyssey.*

18. His daughter was born on December 27, 1974, some five days after the longest day of the year in the Southern Hemisphere.

19. This passage is based on Revelations 10:8–11.

20. Folidol is an organophosphate insecticide used for aphids and thrips. The chemical would need to be ingested in order to have an effect on the individual. There is some question as to whether or not this

is the actual poison that Ross is alleged to have taken. Ross, in conversations with one of us (R. G.), indicated that his father had accidentally sprayed him with the substance when he was very young but his father says that Ross may have accidentally drunk the poison.

21. We can find no evidence that Modecate (fluphenazine decanoate), an antipsychotic medication, is a sex stimulant.

22. Ritalin (methylphenidate) is a stimulant intermediate in strengh between caffeine and amphetamines. *The Soft Parade* is the title of a Doors album.

23. Stelazine (trifluoperazine dihydrochloride) is a phenothiazine tranquilizer with potent antipsychotic properties.

24. The bike was revving past the point that was good for the engine; this is often indicated on one of the gauges with a red line. The term *ton* is 100 mph.

25. Carlos Casteneda wrote in the 1970s on subjects relating to hallucinogenic drugs, shamanism, religion, and mythology. He had a strong following among alternative lifestyles and was influential in the counter-culture of the time.

26. One of Ross's friends remembers him marching around the block sometimes at night, claiming to be a warlock.

27. Reference to Aldous Huxley's *The Doors of Perception.*

28. The "bent-nail effect" refers to a penis with a bend at its end.

29. We could find no evidence relating to the Guzzler Sane story. Uncle Cane Toad doesn't remember, but his memory is not too good around this period, due to his own drug use. He lost contact with Ross from time to time and we have been unable to find anyone who can provide evidence regarding this episode.

30. A feature of some forms of schizophrenia is the phenomenon of "clanging" when the individual involuntarily rhymes material and the involuntary rhyming does not always make sense. The reader will note this a number of times in Ross's story.

31. Pethidine is a narcotic analgesic widely used for the treatment of pain.

32. Mandrax (a combination of methaqualone base and diphenhydramine) was prescribed as a sleeping tablet but was widely abused and is therefore now off the market. High doses had a euphoric effect.

33. Cane Toad confirms that he was admitted to hospital with amphetamine psychosis.

34. Ross's worry about ants was mentioned several times in his notes at St. John of God Hospital.

35. Antipsychotic medications such as Modecate often have side

effects, one of which is tardive dyskinesia. Its symptoms include unusual facial expressions and movements. Ross may have had some of these symptoms and was attempting to hide them, although there was no evidence from his records that this was the case.

36. The pharmacological actions of methadone, or Physeptone, are qualitatively similar to those of morphine. Methadone is widely used in the treatment of heroin addiction as a replacement drug. It is longer-acting than heroin and is taken orally in liquid form.

37. Rainbow Moonfire was apparently a friend of Ross who was not known to Uncle Cane Toad, Elysium Dream, and Magic Star Flower. Ross added her to his story for interest. He did talk to one of us (R. G.) about this woman before he died, but we have been unable to trace her and we do not know any details about her death.

38. Mogadon (nitrazepam) is a sleep-inducing medication.

39. June 21, the winter solstice in the Southern Hemisphere, is the shortest day of the year.

40. Hospital notes show that at this time Ross was obsessed with the notion of destroying the Catholic Church.

41. This is a reference to Ross's claim that he molested some neighborhood children at that age.

42. Jail records show that Ross did stop eating for a few days.

43. Ross actually remained in the prison hospital for seven weeks.

44. Baron Wasteland was also in Morisset at this time.

45. Morisset hospital files indicate that Ross did have this delusional system at this time.

46. This refers to a fire that occurred during his childhood when he and his brother were playing with matches in a shed.

47. During Ross's time in Morisset, his medication was altered and increased.

48. This word play (story/storey) is another example of the loosening of association which is a common feature of schizophrenia.

49. Some individuals develop sensitivity with use of Largactil. It often turns the skin yellow, not "purple-blue."

50. Conversations with Ross's family suggest that his first breakdown with emotional problems occurred when he was about fifteen years old.

51. On May 9, 1980, Ross was returned to Long Bay jail as it was considered that his condition was now under control.

52. Patients on Mellaril (thioridazine hydrochloride), an antipsychotic medication, can remain physically active but tend to react less to stress. It does have an effect on ejaculation but we can find no reports of its causing sterility.

53. "Crown" is Australian slang for members of the police force; that is, they are employed by the "Crown" (monarchy) or the Australian government.

54. John Lennon was murdered in New York City by a crazed fan on that date. Ross was a great admirer of the Beatles' music.

55. In the late 1980s there was serious unrest in the New South Wales prison population, leading to a series of riots, particularly at Parramatta. Shots were fired and 141 prisoners wounded.

56. Baron Wasteland died in April 1982. Pethidine is not a "synthetic heroin" but is a synthetic opiate. Heroin and morphine are also opiates.

57. Another example of clanging, but Ross must also have been familiar with the phrase "See how they snied," from the Beatles' song "I Am the Walrus."

58. Ross's former parole officer told us that the "Aboriginal bodyguard" referred to here was actually a probation officer trainee.

59. Esrevinu = universe spelled backwards.

60. Riverina is a fruit-growing area in southwestern New South Wales.

61. Cobber the Evolutionist was a fellow university student. "Cobber" is Australian slang for friend.

62. Korsakoff's syndrome is a mental condition associated with chronic alcoholism involving severe memory loss.

63. RSL (Returned Services League) clubs are situated throughout Australia. Similar to the American Legion, the clubs are made up of ex-soldiers, sailors, and airmen, and are popular social gathering spots.

64. In late 1982 and early 1983 Ross lived in several halfway houses and was thrown out of two of these because of his behavior. In March 1983 he moved into a flat in Petersham, an inner suburb of Sydney, with two fellow patients from St. John of God.

65. Ross enrolled at the University of New England, Armidale, New South Wales, in February 1984.

66. Terry had suffered a serious accident of some kind at work and was awaiting his "compo," or workers' compensation insurance payment.

67. Cogentin (benztropine mesylate) is used to relieve tardive dyskinesia, the involuntary movements that result from taking antipsychotic medication.

68. Ross did sit up on the awning of the college building, stark naked, during a rock concert.

69. At this point Abraxas is one of the editors (R. G.), whom Ross vis-

ited on a number of occasions, particularly in the florid stages of his illness. This particular conversation occurred not long before Ross took his life but represents his view of what transpired. During this conversation Ross indicated that he had almost finished his book and seemed quite happy about its conclusion.

About Schizophrenia

Ross hoped that his story would give sufferers of schizophrenia and their families a better understanding of the illness. It is therefore appropriate at this point to try to understand the nature of the disorder and how this is reflected in Ross's writing. Ross's story helps dispel the stereotype of those suffering from schizophrenia as somehow "non-human" and therefore frightening, and lets us see the sufferer of schizophrenia as an ordinary person with the needs, wishes, and desires common to most human beings. While cognition, perception, and sense of self may be distorted, the person with schizophrenia may still have the same range of emotional experiences that we all have. Sometimes these experiences are extreme and prolonged and may be both the result of the illness itself and the psychological reaction to having such an illness.

Ross's book is clearly autobiographical. He draws on events in his own life, as well as those of others that were known to him directly. The chapters are filled with drug-related experiences and the beginning signs of a developing psychotic illness. Right from the start, Ross/Sphere realizes he has a problem with his thinking processes. Very early in the book, he says: "I was out of control, lost in my world of confusion. I realized that something was going wrong with my reasoning. I was talking shit again." Many of Ross's unusual symptoms are the result of his drug taking and not of schizophrenia. As the book unfolds, however, his experiences and perceptions clearly reflect an increasingly florid psychotic illness. Ross's family and friends often said they thought Ross's illness might have been caused by the illicit drugs he took, but this is unlikely. There is no scientific evidence that overuse of drugs will produce schizophrenic symptoms of the kind Ross had. Those with schizophrenia and florid psychotic symptoms report that the hallu-cinations they experience are quite different from the hallucina-tions produced by drugs. Individuals with a developing schizo-phrenic illness will often experiment with drugs at a time when they are experiencing unusual, and often distressing, feelings and perceptions. The onset of florid symptoms of schizophrenia is often coincident with the beginning of drug experimentation and there-fore people conclude that the drugs have caused the illness.

Sphere becomes increasingly isolated as the book develops. His relationship with Elysium Dream deteriorates quickly and falls apart. He develops complex delusions about the significance of this relationship and is clearly devastated by its failure. He attaches par-ticular significance to the child that resulted from their brief union. The importance of this relationship and the child were also very clear in Ross's real life and were the focus of his attention until his death.

Ross portrays himself as quite separate from his friends in the later stages of the book. Such isolation is a common feature of schizophrenia and is often the result of the increasingly bizarre behavior of the sufferer, as people become increasingly wary of him. Ross's loneliness may also be a reflection of his time in jail, where some degree of personal isolation or distancing may have been important for survival. Friends and family often commented in interviews that Ross was not the same person when he came out of jail. Part of Ross's pain in life and in his story is a reflection of his loneliness. He wanted to be close to people but his sometimes strange behavior and perceptions tended to scare people off.

Unfortunately, neither of us knew Ross before his time in jail, so it is difficult to know to what extent the change in his behavior reflected this experience. It is conceivable that it did not represent the effects of incarceration but rather reflected an unfolding psy-chotic illness. It is most likely both factors played a part, but espe-cially his developing schizophrenia.

Overall, Ross's story is about the personal experiences of some-one who is developing, and finally develops, schizophrenia. He shares with us his delusions and distorted perceptions of the world and his attempts to obtain relief through illicit drugs. He shares with us his loneliness and emotional devastation over his failed relationship, the nightmares, harsh experiences, and despair that often characterize the lives of those with a psychosis. He shares with us some of the funny side of his experiences and his sense of humor. His story is insightful and devastatingly frank. Ross tells us how it really is for the sufferer. Having schizophrenia—like any serious illness—is tough. There is no escape from the symptoms; they are always there, chronically there. The problem is aggravated by the fact that schizophrenia is a disorder of the brain and so the very organ with which one thinks about illness is affected by the illness. This is the message Ross conveys. While some appear to recover fully from schizophrenia, for others there is often no escape except through death, a solution Ross finally chooses unhindered. Even the prescribed medications did not relieve all his symptoms but rather left him with nasty side effects and unresolved psychological problems such as isolation and loneliness.

Ross's story is not without hope. He keenly sought out solutions to his illness but unfortunately was not prepared to wait any longer for such solutions. Our growing knowledge of schizophrenia is helping us to find more gentle answers to the problems than were available to Ross. The legacy of Ross's book is that it sensitizes us to the intense suffering that those with schizophrenia experience and acts to spur us on to further research, reflecting one of Ross's main interests in life: finding a decent treatment for the illness.

There is considerable evidence that although schizophrenia affects people from all levels of society, it tends to occur more frequently among the lower socioeconomic groups. Some studies suggest that the ratio may be as high as eight to one. One interpretation of this disproportionate representation is that sufferers of the disease are more likely to slide downwards because they are unable to maintain themselves at higher economic and social levels. There is some evidence to support this idea based on an examination of the occupations of fathers of children with schizophrenia and on the occupations of the children themselves. A far greater proportion of the children with schizophrenia have lower-status jobs than their fathers than is found in a control population of children without schizophrenia. It seems probable that the illness pushes individuals into a lower socioeconomic status, rather than their coming from such status to begin with.

As with many sufferers of schizophrenia, Ross had trouble holding down a job and changed occupation frequently. He worked variously as a postal clerk, machine collator, and laborer, and spent a great deal of his time unemployed. It is noteworthy that the rest of Ross's family have stable employment histories and in some cases have been engaged in jobs of considerable responsibility. His father worked as a customs officer and also was successful in real estate ventures and became quite wealthy as a result. One brother is an international airline pilot, another a senior manager of mining operations, and another brother works as a mechanic. None of them shares Ross's checkered employment career.

Schizophrenia Defined

Schizophrenia is a common form of mental illness. Various surveys of large populations suggest that between 1 and 2 percent suffer from this disorder. The term schizophrenia was coined by the Swiss psychiatrist Eugen Bleuler in 1908 (see Davison & Neale, 1986). Meaning, literally, "a splitting of the mind," the term describes the way that schizophrenic language, thoughts, and feelings are often disconnected or split from each other. Bleuler believed a person suffering from schizophrenia was unable to connect up or associate thoughts, feelings, and so on, in a coherent way. So an individual might have appropriate thoughts about a sad event, such as the death of a close friend, but express emotion inappropriately by laughing instead of crying.

Contrary to a common misconception, schizophrenia does not refer to "split"- or multiple-personality disorder. In that disorder, the person has two or more distinctly different personalities, each of which is dominant at different times. In many cases these personalities may not be known to each other and are quite often opposite in character. Almost invariably, a person with multiple-personality disorder has had a very traumatic childhood. This is not the case with individuals with schizophrenia.

Bleuler viewed schizophrenia as a disorder with an organic or physiological basis that could be provoked and influenced by psychological factors. This view holds wide currency today and we will return to this point later. As we have noted, Ross certainly had some traumatic events in his background that might have been seen as the "cause" of his problems, but given current opinion on the causes of schizophrenia it is most unlikely that his schizophrenic illness was associated with these traumas.

At the same time Bleuler was developing his theories, the German psychiatrist Emil Kraepelin offered quite a different perspective on the disorder. He referred to schizophrenia as *dementia praecox*. The term literally means a progressively deteriorating illness (*dementia*) with an early onset (*praecox*). Kraepelin believed that the symptoms of schizophrenia reflected an intellectual deterioration such as that seen in Alzheimer's disease, although current evidence suggests that there is no degeneration with schizophrenia. Like Bleuler, Kraepelin believed schizophrenia had a biological basis. It is clear now that both Bleuler and Kraepelin were correct in this belief. There is now substantial evidence that schizophrenia has such a basis and that events which occur during development of the brain lead to schizophrenia. These events are not yet well understood, and it is beyond the scope of this book to review them in depth. However, we can offer a brief outline of the causality of schizophrenia.

What Causes Schizophrenia?

When Bleuler and Kraepelin first described schizophrenia, they suspected it had a strong biological basis. Anatomical studies of the brains of those with schizophrenia suggested that there were genuine brain abnormalities in those who had the illness. Over the years, and with the rise of behaviorism, this explanation of schizophrenia lost its potency, and theorists in both North America and Europe speculated independently that it was the individual's social circumstances that created or generated the schizophrenic illness. These views were espoused particularly by the antipsychiatry movement, but very little evidence was produced to prove that it was social upbringing or environment which caused the schizophrenia to occur. The antipsychiatry movement was at its strongest in the 1950s and 1960s and into the early 1970s, but lost its momentum when evidence emerged that many of the psychiatric illnesses had a strong biological basis. This evidence came from anatomical study as well as pharmacological experimentation.

There has been a return to biological theories of schizophrenia in recent years, and with the advent of new technologies for studying the brain (CAT, MRI, and PET scanning) we have been able to get a more accurate picture of what is happening in the brains of those who suffer the disease. It is clear now that schizophrenia has a neurodevelopmental basis. Evidence suggests that events occurring to the fetal brain during pregnancy lead to the brain not being structured in a normal way. The development of the brain is a complex process and it is not surprising that things may go wrong in the sequencing of developmental processes that lead to normal function. There appears to be a genetic basis for the development of these abnormalities, but it is not clear whether the mechanism operates directly or indirectly to produce the abnormality.

Nasrallah (1990) and others have demonstrated clear evidence of differences in brain structure and function between those people with schizophrenia and those without. Electrophysiological evidence, that is, evidence obtained from electrical recordings of the brains of those with schizophrenia, shows that the electrical rhythms of their brains are quite different from those without the illness. Those with the illness tend to have greater variability in their electrical rhythms. Studies have shown that if a "normal" person carries out a certain cognitive task, the electrical activity evoked by the cognitive task changes and settles over time to a particular pattern. With the schizophrenic individual, however, the variability does not settle into a particular pattern and the brain continues to present a much more variable pattern than one sees in normal people.

Current studies suggest that the effects of schizophrenic illness relate to temporal and frontal lobe dysfunction of the central nervous system. These regions of the brain play a major role in self-monitoring, emotional processing, and willed activity. It would appear that schizophrenia disturbs both monitoring functions and emotions to varying degrees. The changes in symptom patterns from one set of individuals to another may reflect the differential neurodevelopmental effects in the brain, with some areas being affected more than others and this pattern changing in individuals depending on the time of insult to the brain.

Numerous hypotheses have been proposed regarding the neuroanatomical and neurochemical bases of schizophrenia. A number of neurotransmitter substances (the substances that allow neurons, the basic building blocks of the brain, to communicate with each other) have been implicated in schizophrenia, but in particular the neurotransmitter dopamine has been identified as an important agent in the disease. A number of the drugs that have been prescribed for the treatment of schizophrenia have effects on dopamine. Once alterations to dopamine occur, so the symptoms of schizophrenia change.

There are a number of dopaminergenic pathways in the brain, and schizophrenia may affect only some of these. The drugs that are given to alter dopamine, however, affect not only the abnormal pathways but also the normal pathways, making the latter abnormal. The individual may thus be relieved of some of the symptoms of schizophrenia, but abnormalities in the once-normal pathways created by the drug may cause some of the side effects one sees with drug treatment.

It is conceivable that schizophrenia is a result of both alterations to the biochemistry of the brain as well as to neuroanatomical pathways, so that circuits are somehow impaired. These circuit changes produce alterations in the way information is processed. Depending on which part of the brain is affected, particular symptom pictures emerge. If temporal lobes are involved, it is possible that hallucinations will occur. If frontal lobes are affected, some of the changes in the individual's drive and initiative may be affected. A number of neuropsychological models encompassing these different patterns of schizophrenia have been described in the literature. The metacognitive approach of Frith, described below, is one such model.

Symptoms

The symptoms of schizophrenia are complex and in many cases may be very frightening, both to the victims and to those involved with them. Schizophrenia is unlikely to be a unitary disease (one in which all individuals have the same symptoms). In fact, there is very good evidence that schizophrenia probably covers a number of disorders or symptom complexes with quite different manifestations and features. Five subtypes of schizophrenia have been described in the psychiatric literature; we will look at these later.

There are also some additional disorders that have schizophrenia-like features but that are regarded as separate disorders because they have a time course, or natural history, different from that of "conventional" schizophrenia.

Before discussing the different subtypes, we will look at some of the major symptoms of schizophrenia. These may be divided into four categories: motor, somatic, cognitive, and mood or emotional symptoms.

Motor Symptoms

The variety of motor symptoms is quite large. Some individuals with schizophrenia become very excited and agitated and may engage in excessive motor activity to the point where it becomes life-threatening because of overexertion and related heat stress. These individuals need to be cared for so that they get adequate nutrition and fluids. Some limitation may be placed on activity, and quite often drugs are used to stop the agitation. These drugs are the neuroleptics, or major tranquilizers. Other individuals may engage in unusual facial expressions such as grimacing, or repetitive motor activities such as unusual hand or finger movements. Many of these behaviors appear to be random or without purpose, but some may be related to the patient's delusions. For example, one of the first schizophrenic patients I ever saw spent his days marching endlessly up and down the hospital quadrangle. It transpired that he was a sergeant-major who had delusions about a need to have everyone prepared for combat against an imaginary enemy. The hospital initially refused to give him the "troops" he wanted (other patients that he tried to recruit for training) but subsequently released some "troops" to him for purposes of training in order to give the patients, who normally sat around doing very little, some exercise! While eyebrows might now be raised about this transgression of civil liberties, it is clear that all concerned benefited and the general health and state of many of those involved in the "close order drill" program improved considerably. In fact, many of the patients looked forward to their daily outing, and they progressed from the hospital quadrangle to "reconnaissance" walks through the countryside. Needless to say, the "training" program was carefully monitored to prevent damage to patients and to keep down the cost of footwear. The line was drawn at 20-kilometer forced marches!

On the other end of the motor continuum are those persons who remain immobile in one position for long periods. In some cases they will sit in unusual postures or positions. This condition is referred to as **catatonia** or **catatonic schizophrenia**. These individuals may also exhaust themselves and so need to be managed carefully. Some are very resistant to change and are difficult to move, while others can be moved to new positions and will remain so until moved again. This "waxy flexibility," as it is called, was once commonly seen in schizophrenic illness but is now rare because of the advent of drugs that are very effective in controlling such symptoms.

Some of the unusual motor movements and activities one sees in schizophrenia are not always a direct result of the illness. In a number of cases, they may be caused by the side effects of the drugs used to treat schizophrenia. Some of these symptoms include motor tremors, facial grimacing, including unusual chewing movement, and a stiff-legged gait (sometimes referred to as the "Stelazine shuffle" after the drug that sometimes produces this side effect) where the person hardly lifts his or her feet. Many of these side effects can be counteracted with other medications, but unfortunately some cannot and so the patient may have to be withdrawn from the drug, with consequent return of schizophrenia symptoms. For some patients, long-term exposure to medication may produce motor side effects that cannot be reversed with drug termination. In some cases patients taking medication will develop unusual motor symptoms that are not the result of the medication, but a manifestation of the illness itself.

Ross did not suffer from the motor abnormalities one sees in particular forms of schizophrenia. However, he complained of the side effects of the drugs used to treat him. In his hospital notes in 1977 he is described as having "postural changes and Parkinsonian stance." He was treated, successfully, with Cogentin to counteract these side effects. We can find no evidence in his files of tardive dyskinesive symptoms, such as motor tremors or facial grimacing, which often accompany the use of antipsychotic drugs.

Somatic Symptoms

These are also seen in schizophrenia, although not as commonly as other symptoms. The somatic symptoms that have received the most attention in research include physiological symptoms of under- or overarousal. In some cases the individual may be hyper-aroused, with sweaty palms, high heart rate, and elevated blood pressure. On a number of occasions when we shook hands, Ross had sweaty palms, but in many cases he had also consumed a number of beers, which can induce similar symptoms. So it is difficult to disentangle symptoms of the disease from those of self-medication. Different levels of arousal may be associated with different phases of the illness or with different subtypes of the illness. The nature of the apparently contradictory findings is not well understood and research is continuing into this area.

Some somatic symptoms are clearly related to the hallucinations or delusions that the person is experiencing, while others are the direct result of physical illness quite independent of schizophrenia. For example, an individual may believe that parts of the body are rotting away or distorted, or there may be unexplained pain (Pridmore, 1984). It is absolutely crucial that these symptoms be examined carefully so that real somatic symptoms of physical illness may be identified and treated. As with motor symptoms, a number of somatic symptoms are caused by the medications the patients take. For example, common side effects of the major drugs used to control schizophrenia are a dry mouth and increased sensitivity to sunlight.

Ross certainly had somatic symptoms when he was suffering from his schizophrenic illness, but it is not always clear whether these were the direct result of the illness itself or the result of medications he was taking at the time. He often complained of a dry mouth, and a family member confirmed that he frequently drank huge quantities of water to try to relieve this symptom. The tendency to drink huge quantities of water, called **polydipsia,** is seen in some forms of schizophrenia in the absence of medication. It would appear, however, that Ross's intake was related to the side effects of the drugs.

We must also bear in mind that, given his time in psychiatric hospitals and exposure to other patients, it is possible that some of the symptoms he reports in the novel are a reflection of poetic license, whereby he draws symptoms from others and attributes them to himself in the persona of Sphere.

Cognitive Symptoms
These are the most obvious, and often the most disturbing, symptoms of schizophrenia. They include hallucinations, delusions, and disturbed thinking and attentional processes.

Hallucinations are perceptual or sensory experiences that are perceived as if they really exist but do not, on careful examination, have a basis in reality. The most common of the hallucinations in schizophrenia are auditory. Sometimes the auditory hallucinations may be of machine or animal noises, but these are far less common than voices. A person may hear voices that issue instructions, or criticize the individual in some way. Sometimes they can be recognized as the person's own internal voices, but on other occasions the voices may be those of other significant persons or characters. To the person experiencing the hallucinations, the voices may be very real.

Ross's records show quite clearly that he heard voices, but he appeared to recognize that it was "himself talking to himself." In some cases the individual with hallucinations may act on the voices and sometimes these acts may be dangerous to others, although in most cases the acts are dangerous only to the individual with the schizophrenic illness. Some sufferers feel that their thoughts are being controlled by the hallucinatory voices.

In addition to auditory hallucinations, individuals may experience tactile, somatic, olfactory, and visual hallucinations. Tactile hallucinations may take the form of an experience of something, such as ants, crawling over the skin. This phenomenon is referred to as **formication.** The individual may also have a sensation of something occurring inside the body, or may experience tingling or burning. Some people smell things that are clearly not present, such as perfumes or someone else's body odor. Finally, persons may see things that are not there or have distorted impressions of objects that are present.

In all cases it is important that people with hallucinations be investigated for other diseases besides schizophrenia. It is well known that hallucinations may be part of temporal lobe epilepsy, delirium, various drug states (including drug intoxication and withdrawal), and multiple sclerosis.

Ross certainly suffered from auditory hallucinations. For instance, he thought a television commentator had instructed him to rob the bank. Sphere also demonstrates evidence of auditory hallucinations in this book. For example, when Sphere visits his brother's home to watch television he reports that the radio and television are speaking to him:

> *The fact dawned on me as I watched the TV. The radio was telling me also. Like a prophet, I was becoming more aware I would have to be ready for the day when they would confront me with the tapes of my conversations. The day they recognized the inventor of rock and roll. The world would show up with its bigotry, greed, pride, and hate and also with its reason, compassion, and intelligent perception. It was a painful fate that had chosen me, but it would be my own ingenuity that would rescue me. I was gravely concerned for Eternal. I could die alone. I would have to face them alone.*

In this case, his auditory hallucinations are also mixed in with his delusional system, a not uncommon event in schizophrenia. There are examples of this throughout the book. As the story progresses, the extent and development of the auditory hallucinations and delusional systems become more complex, more frequent, and more distressing.

Delusions are false belief systems that are held by an individual without any basis in fact. In many cases, the false belief system continues to be held in spite of strong evidence to the contrary. Some delusions are very potent and may lead the person to act upon them. In most cases, the actions are harmless, but in a minority of cases the delusions may lead to self-inflicted damage or damage to others. In most cases, however, the damage is to self. The most common delusions are persecutory in nature; that is, individuals believe that others intend to harm them in some way. Such paranoid delusions may cause the afflicted persons to be very guarded in what they say to others, which can then lead to social isolation and avoidance of contact with others. In notes concerning Ross's hospitalization at St. John of God, he is described as "quite psychotic with thought broadcasting, delusional thinking, marked thought disorder, and disordered affect" on each admission. It is further noted that "on most occasions there has been a somewhat mythical quasi-religious quality about his delusions which also somehow encompass pop groups." The theme of isolation from others is clear in Ross's book, particularly toward the end of the story.

Some individuals suffer from delusions of grandeur. They believe they have a mission in life to control or regulate the behavior of others, and attach special significance to events that most people would regard as quite ordinary. Many suffer from delusions of reference and may see significant signs everywhere. For example, the way someone opens a briefcase may be taken as a sign that the schizophrenic person is being spied on or that a special message is about to be delivered. Some individuals have delusions of identity and believe that they are famous characters. They may act as they believe that person should or would have acted, sometimes with dire consequences, usually for themselves.

It is clear from careful reading of the clinical notes on Ross from St. John of God Hospital, from Morisset Prison Hospital, and from the Long Bay jail medical records that he had a very substantial delusional system. There were some paranoid features, and he had delusions of grandeur in his belief about being in control of certain situations which, of course, were not based in reality. A number of these same delusional features show through in the text of his story. In some cases, it is clear that these psychotic features are the result of the schizophrenic illness and not the result of the illicit drugs he was taking at the time, although some of the drugs he took, such as the hallucinogens, may have added to the intensity and extent of his hallucinatory and delusional experiences.

Ross believed that the Catholic Church needed to be destroyed, that ants would take over the world, and that he was a sorcerer. Both in his story and in real life, Ross said he invented rock and roll. In fact, when Ross first came to me with his schizophrenic illness in full flight, he told me confidentially that he wanted me to know he was the inventor of rock and roll and also the Holy Ghost.

On that first occasion, it was clear that his symptoms needed treatment and I took him to the local hospital in Armidale. Ross, at this stage, had not taken his major tranquilizers for some time. While driving him to the hospital, I was concerned because of his poor mood state that he might undo his seatbelt and throw himself out of the car.

I took Ross straight to the psychiatric wing of the institution and introduced him to the nurse in charge of the ward. When I asked him how he wished to be known, he said that he didn't mind if I introduced him as the Holy Ghost. It is an interesting comment on Ross, here, that while he was in the florid state of his schizophrenia he had enough mental wherewithal to appreciate that what he was saying was not quite right; when I introduced him to the nurse as the Holy Ghost, both the nurse and Ross burst into laughter at the bizarre nature of the introduction.

Delusions and hallucinations are also reflected in his book, for instance in Chapter 35, where Sphere says:

> I was alone now. Dire consequences began to eventuate. Tropical monsoons were altered by the increased wavelength of my mind. Storms of uncontrollable fury devastated towns and these were sent by God. Lightning flashes illuminated the sky, earthquakes shook continents, and these were sent by God. I watched on TV the destruction sent by God. I knew that, in my insane frenzy, I was killing more and more people—innocent people who had never hurt me—and every death brought me closer to the point of no return, of a mind on fire with grief. The weather chart showed the highs and lows which corresponded to my various moods. . . . The late movies were driving me mad as they showed my reflection as the Creator.

It is true that many of us have belief systems that are not quite based in reality; what sets those with schizophrenia apart is that their delusional systems often have a bizarre quality and are all-pervasive in terms of the effects they have on their lives and the lives of others. Moreover, most of our "delusions" will change when new evidence comes to light, whereas the delusional systems of those with schizophrenia are somewhat intransigent.

Other deviations of cognition in schizophrenia include disturbances in language. These are often called **formal thought disorders.** A common feature of formal thought disorder is what is referred to as **derailment.** Here, the individual has ideas that shift from one subject to another. In many cases the subjects are unrelated or lack proper connection. The speaker appears to be unaware that the topics are disconnected or unconnected and appears to shift from one frame of reference to another. To the speaker, the connection may be perfectly clear, but it is only after some discussion that it becomes clear to the listener. When derailment becomes severe, the person often becomes incoherent and speech may be totally incomprehensible. For example, in response to the question "How are things at home?" the individual, in stream-of-consciousness fashion, may say something like this: "What I'm saying is my mother is too ill. No money. It all comes out of her pocket. My flat's leaking. It's ruined my mattress. It's Lambeth Council. I'd like to know what the caption in the motto under their coat of arms is. It's in Latin" (Gatting, 1985, cited in Frith, 1992).

Another form of cognitive deficit with schizophrenia involves poverty of speech content. With this symptom, speech is sufficient in amount but the speaker has little information to convey. The information is often vague and overly abstract, or may be concrete, repetitive, and stereotyped.

A less common form of cognitive disorder is the use of **neologisms,** invented words: for example, *faratoto* for father and *flopateto* for fish (Le Vine & Coulard, 1979, cited in Frith, 1992). Another is **perseveration,** where the same material is gone over and over again. The way it is said often indicates that the speaker attaches great meaning to it, but to the listener there is no obvious meaning involved.

Clanging is another less frequent symptom. Here, the sounds of the words, rather than their meaning, govern word choice. In this form of disorder there may be rhyming and punning. There are many examples of clanging in Ross's book, such as: "I am Sphere, and this is the book of fear" (page 25); "I am not a woman. / I am a man. / Yes I am." (page 26); "The cosmic room is my cocoon" (page 123). It is clear that Ross had a predisposition to clang.

Finally, there is **blocking,** or **loss of goal,** which is interruption of speech before a thought or idea has been completed. Often the speaker will indicate that he or she is unable to recall what has just been said or what was meant. It is as if the train of thought has been lost.

Mood or Emotional Symptoms

Those who have cognitive symptoms also often experience changes in mood or emotional state. They may be profoundly depressed and have a sense that nothing is worth doing, that life is not worth living, and that they cannot stand the emotional pain they are experiencing. Alternatively, they may experience euphoria that is out of keeping with their circumstances. They will be very delighted or pleased with everything that is happening in the world and attach positive emotional significance to even the tiniest of changes to their environment. These euphoric states are often congruent with the delusional systems in operation at the time.

Depression, however, is the predominant mood symptom associated with schizophrenia. Ross certainly suffered from profound depression and often sought relief in alcohol. While the major antipsychotic medications he was taking did counteract the more florid symptoms of the disease, the hallucinations and delusions, the drugs did not alleviate his depressed mood. Alcohol was one of the few things that gave him relief, and Ross came to see me from time to time when he was in an inebriated state. He would indicate very clearly that the reason he was drunk was to escape from the dreadful mood he found he could not endure unaided.

It is likely that depressed mood is not a response to having the schizophrenic illness, but rather the direct result of the illness; that is, the biochemistry of the brain has been altered in such a way as to make the person depressed. In some people it is this depressed mood that leads them to take their lives. Ross was no exception here. The intensity of his symptoms was such that he often felt he could not go on. Ross would also have euphoric periods occasionally, associated with his illness. At his university class barbecue at Dumaresq Dam, a picnic spot near Armidale, Ross was "high," without the aid of illicit drugs, and busy trying to pursue and chat up all the women there. His mood resembled the kind of mania that one sees in manic depression, or bipolar illness. There is also a report in his medical records of 1982 of an incident where Ross was described as being "very high." On this occasion he had stripped to his underpants and socks and had done a "wild dance" around the hospital room, egged on by the other patients. Ross was not a bit disturbed when requested to "get his clothes on and to tone down his antics." But he was not in this euphoric state often.

There is a common theme running through Ross's book of significant, often abrupt, changes in mood state. One moment Sphere will be manic and exhilarated; the next, he reaches the depths of despair. He reflects often on his "dark" state and how life apparently holds little hope or meaning for him. He says (page 85): "My elevated mood was alternating from depression to manic high. I hated myself . . . " (a common feature of depression). He later says: "I was rotten drunk and full of pity for myself." In his hospital notes it is recorded that Ross "could not find anything positive to say" and was "ridiculing himself constantly."

Classification of Symptoms

Since 1980, attempts have been made to explain the wide variety of symptoms seen in schizophrenic illness in terms of two classes of symptoms, positive and negative (see Crow, 1980, for detailed classification). **Positive symptoms** are those such as hallucinations, delusions, disorders of thought and language, which are viewed as "abnormal by their presence," whereas **negative symptoms** include poverty of speech, social withdrawal, and lack of initiation. Unfortunately, this scheme does not explain all symptoms of the illness, but it tends to be used widely now.

More recently, Frith (1992) has developed a symptom classification scheme that covers all symptoms and that avoids the shortcomings of Crow's approach. Basically, he defines positive symptoms, such as hallucinations and delusions, as **abnormal experiences,** while negative symptoms, such as social withdrawal, are defined as **abnormal behaviors.** Frith views the various features of schizophrenia as reflections of different impairments in the single cognitive mechanism of **metarepresentation,** a fundamental process central to conscious experience. It is the process of thinking about or reflecting on one's inner experiences—the process of thinking about thinking. According to Frith, impairments in metarepresentation relate to disturbances in the brain. It is not clear which brain structures are involved, but evidence supports the notion that the frontal and temporal lobes are significant in the production of these symptoms. The three principal abnormalities that account for all the major signs and symptoms of schizophrenia are impairment in willed action, self-monitoring, and monitoring of the intentions of others.

Frith's ideas are gaining considerable support, and further research will confirm whether they are correct or not. For the time being, his approach to the symptoms of schizophrenia is an interesting one, deserving research attention, but we are clearly a long way yet from understanding the brain–behavior relationships underlying schizophrenia, and from understanding the symptoms of the illness itself.

Subtypes of Schizophrenia

As mentioned previously, schizophrenic illness has been classified into subtypes on the basis of clinical symptoms and life history of the disease. This long-standing approach to classification, which is quite different from the cognitive approach taken by Frith and the negative–positive symptom view of Crow, is not without its critics. Some of these subtypes are less stable than others, and their prognostic and treatment implications are variable. The subtype ascribed to a particular individual depends on the predominant symptoms that person presents.

Five subtypes of schizophrenia are described in the widely used *Diagnostic and Statistical Manual of Mental Disorders* (the DSM-III-R) of the American Psychiatric Association.

Catatonic type. The essential feature of this type is "marked psychomotor disturbance," which may involve "stupor, negativism, rigidity, excitement or posturing." Sometimes there is "rapid alternation between the extremes of excitement and stupor." Associated features include stereotyped behaviors, "mannerisms and waxy flexibility. Mutism is particularly common." Individuals with this particular form of illness need careful supervision to prevent harm to self or others. They often need medical care because of malnutrition, exhaustion, elevated body temperature, or self-inflicted injury.

Treatment with modern drugs means that most of the symptoms are negated.

Disorganized type. Individuals with this condition are incoherent, have marked loosening of association, and show grossly erratic behavior. In many cases they also show flat or grossly inappropriate affect. They do not exhibit systematized delusions as in the paranoid subtype (see below), but fragmentary delusions or hallucinations may be present. With these fragmentary systems there is no organized or coherent theme. Associated features with this condition include grimacing, unusual mannerisms, complaints of various forms of medical illness, and extreme social withdrawal. Other oddities of behavior may be present. These individuals are extremely socially impaired. Many of them had a poorly integrated personality before their illness developed. The onset of the condition is slow and insidious, and this condition tends to be of a chronic nature without significant remission. In older classifications, this form of schizophrenia is referred to as **hebephrenia.**

Paranoid type. A small percentage of sufferers in this subtype can be dangerous. Its essential feature is preoccupation with one or more systematized delusions; or the individual may have frequent auditory hallucinations related to some sort of single theme. "Symptoms characteristic of the disorganized and catatonic types, such as incoherence, inappropriate affect, catatonic behavior or grossly disorganized behavior, are absent." Associated features include anxiety, anger, argumentativeness, and, occasionally, violence. These individuals often have a stilted, formal quality or extreme intensity in interpersonal interactions. As many of them are very intelligent, they may argue at a high level and be difficult to deal with because of the seeming rationality of what they are saying. Impairment in their social and occupational functioning may be minimal, provided they do not act upon their delusions. Onset for this condition is later in life than for the other forms of schizophrenia; some do not develop it until they are well into their twenties. There is evidence to suggest that the capacity for independent living and work is better for this type than for others.

Ross was classified in hospital records as having paranoid schizophrenia. He certainly had systematized delusions and hallucinatory experiences, and he was able to function in the community. When not suffering from the illness in a florid way, he was regarded by people as being a gentle soul, but when he did have episodes or outbreaks of violence they were significant, and might have been regarded as being life-threatening. He attempted to strike his father with heavy objects with the avowed intention of causing serious harm. He physically assaulted his mother on one occasion, and there were other reported incidents involving a ticket inspector, a prison guard, and a parole officer. As a young boy he occasionally alarmed and puzzled his friends with uncharacteristic outbursts of aggressive behavior. In the hospital in 1982, he was reported as being "easily provoked and aggressive." A later report from this time found that Ross was "not acceptable to the halfway house because of his history of violence."

Throughout his story, Ross shows evidence of paranoid delusions, for instance "Society is out to kill me . . . " (page 26); "I'll still have to destroy my mind or they'll find me" (page 90); and in some places he comments, through the character of Sphere, about his paranoid personality. Sometimes his delusions are drug-induced, but mostly they are the result of his psychotic illness.

Undifferentiated type. Individuals with this condition have prominent psychotic symptoms such as delusions, hallucinations, incoherence, and grossly disorganized behavior that cannot be classified in any of the subtypes described above.

Residual type. Finally, this type is reserved for cases where there has been at least one episode of schizophrenia but "the clinical picture that occasioned the evaluation or admission is without prominent psychotic symptoms though signs of the illness continue to persist." These individuals are often described as emotionally blunted, socially withdrawn, and eccentric in their behavior. They also have illogical thinking and mild loosening of associations. They may have delusions or hallucinations, but these are not very prominent and are not usually accompanied by strong affect. The course of this subtype may be chronic and there may be acute exacerbations from time to time. Occasionally the person will be in remission.

There is some disagreement about the subtyping described above, and a number of other schemes have been proposed. The classification scheme presented here is widely used in Western circles, however, and certainly makes for ease of comparison between clinics and laboratories interested in research into this form of psychiatric illness. Of all the alternative schemes that have been proposed, the cognitive metarepresentational model of Frith is most likely to supplant the subtyping approach.

Overall, there are many symptoms associated with schizophrenia, and the complex picture of the illness is far from clear. By examining the range of symptoms and mapping this information on to existing knowledge of brain function, we may be able to develop a clear picture of which neuroanatomical substrates are involved in the disease process.

As stated earlier, schizophrenia seems to be a biochemical or neuroanatomical disturbance; the theory that schizophrenia is caused by social circumstances is no longer valid. It needs to be pointed out, however, that the illness does not occur in a vacuum. It is clear from a great deal of research that individuals' social circumstances very much influence the outcome of the illness and particularly whether or not there are exacerbations of the illness. The evidence shows that appropriate social environments can have a considerable effect in reducing the expression of the disease. In some chaotic social environments the schizophrenic symptoms may be exacerbated.

Treatment

Many treatments have been described for schizophrenia, but the clear choice at present is for medication combined with well-designed social education and management. The major tranquilizers and neuroleptics available at the time of Ross Burke's illness, Stelazine and Chlorpromazine, which are still widely used, have significant effects on the positive symptoms of schizophrenia, hallucinations and delusions, but leave the negative symptoms in place with depressed mood. Treatment with mood-related drugs, such as the antidepressants, is often indicated with the older antipsychotic agents, and many individuals continue to benefit from poly-drug therapy.

Unfortunately, many of the traditional drugs are very broad in their effects—somewhat like shooting a sparrow with a shotgun. There are many side effects from the major tranquilizers, including tardive dyskinesia (lip-smacking and chewing movements), which are distressing to the patients and to those around them. In many cases the side effects become chronic and do not disappear once the drugs have been discontinued. Some additional medications such as Cogentin can be prescribed to remove some of these side effects, but the problems of dry mouth and so on will always remain. Some of the motor symptoms that are ascribed to the drugs may be present in patients who have never had such medication, particularly as the disease develops and becomes chronic. The pre-drug literature reports many examples of this kind. The move is now towards finding pharmacological interventions which are much more targeted and specific in their effects and which do not leave the patient with so many side effects. In recent times, two new effective antipsychotic drugs have been developed for the treatment of schizophrenia. They have far fewer side effects and are better tolerated than the older medications. One of them, Risperidone, is particularly effective in combating the negative symptoms of schizophrenia as well as the positive. The other, Clozapine, has proven effectiveness in the treatment of those who normally respond well to other medications as well as longer-term, intractable patients who have not responded to other forms of drug therapy. These newer drugs offer considerable hope for symptom relief, with minimal side effects, to the vast majority of those suffering from schizophrenic illness.

Ross was given the standard drug treatment for schizophrenia. For example, the Stelazine and Chlorpromazine listed in his medical records are often given to patients with psychotic symptoms. A number of these drugs provoke idiosyncratic responses, so the prescribing physician will change medications in order to find the best "fit" for the individual. Ross was receiving medication both for the florid symptoms of his psychosis and the depression that accompanied it. His treatment with both the antipsychotic and antidepressant drugs seems appropriate, as psychological studies of individuals with paranoid schizophrenia show that depression is a common accompaniment of the disease.

A frequent problem with the treatment of schizophrenic illness is that many patients stop taking the drugs once they feel better, in the mistaken belief that they are cured of the illness, not realizing that drugs will give them relief from the symptoms only as long as they continue taking them. The mistaken belief that they are cured may come partly from the fact that symptoms do not recur in any florid fashion for some time after cessation of drug therapy. Because there is a lag between cessation and the return of symptoms, there is a natural human tendency to conclude that the drugs are not having any effect on the illness and are therefore not important. Sometimes it may be a few weeks before the psychotic state returns. This may be because it takes a while for the drugs to leave the system and the illness may not be active at that point.

Another reason some individuals give up drug therapy is that the side effects appear to be worse than the disease. These may increase with time and dosage, and because the florid symptoms of schizophrenia are subsiding as a result of the drugs, the side effects appear to be more prominent.

Ross had considerable problems with drug side effects. He tended to put on a lot of weight, which he did not like, and also complained of a dry mouth, poor concentration, reduced sexual performance, and low motivation. The other reason he gave up the medications is that while they reduced his psychotic symptoms, they offered him no relief from his depressed mood state, leading him to believe they were ineffective. He also thought he was cured.

The move to more specifically focused drugs should help us target more particularly the symptoms of schizophrenia, and I believe an appropriate reduction in side effects will occur as a result. These new drugs are coming on the market. Drugs, however, may not be the whole answer. If there are neuroanatomical substrates that are affected in schizophrenia, or some forms of schizophrenia, our knowledge does not extend to changing these substrates to a normal state. We are a long way from understanding what happens in this area, and it is unlikely that in the near future there will be therapies available to change these neuroanatomical structures to normal.

As suggested before, the social circumstances of the individuals with schizophrenia can exacerbate or reduce the expression of symptoms. It is important that their families and significant others learn about those things that make the illness worse, and those that help to contain it. Appropriate training and counseling are required to help both individuals and their families cope with the symptoms. There is recent evidence to show that some sufferers may benefit from some forms of therapy, but in severe cases it is unlikely that social interventions will be particularly effective in helping the individual deal with the illness.

In summary, schizophrenia is an illness of the mind and not merely a response to social circumstances. Because it is an illness of the mind, the behavior, cognitions, affect, and activity of the individual are influenced by the illness.

RICHARD GATES

References and Further Reading

Books and Articles

Crow, T. J. 1980. Molecular pathology of schizophrenia: more than one disease process? *British Medical Journal* 280: 66–68.

David, A. S., and Cutting, J. C. (Eds.). 1994. *The neuropsychology of schizophrenia.* Hillsdale, N.J.: Lawrence Erlbaum. A thorough review of the psychology of schizophrenia from a neuropsychological perspective. Very academic.

Davison, G. C., and Neale, J. M. 1986. *Abnormal psychology.* New York: Wiley.

Deveson, Anne. 1991. *Tell me I'm here.* Melbourne: Penguin Books Australia. A powerful story written by a mother about her son's tragic battle with schizophrenia.

Frith, C. D. 1992. *The cognitive neuropsychology of schizophrenia.* Hillsdale, N.J.: Lawrence Erlbaum. A straightforward account of schizophrenia and recent attempts to understand it. It is aimed particularly at those engaged in a professional or academic capacity.

Hofmann, A. 1961. Chemical pharmacological and medical aspects of psychotomimetics. *Journal of Experimental Medical Science,* 5: 40.

Huxley, Aldous. 1954. *The doors of perception.* London: Chatto & Windus.

McFarlane, J. 1976. The mind of modernism. In *Modernism 1890–1930,* ed. Malcolm Bradbury and James McFarlane, 86. London: Penguin, 1976.

Nasrallah, H. A. 1990. Brain structure and function in schizophrenia: evidence for fetal neurodevelopmental impairment. *Current Opinion in Psychiatry* 3: 75–78.

Pridmore, S. 1984. *The case of Joshua Kirk: an episode of schizophrenia.* Melbourne: The Schizophrenia Fellowship of Australia. The story of a university student from South Australia who suffered a single episode of schizophrenia from which he recovered.

Sechehaye, Marguerite. 1951. *Autobiography of a schizophrenic girl: with analytic interpretation.* New York: Grune & Stratton.